THE CURSE OF THE FATHER

BY
CHAD DANIEL

The Curse of the Father
Published by: Chad Daniel Ministries
P. O. Box 2151
Redlands, CA 92373
www.chaddaniel.com
314-422-4389

Unless otherwise noted, Scripture quotations are from the King James
Version of the Bible.

Scripture quotations marked NKJV are from the New King James
Version of the Bible Copyright © 1979, 1980, 1982 by Thomas
Nelson, Inc., Publishers. Used by permission.
AMP-NKJV-KJV NLT-NIV

ISBN: 978-1-7333398-0-3
Copyright © 2019 by Chad Daniel / Chad Daniel Ministries
First Edition Printing: July 2019
Printed in the United States of America

To Paul Black:
Every Oz needs a man behind the curtain.

Special thanks to Contributor and Editor, friend, international travel companion, and senior producer, James Paul Vincent Arthur Black, for your help in making this book a reality. You have dedicated so much to this work and to every project we have created for the past 12 years; I am eternally grateful.

FOREWORD BY
JOYCE MEYER

In our present day, people are facing challenges that past generations never had to deal with. The temporary issues of identity, acceptance, and peer pressure are forcing people to make *eternal choices*. We need to be equipped through the word of God with the tools and mindsets to make right decisions.

I've known Chad Daniel for over twenty years. His desire to reach people on a global scale has personally impacted my family, and he is someone we know and trust. His ministry products are thought-provoking and engaging with relevant messages to people from all walks of life, always utilizing the power of God's word.

I was compelled to write the foreword to Chad's first book, *The Curse of the Father*, because I strongly believe that this story illustrates the truth behind the spiritual battle that rages in the mind of so many people.

The Curse of the Father is a nontraditional approach to a topic that is rarely discussed in an open forum. This is a unique and compelling story of Chad's direct experience of losing his father to suicide. This event has been a pillar of his global ministry, and it communicates the value of the life we have been given.

Chad has always used object lessons and supernatural analogies to communicate spiritual truths. This story is no exception, and I would expect nothing less from him. *The Curse of the Father* is a revealing look at the insidious nature of suicide and how shame and unforgiveness can prevent us from living a life of freedom and joy.

I personally know the pain of losing a loved one to suicide. Many years ago, my brother took his life after a long battle with depression and addiction. The pain that I felt over this loss is a universal experience. It will always provoke a multitude of questions with very few answers. These are the questions that Chad opens for consideration in *The Curse of the Father*.

Chad takes us through the tragic series of events that caused his father to take his own life, his journey to confront the demons of his past, and the grace of God that turned his mess into a message.

Joyce Meyer

There is a forest that leads to demise.
Two books await—one of life, one of lies.

You must uncover what was left behind,
And face the shadows in your mind.

Alive will become the thoughts you hold,
And turn your soul dark with cold.

In the forest, how long you will toil,
Confined by my prison of roots and soil.

What lies in wait, it shall be birthed.
Yet, from the darkness, you may find your worth.

Your burdens so light, should they be shared,
So come with your friends if you so dare.

Rest in my kingdom, you won't be a bother,
But here you must face The Curse of the Father.

INTRODUCTION

The story you are about to read is one of mystery, intrigue, and darkness. If this type of tale is not for you, I suggest you return this book immediately. However, if you are one who enjoys a good ghost story, the likes of which you would find in any horror film, welcome.

My name is Chad Daniel. I'm a youth specialist, writer, and television personality. For the past 30 years, I've traveled the world ministering to young people. During that time I've learned an important truth: what is commonplace in one part of the world may not be so in another. I believe that in order to live life and live it fully, you need to take yourself away from the familiar and venture into the unknown. Sometimes that can be uncomfortable, sometimes it's scary, but know this: it will always be an adventure.

Ten years ago, I met a man I now consider a close friend and mentor, Dr. Berin Gilfillan. Berin challenged me to begin documenting my global adventures in hopes they could be used to communicate the excitement of following God into the unknown. This charge has put me in harm's way countless times. Over the years, I climbed the pyramids of Giza, chased down rhinos in the African bush, swam with sharks in Cape Town, explored the ancient empires of Cambodia, followed the footsteps of the Apostle Paul in Syria, searched for endangered species in South America, and what's even better is that I've captured *all* of it on video. I've produced television content for twenty nations around the world. And I did this for one reason only, to communicate the love of Jesus to people just like you!

It was this passion, along with a tragic event from my past that brought me to Japan. My destination was an area at the base of Mt. Fuji, commonly referred to as the Suicide Forest. There, along with my television producer and friend, Paul, we set out to create a documentary that addressed the topic of suicide, hoping that this small act could possibly reach hurting people around the world. We were unprepared for the hardships that would confront us, and couldn't have imagined the adventure that awaited. I never thought that 15 years of repressed emotional pain would rear its ugly head there, in the middle of the Suicide Forest. Over the years, Hollywood and YouTubers have taken stabs at capturing the grim nature of the Aokigahara and the heinous acts committed there every year. I have personally seen many of these videos, but their absence of any spiritual truth left me disappointed. So I set out to write my own creative tale, *inspired* by my personal experience in the Aokigahara and the spiritual warfare that raged in my mind while navigating the forest's mysteries.

The Curse of the Father is that story.

Before we begin, I must advise you that there are metaphorical elements in this tale that I have taken creative license with. Hints of ancient cults, demonic entities, and reapers of death are woven throughout this story. These fictional elements are present in order to serve as allegorical devices, provoking you to consider the unseen realms of the spirit and the vicious battle raging for your heart, mind and soul.

Now, if you're still game to join me, prepare yourself for an exciting ride. The first chapter details a scene of me standing in Tokyo Station, awaiting the arrival of my train to whisk me away on this adventure. This is my official invitation to *you*, to join me on my journey into the Suicide Forest. What awaits us is grim and, at times, uncomfortable. But I promise you now, by the end of this story, the train will bring you and me back here safely with a new insight and appreciation for our lives and the lives of others. At the conclusion of this story, I will examine some of the spiritual metaphors contained throughout these pages. Please hold all questions until the end, where I have done my best to answer them.

The train is about to pull into the station; there is not much time left. Make sure you have your ticket and nerves of steel.

Are you ready?

ONE

THE COMPLETE
MANUAL OF SUICIDE

Even before arriving in Japan, and long before I took my first step into the Suicide Forest, I struggled to erase the nightmares I had contrived of it. No matter how many times I told myself that it was all just a dream, a small voice in my heart continued to caution me otherwise. Every mental replay of those horrific mental images persisted to twist those wicked dreams into dreadful memories.

An infinite expanse of corpses hung inches above my head, slowly oscillating in pendulum-like movements from the forest canopy. Their lifeless eyes slithered into my very soul. The earth heaved and groaned beneath me, as if the forest were not only alive, but also nourishing on the decay of those lost souls. Adrenaline-igniting fear shot into me as a malicious voice filled my mind, tormenting me with one thought: *You are going to die here as well!*

My body tensed, as if a noose had flung around my stomach and tightened itself into a fatal degree. Before I knew it, my feet lurched forward of their own accord as howls of rotting cadavers grasped at my heels.

Where was I going?

My mind could not keep up with my pace as I raced towards the fading sun. Darkness crept in through the forest as its hallowed expanses, fatal ravines, and spirits of past guests, grew as recognizable as my own heartbeat.

I stumbled over the personal belongings of previous visitors discarded along the path. I was not the first to tread this unholy terrain, and an ache in my spirit told me that I wouldn't be the last. My feet crashed through a myriad of soiled pages littering the forest floor. Step after step, page after page, all handwritten. Countless lives and untold pains endlessly cried out to be read, desperate to be remembered. But there was no time to remember lost souls. The overpowering pull on me wouldn't waver.

I pressed deeper into the forest, deeper toward the source of the darkness: the Clearing and the Ancient Tree in its center. I innately knew I was destined to find it. What wicked mysteries festered deep within its organic womb? It's where all this started and where all of this would end.

I would soon know the answers I sought, as my feet finally seized their unrelenting pace and my eyes took sight of the ominous clearing. I pressed deeper into the expanse, to the source, the origin of the terror in my heart: the Ancient Tree, the sole inhabitant at the center of this domain. That tree, it was the beginning of all things, and the end of all of things.

As if in the eye of a raging storm, I whirled about in the Clearing, the ground pulsing with life under my feet and the surrounding woods breathing and quivering with malicious intent. Unearthly lights glimmered in the wooded expanse as a cacophony of echoed voices reverberated with high pitched shrills and gruesome laughter. Were they beckoning me?

No.

They announced the arrival of another… an undisputed curator of this wicked domain.

A devilish spirit electrified the expanse with infernal power.

"You are never leaving this place," a perverse, beast-like voice snarled.

Rotting odor assailed my senses and panic flooded my weakened frame as It manifested, violently crashing into the clearing from an unseen realm.

The creature flexed its colossal frame and gnarled its long, sharp face, fiendishly sneering. Its sunken, lifeless doll-eyes narrowed at me. Black scales armored its ogreish form and insect-like appendages extruded from its body, disgorging liquid fire from gaping fissures. Its razor-sharp spades gouged at the ground as It pulled itself through the clearing, like a predator approaching a prey.

This couldn't be real! I had to wake up!

The creature's foul rancid breath stung my face as darkness radiated from its eyes in a black triumphant glow. It was relentless, consumed by an insatiable hunger, as unyielding as the grave.

"You are marked for death!"

Wake up! Wake up!

The creature lunged and my legs buckled.

No! I had to do something! I had to *say* something! But ... what?

I opened my mouth to cry out. But a foreign tongue poured from me. Words emanating from an unknown source shot off my lips.

And the creature flinched, seeming to recognize the adversarial divinity of those words.

Or was it something else that provoked the wicked demon to hesitate?

Yes, I heard it as well now. Accompanying my rhetoric was a deeper tone, ever rising, engulfing my senses. The unmistakable warning of a train's horn reverberated through the shadows of the forest. An indisputable sound of a locomotive hurtling down an unseen track, tearing the veil between two realms.

In a heartstopping stalemate, a vicious smile fractured the bones of the demon's beak-like mouth; then cheeks ruptured, revealing the hideous decay behind its scaled flesh.

"See you soon ... Son," it scowled.

The lights of the train ripped into the scene, finally releasing me from the nightmare, leaving me with a single, disconcerting thought:

Dad?

The siren of the approaching train swallowed up this exclamation as my eyes shot open. Was that just a dream?

Tokyo, Japan.
March 10th.

Stifling heat and hot, creosote and diesel soaked air blanketed us as we stood on the noisy train platform, waiting for our guide to arrive.

A sea of business-dressed professionals stood and waited for their trains. As if on cue, after the locomotives halted, they moved together in one fluid motion. They looked ahead or down, not smiling, not talking, not noticing anyone, especially us: two American outsiders. Today of all days, I didn't mind others ignoring us; we were out of place. We lumbered our personal bags along with two large camera cases packed full with video equipment.

"You ready for all this?" I asked Paul, my producer. Paul Black was twenty years my junior at twenty-five. Unlike my shaved head and goatee, he had short brown hair and wore his full, dark beard closely trimmed and neat.

In many ways, this visit to Japan was much like any other production trip Paul and I had taken. There were, however, some key differences this time. Japan was not our intended destination. We were supposed to be flying home to California. However, days ago while wrapping a week-long television shoot in Thailand, I received an odd request from my friend, Berin.

"On your way back to California, would you mind stopping off in Tokyo for a couple days and documenting what's happening in the forests around Mt. Fuji?"

I soon learned that hundreds of people had been traveling to a specific wooded area at the foot of the mountain and committing suicide. The area in question was named the Aokigahara Jukai, or more recently dubbed, the Suicide Forest. Even more unsettling than the deaths occurring there, was the rumor that these people were killing themselves because a *book* told them to do it. Although my stomach turned at the thought, I had to admit, my interest was piqued. I agreed, pushed our connection back two days, and arranged with Berin to connect us with a local guide in Tokyo. So there we were with packed bags, a 48-hour countdown and no script or plan. Everything about this project was rubbing me the wrong way.

"You up for this? You alright?" I pressed Paul again.

He gave me a steady look before continuing to manage his equipment. "I was alright when we got arrested in Rome, or when I filmed you jumping out of an airplane." He lightheartedly shrugged his shoulders. "And I was alright when you wrestled that thirty-foot python in Brazil." Snapping the buckle on one of the bags he added, "Besides, what's there to be nervous about? It's just a forest, Chad."

Just a forest? His upbeat attitude produced at least ten retorts in my mind. But those quips couldn't come, not with the rumbling of our long-awaited train. As it pulled into the station, I scanned the crowd. Through the sea of humanity, I spotted not one, but two Japanese women in their mid-twenties, one leading the other in a firm handhold. The leading girl caught sight of me and made a beeline towards us.

Two guides?

"You must be Chad," said the shorter of the two, letting go of her companion's hand. "I couldn't miss your shaved head! You look just like you do on TV! I'm Asuka! A-S-U-K-A, Asuka! Not 'Asooka,' but 'Awws-ka!'" The petite young woman with big, wavy hair and a personality to match drilled over her spelling and pronunciation in a way that told me she had to clarify her name for most foreigners. Her words rung with a familiar Midwestern accent, augmented by hints of a Japanese melody and sentences ending on high notes.

"Hey, Awwska!" I said, mimicking her pronunciation.

Asuka nodded to her companion, who stood slightly taller with straight black hair. "This is my friend, Miku. She's an actress."

"Oh, no, no ..." Miku nervously fiddled with a silver cross around her neck as she laughed uncomfortably.

Asuka rushed us along the platform, pointing to another newly arrived train. "We need to get on this one quickly! Come on! We can talk after we board, okay?"

Paul and I hoisted our bags and followed Asuka and Miku through the station, ready to assume the leadership offered by our guides.

We barely made it through the steely doors of the bright yellow locomotive before they slammed behind us.

The floor under our feet vibrated with power as we made our way down the aisles of the cars until we found our seats. The large windows let in the passing scenery and soon the fleeting landscape turned into a blur of motion. The train hummed, soothing our uncomfortable silence.

"Is this your first time in Japan? I imagine you will want to put on your yukatas," Asuka smiled.

"Our what?" I asked.

She grinned, "It's like a kimono, only cotton. You *do* know what a kimono is, right?" She turned to Miku, raising a hand over her mouth and trying unsuccessfully not to giggle.

I humbly smiled, then searched my memory for the brief amount of tourist information I absorbed during the flight. "Only if I get one from Jotaro Saito in Roppongi, I heard those are the best!"

Asuka's mouth fell open as she tilted her head. "So you've done your homework on Tokyo," she smiled. "I'm impressed, but I guess I shouldn't be surprised."

"Actually," I had to admit, "it pretty much stops there ... unless you want to take me to Tokyo Tower to see Godzilla destroy it! I'm always up for a good show!"

Miku nodded enthusiastically. "Yes, yes. Me too!" Her spacey expression made me wonder whether she was trying to be agreeable or if she just didn't understand the joke. I gave a quiet laugh, and settled back into the rhythm of the train.

"So how long have you two been guides?" I asked, trying to break the silence that had fallen over us once more.

Asuka shook her head. "No, no, we are not *professional* guides. Dr. Berin asked me to help you as a favor. I just finished university and had some free time."

Not professional guides? That was a bit of a surprise, but in reality, not a big deal. Back when I was a rookie cameraman, I could navigate most areas of the world on my own. However, as my role in television evolved into the person *in front* of the lens, I started needing the guidance of a third party, allowing me to focus on creating content. But the role of a guide could be filled by mostly anyone that had a general knowledge of the area and (hopefully) even a pinch of competency. Noting Asuka's aggressiveness to get us on our train, she would fit the role just fine. "No problem, Asuka! Happy for the help. So you just finished university? What do you want to do?"

Asuka hesitated then answered, "I'm not really sure yet. I'm just kinda figuring it out, you know? My step-dad says that I should go into administration. It's my personality, I guess. But I don't want to be stuck in an office. I'm sure *you* understand that, right?"

"Of course! What about your mom? What does she do?" I asked.

A shadow seeped into Asuka's eyes. "She passed away when I was nineteen, my first year at university. Heart disease," she said glancing out the window, but the strength in her face remained untested. "She was a nurse before she died. Actually, she studied in Chicago, that's where I was born."

There it was! I *did* know her accent. "So how did you end up in Tokyo?"

"When my mother got a job. I was six when I moved here. And yes, the accent stuck!" she said, flashing another smile.

"Well, I take it if you know Dr. Berin," I added, "you must have some kind of involvement in ministry?"

"No, not really," she said, dodging my eyes. "Dr. Berin knows the pastor of the church I *used* to go to, but it pretty much stops at that." Her hands played with themselves. I knew her uneasiness all too well. Her explanation was a common one when some people first discover that I'm involved in ministry.

I changed the subject, wanting to set her at ease from any illusion of judgment. "So, do you know the place we're going?"

"Aokigahara? Yes!" Her eyes widened. "I spent a lot of my summers there with my mom when I was a teenager. It's been a while since I've visited, with university and all, but how much can a forest change in five years, you know?" She poked at Miku's shoulder. "But Miku's never been. She's too scared. Afraid of ghosts!"

"Do not tell them that!" Miku fired back, her English clearly less fluid than her friend's. She folded her arms and turned away from Asuka. But the subtle embarrassment on Miku's face told me that Asuka's tease was based out of truth; Miku *was* a little scared about the secrets inside the Aokigahara, wasn't she?

"Oh!" Asuka erupted, paying little attention to her friend's pouting. "Chad, I have something for you." She glanced around hesitantly and reached into her purse, pulling out a white book wrapped in plastic, masking its black and red details. "It's the book you emailed me to find. I tracked one down for you, but let me tell you, as I was buying it, the store clerk gave me the rudest looks."

I took the book. Though it was small and appeared innocuous, it seemed to weigh a ton. "Yes, I'm sure they did."

I slowly unwrapped it, revealing its front cover. It had two coffin-shaped rectangles, each containing human bodies. The body on the right looked like a wooden peg doll, while the one on the left was less detailed and seemed to almost overflow as if to escape from its confines.

Although written in Japanese, the book's title was paired with bold English words cascading down the edge: *The Complete Manual of Suicide*. Whatever weight the book held seemed to double as I read those words.

"I've heard of this book," Asuka's voice pierced through my thoughts. She looked around the car as if to make sure that others were not watching or listening. "But I don't know much about it."

My mind raced for words to justify the questionable purchase.

Paul stepped in. "This book is a how-to guide for suicide," he explained gravely. "There are various chapters that detail different ways to take your own life, from electrocution to asphyxiation. The final chapter details a forest at the base of Mt. Fuji that is deemed, '*The perfect place to die.*' The name of the forest is Aokigahara Jukai, also known as the Sea of Trees, or the Suicide Forest. We've heard that hundreds go into the forest every year and never come out."

Miku shuddered, one hand returning to her necklace. "I hear that you can get lost in Aokigahara. Phones do not work there, even compasses are useless."

"Why wouldn't compasses work there?" I asked.

"No one knows," Miku whispered, her eyes growing large, her voice hypnotic. "At night you can hear screams through the trees, or sometimes, laughing. Some people say that they have seen *Yūrei!*"

Yūrei: That was a Japanese word I *did* know. It was a word that had multiple English meanings (as many Japanese words do.) *Yūrei* was an amalgamation of the words "dim" and "soul." It was a word that conjured up dark images, ones that for me, felt all too real. My memory flashed dreamy images of running as fast as I could through a forest of sinister intent with It stalking at my heels.

That was just a dream, right?

"Well, I've never heard of the connection between this book and Aokigahara," Asuka interjected, "and I don't recall any suicide scandal around the forest when I was there as a teenager. Of course, I've been away for a long time. But I *do* remember the stories residents would tell about the forest. Ever since I was a little girl, the Aokigahara has had an aura of foreboding. But that's all just for fun, you know?"

"Most likely," Paul agreed. "I think we should plant our feet in the practical realm for this project."

"Speaking of which," Asuka pulled her feet onto her seat, "I wasn't fully informed about what your video project is about." Her eyes fell onto the book. "But if I'm taking you to the Aokigahara, and we have that book, I think I have a pretty good idea now." She frowned.

Paul motioned for the suicide manual. He didn't seem to feel the unnatural weight of the book as I had. He pensively thumbed through its pages. "Yes, we're going into the forest to investigate the suicides there. This book is one of the catalysts; in fact, many corpses are said to be found with this manual beside them. We want to find out why."

Shifting in their seats, Asuka and Miku exchanged cautious looks.

"I don't like it," Asuka bluntly announced. "I should have been told all this beforehand. This project sounds like sensationalistic propaganda!" She struggled to keep her voice low as every sentence ended in a high shrill. "And you aren't the first filmmaker to travel to the Aokigahara. It's an exploitation of our country."

My stomach clenched. "No, that's not the case! We're not here to smear your country and we don't have any intention of sensationalizing death." I paused. "Look, we are only here because Dr. Berin wants the best crew for this project and apparently this means the three of us." I stopped, remembering Miku. "Sorry, the *four* of us."

"I am an actress," Miku interjected softly, "but not a brilliant one." She hung her head with embarrassment. "And I have seen your films. All of them. No, I was not directly asked to be a part of this project. But I begged Asuka to take me with her." Miku's gaze returned to her friend. "The films Chad makes touch people's hearts. They touched mine, Asuka-Chan." She looked back to me. "I cannot say that going to the forest is a good idea, but whatever the subject, I want to help. I do not have to act in the film, but I want to be a part!"

Taking the book out of Paul's hands, I showed Asuka the front cover. "This book has infected the lives of thousands of people. It has planted the seeds that suicide is not only good but that there is an actual 'perfect' way to die."

Asuka's hardened face began to soften.

"Asuka, we're not here to hurt anyone and we don't want to bring shame to your country. We just want to help. Look, I promise you, I'm not the guy you think I am. I'm not a ghost hunter or an internet clown trying to pull in more subscribers. There's really no agenda here beyond trying to help people understand that their lives are precious."

Asuka exchanged a pensive look with Miku, then sighed, letting her shoulders relax. "When we go to the Aokigahara, please be respectful. The residents there never asked for this publicity, and they don't want it, okay?"

"Yes, absolutely," I said.

"Suicide is romanticized by people," she said, dropping her eyes, "until it actually happens to someone you know ... someone you love." Silence once more.

My throat closed for a moment, feeling a familiar pang. I swallowed hard. "Asuka." She lifted her face. "I assure you that I can relate to the seriousness of losing a loved one to suicide."

The solemn silence that now surrounded us became the bond of agreement between the four of us. It was a relief to have the air clear. There was too much work ahead of us, and our time was too short to harbor worry and doubt. I let my mind wander from the confrontation, but had to fight the thoughts that had plagued me since I agreed to this project. *That dream.* It didn't sit right with me, and it just wouldn't go away. I glanced down at the book and forced myself to focus on the task at hand.

"There," Miku's voice broke the silence. "I can see Mt. Fuji now." She looked out the window and pointed. We stared out the window in solidarity, and rounding the corner, the city landscape indeed gave way to a beautiful view of the Japanese countryside.

Proud and majestic, off in the distance, Mt. Fuji stood tall against a dappled blue sky. White wisps of clouds danced a peaceful and languid beat across the tip of the dark looming mass, while a skirted forest of trees framed its base, holding secrets and horrors we would soon discover.

"Welcome to Aokigahara," Asuka sighed.

As the train forged ahead, moving deeper into the lush, green Japanese forest, I could no longer stifle the thoughts I had worked so diligently to ignore.

The greens and browns sped by and blurred into a memory of another lush forest on another hot summer's day fifteen years ago.

* * *

I stood on my estranged father's back porch in Baton Rouge. Estranged. I hated that word. It sounded so ... permanent. While I remained hopeful that one day Dad and I would work out our differences, I had a feeling today wasn't going to be that day. My eyes scanned the southern wetlands, taking in the brush and trees that poked their heads from beneath the water. Browns and greens against the blue sky all reflected on the rippling water, and I was forced to admit that it felt slightly serene.

The smell of my father's cigarette permeated my inward musings. I sighed. To be honest, I was not even remotely serene. Not here at Dad's house, which was why—even though we lived in the same small town—I rarely came to visit. But today, I had something to tell him, something important. I thought I could feel him watching me. But no, as I turned to face him, my father was not watching me at all. No surprise there.

He slumped in a tattered patio chair that had a little glass table next to it littered with a beer bottle, a recently used penicillin needle, and an ashtray overflowing with cigarette butts. He took a drag of his cigarette, looking distantly out at the wetlands. Though he had a good smile and charming disposition, he always seemed to put both on hold whenever the two of us were alone together.

"So how's all that pastorin' going for you?" he asked, perhaps just trying to break the uncomfortable silence between us.

I forced a smile. "It's good. Eager people, lots to be done." I knew he wasn't interested, so I tried to keep my answers short and positive. Moreover, it was best to not get too deep into my faith since he didn't care for God, much less ministry.

"Yeah, yeah, whatever," Dad's voice trailed off as he took another drag and blew the smoke into the humid air.

My eyes followed the rising puff. I had come to ask him for a favor and I took a deep breath, figuring it was time to get on with it. "You wanna come with me to visit Mom today?" He usually turned me down but with the upcoming anniversary of her death, I hoped that this time …

"Nah, can't."

"But she would want you to be there," I said, disappointed that he would just dismiss my request again, without even discussing it.

"She's your wife," I insisted.

"Was."

He was shutting down faster than usual, but as irritated as I was begin-ning to feel, I really wanted him to come with me. There was a greater mo-tivation to talk with him today, greater than asking him (for the fourth year in a row) to remember his wife. Rather, the real reason I came was about my future. Despite the emotional distance between us, I still had an inflated responsibility to let my living parent know about my plan, and hopefully, receive a blessing of some sort.

This would've been a different scenario if my mother was sitting in that chair and my dad was the one buried. I was always much closer to her. She was the parent who raised me in the faith. She would understand. But my dad … that was a different story. "Listen, Dad, it's important that we go together, because this could be the last time we'll have this chance for a little while."

"What the hell are you talkin' about, kid?" he asked.

I looked away not quite knowing how to tell him. My mind rushed to the imaginary scene of telling my mother this news, how proud and excited she would have been. But that thought made the present situation even harder than it already was. Guess it was just best to say it as simply and quickly as possible. "I got an offer to be a full-time missionary. You remember my friend, Pastor Mason? He's been helping me formulate a plan and I think I'm going to move overseas."

"Mason? Oh, you mean that football player that went to jail for attempt-ed murder?" Skepticism and disdain permeated his words. "Once a con, always a damned con, Chad. Typical jailhouse rat who 'found Jesus.'"

Those words bit hard. Despite his attack on my friend, I knew that the

motivation was deeper, more personal. He was attacking me. *He assumed my plan was just a fluke and that it would probably pass in a week's time. He had always thought this way about me, and though he may have had a point from my past track record, this time, I hoped he was wrong. This was important. I felt like for the first time, I had a real direction in my life.*

"*This is serious. It's an exciting opportunity.*"

He shook his head. "Not so exciting to be overseas."

"*But didn't you travel when you were in the Air Force?*" *I couldn't stop the words and wondered why his opinion still mattered so much to me.*

He took another drag of his cigarette. "There's no money in doing work like … whatever it is you do," he scoffed, condemnation ringing loud and clear. I could feel the subtext of his words.

Money troubles weren't unfamiliar to my dad. He was carrying his own financial burdens. After the sadness of losing his wife, my dad had mostly receded into the confines of his house, and the loss of his job followed shortly after. Now, at the age of fifty-six, when others were making retirement plans, my father was facing the intimidating prospect of re-entering the workforce, a task that had only led to dead ends. The lack of employment was getting to him. His credit cards were maxed out, his savings depleted, and even his home was in jeopardy of being repossessed. I hated seeing him like this: no spouse, no friends, and diminishing connections with his family. As much as our distant relationship hurt, seeing my own father in such a helpless situation stung even worse. "You're not in the Air Force, kid. You barely even have a real job at all!"

This was exactly what I knew would happen. He never understood. "I don't know why I tell you anything," I fired back, resentment echoing in my words.

A moment passed.

"*Listen to yourself. You're not a child anymore. Grow up! You've got a wife that you've gotta support now. And that's going to take some cash, kid. REAL cash. News flash: bibles and communion wafers don't fetch a high price, especially in whatever backend country you're thinkin' about running off to.*" He went on before I could get a word in edgewise, "*You have your college degree, why don't you actually use it?*"

He was direct and he was mean. But even though he was shooting me down, at least he was trying to contribute in his own brutal way. And despite his hostility, the underlying criticism echoed in me as well. They were the same doubts I carried since this opportunity had been offered to me. But unlike my dad, every time those doubts came, I locked them away and labeled them as irrational. But hearing them spoken out loud, they struck resonance, even if I didn't want them to.

"*God, you're just like your mother, 'just have faith and everything will work itself out'!*" he practically spat the words.

"*Isn't that a good thing?*" I asked. "*Her faith is what gave her strength. It's what gave her hope.*"

"*Strength? Hope?*" he scoffed. "*Look where that got her—terminal cancer and an early death.*"

The words cut deep but I tried to stay positive, "*But her faith did prove out. She graduated to be with God.*"

"*Stop that, Chad!*" he barked. "*Just stop!*"

Silence.

"*Your mom's reward for her faith was cancer,*" he accused angrily. "*Cancer that killed her too young. Some reward.*"

That was the heart of the matter, wasn't it? My father was a hurt man. Even if he was trying to help guide his adult son, that guidance was unfortunately out of a place of bitterness toward the rest of the world. I swallowed my retort along with the lump in my throat. I knew if I answered, I might say things that couldn't be unsaid. His words severed my heart with a raw, sharp stab. I didn't want to hear anymore, and even worse, I didn't want to admit that I, too, sometimes had those exact thoughts. I didn't want to admit that even I, a minister, couldn't understand the mystery that would take away such a good person when I needed her so much.

"I just can't listen to you when you keep talkin' about all this God stuff, kid. When you start talkin' that way, I just ...." his voice cracked, "I just keep thinkin' about her. And I don't wanna think about her. I don't wanna think about any of it."

I knew this was his way of apologizing. He knew he had gone too far and I was glad I hadn't said the biting words that would have surely turned this argument into a disaster. I folded my arms across my chest and muttered, "I miss her, too."

He rolled his eyes. "Yeah, I'm sure you do, kid. Be sure to tell her 'hi' for me next time you're in church, okay?" He flashed a baiting grin at me. "And tell her another thing for me, too. Tell her that wherever she is, either 'the promised land'... " he exaggeratedly raised his hands like a televangelist before letting them fall to his sides, "or rotting six feet under, both are better than the hell I'm in."

He held his glare, but I refused to bite. He might be looking for a fight. He might be trying to turn this around and make it all about him, but I wasn't going to stoop that low. I turned my back, making a silent pledge that I was never going to come visit this hostile stranger ever again. It was a promise that I had broken a dozen times over, and a nagging in my mind foretold that I would, unfortunately, keep breaking that promise until my dad finally dropped dead.

So as my dad took another resentful drag off his cigarette, I resigned our talk, along with our whole 'father-son' relationship, to dissipate as effortlessly as his tobacco smoke vanished in the breeze. I let the silence hang between us, sharper than the swaying blades of grass and thicker than the humid summer air.

TWO

ECHOES FROM
BEYOND THE VEIL

We arrived at the Kawaguchiko station, gathered our things, and quickly exited the train. I slipped the suicide manual into my bag, and although out of sight, I couldn't help but feel the weight of it growing heavier.

"Is the hotel close by?" I asked Asuka as she led us through the station.

She remained pensive for a moment. "Well, we are not exactly staying at a, um, hotel, okay?" she replied clumsily. "We're going to stay at a ... Ryokan."

"A Ryokan?" Another unfamiliar term.

"A guesthouse?" she asked, uncertain of her words. "A Ryokan is a more traditional inn."

It seemed fine, but, "Why are we staying at a Ryokan instead of a hotel?"

We arrived at the station's exit. Asuka turned to me and grinned mischievously, "Because this Ryokan was built *inside* the Aokigahara Jukai."

Miku crossed her arms and slouched, "Y-you mean, we are going to be sleeping *in* the Aokigahara?"

Asuka grabbed Miku's arm. "Don't be such a baby," she teased, pulling her friend along.

"I am not a baby!" Miku retorted as they darted through the doors and disappeared into the golden light of the evening.

The exterior of the Kawaguchiko building was considerably different from the station back in Tokyo. Tokyo's harsh cement and shades of grey were replaced with lodge-style buildings with wooden square accents. It was warm and inviting with rooftops that sloped in a similar manner as Mt. Fuji clearly visible behind us.

While Asuka hurried away to fetch a taxi, Miku took an opportunity to ask Paul the questions she was embarrassed to express in front of her friend.

"Do you know celebrities like Chris Pratt or Will Smith?" Her hands met in front of her mouth, trying to hide an embarrassed smile.

Living in Southern California and working in television, Paul and I heard questions like this a lot. It was an easy generalization to make.

"Well, I did meet Patrick Stewart at the airport once," Paul said.

"Patrick … Stewart?" Miku asked.

"Yeah, umm, he played a French captain on a show called *Star Trek*," he added.

Miku looked down for a moment, then lifted her eyes in realization.

" 'Help me Obi-Wan Kenobi' ?"

Paul opened his mouth to correct her, paused, then replied, "Exactly."

Miku smiled triumphantly.

Their chatting became background noise as I took in my surroundings. I watched the other people at the station come and go. A group of teenagers exited the building. They were all talking much louder than everyone else and carried pillows and bags as they boarded a large bus. The bus doors closed behind them, muting their cheerful voices.

A group of European tourists stood nearby, clearly mountain climbers, who were preparing for the massive undertaking of scaling Mt. Fuji. I followed their gaze upward toward the grand expanse. How far would they get?

Finally, I noticed a young Japanese man standing alone. Despite his young age and vitality, he slumped with a depressed and defeated look. His business suit was visibly disheveled. But most notable were his shoes, not necessarily the type of shoes he was wearing, rather how the man treated them. He constantly glanced down at those shoes. Were they scuffed? No. Even at my distance, I could see that the shoes were immaculate. Still, after a few glances, the young man knelt down to buff out a scuff—whether real or imagined, I couldn't say.

From my earliest memories, I've always noticed shoes. They tell a lot about a person. Because my father had served in the military, he constantly reminded me to keep my shoes shined.

There is always one thing a person will be meticulous about.

Our taxi arrived along with Asuka, sitting in front with the driver. As Paul loaded the gear into the trunk, Miku and I slid into the back seat. Once Paul joined us, it was a tight fit, but we made it work.

The driver shifted the car into drive and sped away from the station. I glanced back one last time and caught another glimpse of the young man with the depressed, defeated expression and the perfect shoes he could not stop attending to. As we turned onto the highway, he disappeared out of sight, and the taxi made its way into the darkness of the Aokigahara.

Nearly sunset, the dappled, dimming light speckled the road ahead with alternating amber and grey tones. The setting sun cast long shadows throughout the forest, restricting our view of the landscape. The murky forest floor twisted up and down in wild, unpredictable patterns and left very few vantage points to peer inside at its damp and dreadful secrets. We could, however, observe the trees alongside the road, and unlike forests in the United States, the color tones here were all over the spectrum. Intricate details abounded as oranges, reds, greens, and yellows played back and forth with the shadows and light.

This imagery made the forest seem powerful and mysterious, almost as if it were a living entity, and I couldn't hold back the morbid images I had seen while hurriedly researching this place. Images of bodies strewn across the forest floor forcibly filled my mind. Men and women in desperate situations, having no way out, choosing to travel to this nearly unplottable area to end their lives. I could almost feel their pain and hear their cries and whispers through those trees.

You're going to die here as well.

The memory of that chilling voice from my dream sucked the breath out of my lungs as it echoed in my head. As much as I didn't want to accept it, the forest felt familiar, too familiar. I could nearly place myself in it, running, running from that wretched voice from my dream.

"I have been here for thirty years," the driver spoke to Asuka in broken, yet decent, English. "Many people come to this place."

The driver glanced at me through the rear-view mirror and asked, "What has brought *you*?"

Asuka quickly interrupted and started speaking to the driver in Japanese. For a moment, I was almost irritated with her butting in to answer, but I could tell that she merely wanted to explain our reasoning to the driver in a genuine way. When she finished, the driver soberly nodded. He spoke back, this time, his tone was hushed and low-spirited.

"He says he has given rides to many people going to Aokigahara," Asuka translated. "He knew some of these people were coming here to end their lives. He says that those are his worst days. He feels he should try and say something to these people, sometimes he does. But often, they have the same disposition: distant, vacant … hopeless."

"So, is it as bad as they say it is?" I asked.

The man replied with a despondent laugh, "Yes, sir, worse. Locals do not want to talk about it. It's embarrassing, you know?"

Asuka looked back at me, dismay in her eyes. No, Asuka couldn't lean on the side of skepticism anymore- *it was true*. The Aokigahara Jukai, this place from her childhood, had been mutated into a beacon of death, a landmark for the hopeless to come and end their repairable lives.

"You are doing good work here." Again, the driver's eyes met mine through the mirror. "Your video—people need to know, yes? Residents do not want attention on it, you know. But, I think, if no one knows, how will it change?"

The sun had nearly set as we traveled through the deepening darkness. After a moment, the driver added with a playful smirk, "But, you know

…" His eyes danced between watching the road and the mirror which now framed Miku's anxious face. "Not many people are brave enough to stay *inside* Aokigahara." He dropped his voice and whispered, "There is a legend. Sixty years ago, a young girl was on a trip to the forest with her classmates. The girl was bullied and she did not have any friends to defend her. One night, she ran into the forest to die."

Miku whined from nervousness and covered her ears.

But the driver continued, "Her ghost came back to the camp to haunt the kids who bullied her. All the children, good and bad, were so scared that they ran into the forest, trying to get away. They got lost … never came out. Sometimes, even today, you can hear the ghosts of those children, laughing, playing in the Jukai."

Miku was thoroughly spooked! No matter how hard she covered her ears, she couldn't muffle out the story. "It is not true, is it? There aren't REALLY ghosts here, right Asuka?"

Asuka kept her face hidden from Miku's worried eyes. Instead, her gaze fixated on the ever darkening depths of the Aokigahara. How many childhood moments was she reviewing in her mind? How many of those memories were now turning bitter, mingling together with the Aokigahara's recent reputation? Ghost stories were one thing, but *real* suicides were another matter entirely. "No, Miku. There aren't any ghosts in the Jukai." Her distant voice lifelessly rolled over the sentence in a way that indicated she had told Miku this many times before. "But, I think there's something much worse."

Twilight had settled over the forest when we turned down a side road off of the main highway. The taxi's headlights shone brightly as it made its way along a winding dirt path. Then they appeared: the warm lights of the Ryokan, glowing like an ominous beacon welcoming us. Even in the dark, the inn was iconic and beautiful, a cherry wood structure that stood nestled amongst the smoldering lights, lush greens, and watery reflections of the surrounding pools. Lights glowed through curtains and paper sliding doors in varying degrees of soft white, yellow, and a touch of amber. The driver pulled up to the front and parked the taxi. We opened the doors and stepped out into the night air. The smell of soil and greenery greeted us, and I felt a tiny flicker of calm.

Until I saw...her.

My eyes made out a silhouette, the figure of a woman standing in the entryway, backlit by the luminance of the house. She appeared to be an elderly woman, wearing a traditional Japanese yukata, the type of dress that Asuka and Miku had teasingly referred to.

"Is that our host?" I whispered to Asuka.

Asuka's frozen face grew pale. "Yes, the Ryokan's housemother." Her voice stuttered as her shaking hands nervously gripped her small suitcase. After a moment, Asuka took the first of a dozen hesitant steps toward the traditional building and the mysterious owner guarding its gates. Miku and I followed in her anxious wake.

The housemother bowed with stoic reservation, then evaluated us with a fiery judgment in her eyes.

"Asuka." The elder woman spoke my guide's name in a manner so formal, ice-cold chills washed over me.

Asuka dropped her eyes from the housemother, feeling the same frigid sensation. Asuka opened her mouth as Japanese words hummed and curved from her quivering lips in slow, apprehensive patterns.

The elderly woman suddenly snapped back at Asuka, rebounding with her own foreign words, only her words fired off in a bullet-like rhythm. Asuka's face grew even more pale as her posture steadily sunk into a defeated stature of humiliation. Whatever the woman was saying, Asuka was her target and the shots seemed to hit their mark with lethal accuracy. Then the elderly woman's barrage ceased, leaving only uneasy silence to further glaciate my chills. In an apologetic bow, even Asuka's big wavy hair seemed to have lost its volume as it veiled her repentant face.

Stepping past the girl, the housemother turned her sights on me.

I braced.

Her aged eyes exposed a fierce battle between contempt and life-long self-discipline. Her porcelain skin wrinkled as her mouth formed words in a language that she might have considered a chore to speak. "You are the American from television."

Was it a question, or an accusation? Either way, I walled up my defenses, armoring myself with the singular weapon I had to combat suspicion: Southern charm. "Yes, ma'am! I'm Chad Daniel from California, and it's great to meet you. You have a beautiful home!" I boldly thrust out my hand and offered my signature grin, hoping to God that she didn't detect the turbulence just behind my teeth.

But ... nothing!

The elderly woman gave none of the warm reactions I had grown accustomed to when deploying my volley of perfunctory charisma. That charm had rescued me from heaps of ambiguous foreign situations before, some social, some more perilous. Was this housemother not going to bite? Was she going to drown me in the same pool of shame Asuka still was treading in? With each passing second the woman glared into me, the forced friendliness in my eyes diminished more and more, though my superficial smile remained absurdly intact.

A slight bow from the woman made it clear that she had won whatever contest we had engaged in. She spun, standing taller as she directed herself back into her home, her fortress, and seemed to convey that we were in her territory. Her regulations were strict, and her reign: absolute.

The elderly woman paused at Asuka once more, although her eyes didn't diverge from the Ryokan's threshold and the uninhabited halls beyond. After one more foreign remark, the formidable housemother disappeared through the doors, now matching her physical distance with her chasm of civility.

I exhaled a much overdue breath of relief as all of our eyes communicated a dozen thoughts within seconds, save for Asuka. Asuka's eyes sought none of ours; they were heavily preoccupied with taking in the ominous sight of the Ryokan.

"Hey, you okay?" I asked,

Asuka blinked back into the present moment, but an echo of embarrassment restrained any of her melodic tones. "Yeah, I'm okay."

"What ... umm ..." A blizzard of inquiries and complaints piled over one another in my mind. I couldn't pick out which one to voice first. But nonetheless, a seemingly inconsequential one rose above the others. "What did that woman just say to you?"

Asuka took a few steps on the stone walkway, then stopped at the door. "She said... 'Welcome back.' " Then Asuka, like the housemother, vanished into the warm light of the Ryokan.

I exchanged weighted glances with Paul and Miku with another question filling my mind. What exactly had we gotten ourselves into?

There were no other guests at the Ryokan and the inn had a stale, haunted feel. The only sounds were those of the water fountains which stood out in the traditional Japanese garden, the ticking of various clocks through the halls and our shoeless feet padding down the wooden floors. We arrived on the second floor where Asuka and Miku would share a room. Miku disappeared into it. I found my own room just down the hallway and dropped my bag decidedly onto the floor. The guest room was classically Japanese in every way: no TV, no dresser, no bed. Just a tatami mat and a thin, rolled mattress occupied the far corner.

Asuka appeared in the doorway, her back resting against the frame. "Will this room work for you?" she asked, her eyes scanning the simple room. "The Ryokan doesn't get many guests anymore, maybe because of the Aokigahara's reputation nowadays. Does it have everything you need?"

"Yeah, it'll be fine. Are you alright? What the driver said … it seemed to have bugged you," I asked, still remembering Asuka's distance during the ride. "And now, that housemother. She doesn't seem happy to see us."

Though the color in Asuka's cheeks had returned, I could still see an echo of trepidation in her eyes as she said, "This isn't going to be an easy experience for any of us. Opening old wounds, either culturally or personally, isn't usually welcomed, you know? But I'm glad I can help Dr. Berin on this one. Speaking of which, have you been able to contact him?"

"No," I said. "I haven't had any service since leaving the station."

Asuka pulled out her phone, a pink flip phone with a panda bear charm dangling from the end of it. "Same. I guess it's just the four of us

for now. But I shouldn't leave Miku alone for too long, especially after that ghost story." She crossed her arms. "I'm sorry that I didn't let you know ahead of time that I was bringing her. But as you've seen, she was anxious to meet you."

"It's no problem. I'm just surprised that she was okay to come to the Aokigahara in the first place. Is she really that superstitious about the forest?"

Asuka gave a courteous smirk. "She's superstitious about everything!"

"You two just seem like such polar opposites, how did you become friends in the first place?"

Asuka sat in the doorway in thought, tracing invisible lines on the tatami mat. "Elementary school. I'd just moved to Tokyo. I didn't have a lot of friends in my first year, and I usually just kept to myself. Miku was the same, she didn't talk much. But Miku has always been … a little gullible," Asuka admitted. "One day at school, I overheard some of the other girls planning to play a trick on Miku, knowing she was dim enough to fall for it. They were going to steal her shoes from her locker and hide them. When Miku found out they were missing, the other girls insisted that Miku didn't bring shoes to school that day, had she forgotten? Miku was confused at first, but sure enough, Miku left school without shoes, convinced that she never brought them at all.

"Seeing the poor girl walk out barefoot, I couldn't stand by and let that happen. So I confronted the girls and demanded that they hand the shoes over. Of course, they refused at first. But after a punch to one of those stupid faces, Miku's shoes 'magically' appeared, and I ran after her. She was halfway to the station before I caught up, and her feet had already become black and bruised. When I showed her the shoes, she was so relieved that she hadn't forgotten them at home!" Asuka laughed. "But then I scolded her! She was too naïve, and she needed to understand that some people will take advantage of her good-natured trust."

Asuka stood to her feet and said, "After that I left her, thinking that would be the end of it. But the next morning on my way to school, there was Miku, waiting for me at the station. I tried to ignore her, but she just kept following me like a lost puppy. Every lunch period, every festival, every walk to and from school, she was there. She didn't say much, just followed me like a shadow. I don't think she trusted herself enough to discern friend from foe. I think she just wanted someone to look after her. It's been that way ever since."

"She'd be lost without you," I added, the picture of their relationship now becoming clear.

"I don't know if that's true. Miku is stronger than she thinks she is." Asuka glanced down at her phone again, noting the time. "Okay, I'm going to bed. Tomorrow's going to be a big day for all of us." She turned and slid into the hallway.

But I was not ready to sleep. There was no way I could rest until I had put a punctuation to all of today's events. For that punctuation, I needed Paul as a sounding board.

I walked to the window and looked out at the forest. In that moment, it seemed as if there was nothing more than a great black entity in every direction. I felt almost as if the forest had swallowed me, and this place, whole. I glanced down from the window to the entrance of the Ryokan where we had our confrontation with the elderly woman. She was no doubt roaming the halls of this place, tending to her nightly duties as the inn's caretaker. Then I caught sight of Paul as he leaned against a lamppost in the garden.

I headed down to meet him, and as I neared, I spotted the camera in his hand. He casually took pictures of the silhouetted forest, backed by a star-filled sky and a full moon. He wasn't necessarily taking the photos for the documentary; rather, much like me needing him as a sounding board, this was Paul's means of placing finality on our day of travel. His punctuation.

"Do you have any service?" I asked, holding out my phone.

"No," Paul replied. "You?"

"None." I shoved the useless phone into my pocket and we stood in the quiet, save for the snap of a photo here and there.

"Big day tomorrow," he muttered, not looking at me.

Something was bothering him and he was trying to sort out whatever that thing was. I could tell by his expression he was trying to decide if it was worth bringing up or if it was something a good night's sleep would fix.

"You alright?" he asked.

"Yeah, there was something I was going to ask you." I looked down at the ground as if to search my thoughts. The truth was, there was nothing I needed to ask him. It was just my routine way of starting a much-needed conversation. It was Paul's cue to fire off a handful of reminders of things we might need to discuss. I would then pick one and we would continue. But not this time. Paul was not interested in playing our usual game.

"If I remember, I'll just let you know," I said resigned.

"Yeah, okay ..." Paul replied, returning to his camera's viewfinder.

I frowned, not liking it but accepting *my* cue. I started to walk back into the inn when he spoke up.

"What Asuka said on the train today … I just want to make sure. We're in a very grey area here, culturally and morally. Being here, making this piece … I'm concerned about what this project is going to stir up."

I turned. "Stir up what? Are you talking about how people will react to this piece?"

Paul looked out into the emptiness of the sky. "Maybe something greater than that. This project is different, I can feel it. Maybe it's the place, maybe it's the subject, or maybe it's the people. I don't know. But it's different."

Aha! Maybe he was finally feeling what I had felt back in Tokyo. "Different good? Or different bad?" I asked.

"I'm still undecided." He took one last look out over the Aokigahara before heading back inside the Ryokan.

Yes, Paul *did* feel it.

I sighed, contemplating the events of the day. I thought about the people I had met, the taxi driver, the house mother, the things people had said about this place.

What was true? Was any of it true? What was I going to say about this mysterious forest when Paul's camera started rolling tomorrow?

It seemed like I was no closer to any kind of revelation about the Aokigahara than when I agreed to do this. In fact, everything had become more muddled and convoluted since I started this journey.

A sudden ripple on the nearby pond caught my eye, the dark water trembling from the disturbance. But the source of the disruption was nowhere to be found. Only a handful of shallow, flattened rocks poked out from the pool, large enough to walk upon. The rocks made a trail across the water. The pond, a black abyss, and those slippery rocks, a vague pathway across the void. One wrong step and you'd fall into the dark unknown below. Every jump had to be so precise. It was a lot like how I was feeling about this project. Paul was right, we *were* in a very grey area here. There was a reason why suicide wasn't a subject commonly addressed; there was so much unknown, and darkness of shame and discomfort loomed all around it. Could we find our footing in all of this? Could I lay out those stones to help guide hurting people out of their own darkness? Or would I take a wrong step, and plummet into the void of doubt?

Shivering, I returned to the house which was now dark, all the lamps out.

The ticking of the clocks decorating the entrance of the Ryokan brought a steady rhythm back to my mind. I froze, letting the calmness and warmth of the house give me the respite I needed. My eyes burned as I closed them tightly, and I could feel fatigue setting in; it was an exhaustion so great that I could have easily started dreaming. Best to head back upstairs and catch a solid night's sleep before the (undoubtedly) eventful day tomorrow.

But then ...

SWISH!

My eyes flashed wide as the sound of a sliding door hurled open beside me, giving a clear view of the Ryokan's garden and the Aokigahara beyond. With the housemother absent from view, I composed myself, readying to greet whomever was arriving at the inn at such a late hour. Was it a Japanese guest? An employee? With either option, I was certain I wouldn't have the language skills to help them appropriately.

But the newly opened door revealed no visitor beyond the frame. Only a chilling stillness hung beyond the paper door. I poked my head outside. No one. Was it the wind that slid the door open? No. There was no breeze to be felt. I forcefully tugged at the sliding door, using a bit of strength to unwedge it from its hold in the frame.

Then a voice called out to me from the darkness of the Ryokan's garden.

"Sumimasen!" a soft, youthful, female voice cooed.

I caught sight of her form. Sure enough, a young girl called out to me as she made her way onto the stone path. The glowing lights of the inn began to illuminate her as she approached. The girl wore shiny black shoes with satin bows on her buckles, both the buckles and her shoes soaking wet. Bits of leaves and soil clung to them, creating sloppy footprints in her wake. She donned a black, frilly dress which fell to her knees, European in style, but a fashion clearly from an earlier century. Oddly, the immaculate dress did not share the same dirty condition as her shoes.

The young girl halted at the door, carelessly occupying herself with tying her flowing blonde hair in a long ribbon which matched the bows on her soiled shoes. Black gloved hands gathered wavy strands of stray hair. Her eyes made no contact with mine. Rather, they darted rapidly around as she began to speak hastily, Japanese words spilling freely from her mouth despite what sounded to me like a very un-Japanese accent. Then she paused, as if waiting for a reply to a question.

"I'm sorry, I don't speak Japanese," I awkwardly responded.

Her eyes widened with a twinkle as a playful smile spread over her face. "Ah! English! Yes! I know English very well!"

It took me a moment to rewire my mind to the familiar language. I chuckled nervously, "Yes, English. I'm sorry."

The peculiar girl nodded, but let her big smile fade, replacing it with a tightly closed smirk. "Shall I come in or shall we stand here all night?" she asked.

I realized I was blocking the threshold, but yet I hesitated. Who was she? What did she want at this hour? And did she *really* need my permission to come inside?

"Oh! Right! Sorry, please come in!"

She glided passed me, seemingly familiar with the Ryokan's interior. Her shoes continued to leave muddy prints on the polished wood floors as long, black ribbons trailed behind her in a nearly gravity-defying manner. "Visiting Aokigahara?" she asked, removing her black gloves and slipping them into the folds of her dress.

What was this little girl doing out in the forest this late at night? And in that costume? "Umm, yes, Aokigahara. Visiting." I was dumbfounded.

She nodded, her eyes scanning the inn's foyer. She slid a finger along the cherry wood walls then inspected the pale tips of her skin. "Business or pleasure?" she asked, continuing to stroll the room.

Business or pleasure? I don't think many foreigners would find much pleasure in flying to Japan to visit a suicide forest. "Business," I answered. "And … you?" I asked, curiosity overtaking me.

"Same," she said with a grin, her eyes intently focused on mine. "Eager people, and lots to be done."

Her dagger-like stare induced an anxiety in me that nearly matched the ambiguity of her words. And her accent: deep, almost … archaic. What was that accent?

Her attention drifted to scrutinize one of the clocks on the wall. "Did you come all this way alone?" she asked as her hands joined themselves behind her, her petite frame teeter-tottering on her rhythmically shifting feet.

"No, I'm here with some colleagues."

"Oh, I see! Here to investigate the mysteries of Aokigahara?" She shot a glance and a smirk back at me, both laced with an unsettling mischief.

Me? Investigating the Aokigahara? I couldn't be *that* obvious, right?

She delicately opened the glass door to the clock and, like a skilled surgeon, moved the hour hand forward with exact precision. "This one has a bad habit of losing time." She snapped the cover closed. "The hour is later than you think." The clock chimed as she glanced back at me with a look of undeniable satisfaction. A lively melody echoed through the hall and soon the other clocks joined in, sounding off in their own distinct themes. "These modern timepieces are very useful when they have someone to watch over them." She reached back into the folds of her dress, fetching her gloves. "Now, I must get back to work. Much to do at this time of night."

Work? At this hour? My exhausted mind couldn't make sense of the encounter even as the girl headed back out the door.

I followed her to the doorway, watching her dark visage begin to dissipate into the night.

She stopped abruptly, "How many people did you say you came with?" she asked, slipping her gloves onto her hands.

"Me? Three others," I stuttered.

She remained pensive, contemplating my words. "So four in total?" Her question wrapped in contemplative interest.

"Yes."

The visible breath of a confirming sigh filled the air around her. "I see. Four is an unlucky number here in Japan." She turned to face me. "The word 'four' in Japanese is 'shi.' " She paused, clearly waiting for a revelation that my drowsiness wouldn't allow. " 'Shi' is also the word for death. Any man of God should know this."

My heart stopped. Her words hung in the air between us.

"There is an old proverb," she continued, lifting her gaze skyward as if speaking to the stars, unseen from my vantage point. "It was a proverb told to explorers of the ancient world: 'When four travelers venture into the unknown, only three will return. For the scar of revelation first requires a sacrifice.' " Another sly smile crept across her face. The girl bowed, turned and receded into the darkness of the forest.

Was this a dream? Who was she? What was her business in the Aokigahara? More questions, but no answers. My body froze as my mind raced. *Four* will venture into the unknown, but only *three* will return? Was she referring to us? She couldn't be!

No. These words were simply ominous warnings from a teenager with nothing better to do than to harass foreign guests. That had to be it, right? That girl is probably laughing with her friends about it now as she changes back into clothing from the 21st century. Well, this is one prank that I'm not going to fall for. Superstitious nonsense!

I hoped.

As I made my way back up the flight of stairs, I came across Miku standing in the hallway. She nearly scared me to death! She was looking out the window, frozen in fear, her face pale, and her body trembling.

"Are you okay?" I asked, anxiously creeping closer to her.

Miku said nothing. She remained stoic, staring out the window, the moonlight bathing her frightened face. She lifted a trembling arm and pointed into the forest. "It's *them!*"

"It's who?" I joined the terrified girl at the window and I couldn't believe my eyes. But there it was, right in front of me, a sight I would never forget.

In a distant pocket of the blackened forest, giant flickering shadows danced to and fro. The ominous shadows were eerily human-like in form. They flickered in and out of view in what seemed like thousands of small unearthly pulses of light, blinking with unpredictable rhythms. Worse, what accompanied this were the sounds of high pitched, haunting laughter.

Visibly trembling, Miku whispered in cold terror, "It is the ghosts of the children!" She couldn't stop shaking, one pale hand clenching her silver necklace. Her breathing turned into gasps of fear that echoed down the halls.

I regarded Miku for a moment then peered back to the anomaly in the forest. The oddity was much too far away to make out clearly. Those glowing shapes could be justified by several factual excuses, right? But that laughing, it voided all practical explanations. After just rationalizing the encounter with that strange girl in the black patent shoes, did I still have enough fortitude to ignore a *second* inexplicable phenomenon tonight? I wasn't going insane, was I?

Was Miku right? Were those the sounds of laughter from little children haunted by their ghostly schoolmate? Do I even believe in ghosts?

But just as the tidal wave of questions crashed into me, those ghostly flickering lights, along with the eerie laughter, vanished! The distant pocket of the darkened forest, which hosted the ethereal scene, immediately faded into nothingness, leaving my questions unanswerable and poor Miku's mouth gaping wide.

"What's going on?" Asuka burst from her room just moments too late, rushing to her friend's side.

"The children!" Miku insisted, grabbing Asuka's arm and pulling her to the window. Miku clenched Asuka's hand and expectantly held her breath.

Nothing.

Asuka incredulously waited beside Miku, but I could tell she was quickly piecing together the source of her friend's dismay. "Miku …" Asuka sighed, "the ghost story? Really?" Her empathetic eyes found Miku's hysterical ones. "Come to bed, okay?"

"But," Miku started, still scared and confused. She looked to me. "But he saw them, too!"

Asuka found my gaze in the hallway's darkness, expecting a response. "Well, Chad?" Her eyes widened, almost as if to communicate that Miku needed one more push to lull her panic. "Well? Did you and Miku see ghosts in the forest?"

I glanced back at the window framing the empty forest, both the night and Asuka's patience wearing thin. "Let's … let's all just get some sleep," I said, knowing Miku would feel betrayed.

Asuka gave a proud smile. Miku closed her eyes tight, dejected by me. Whisking Miku into their room, Asuka shot an inquisitive look back at me before closing the door behind her. The paper thin walls gave little muddling to Miku's weeping and Asuka's soft, consoling voice.

For a moment, it felt as though the window and its fleeting mysteries beckoned for my return, and I almost complied. But no, there was so much to be done in the morning.

As I made my way down the darkened hall, one thought continued to plague my mind: The Aokigahara Jukai was not empty. Not empty at all.

* * *

I paced the floor of my living room, last week's argument with my father still on replay. My wife, Shay, sat on the couch behind me watching TV. Shay was slim, stylish and had lots of long curly, light brown hair and a soothing southern drawl. She was watching a travel show set in Southeast Asia; the host was explaining the importance of some ancient ruins that had recently been unearthed. Although it had a cheese-ball tone to it, my wife loved this show.

"You could totally do something like this," she said, her eyes not leaving the screen, "host a travel show."

I scoffed, "Yeah right, it takes a lot of time and money to do something like that, and even this stinks."

"Well then, do something better!" she shot the playful retort and smirked. "We should go back to Malaysia sometime. That was fun."

On any other day, Malaysia would have been a welcomed conversation, reminiscing about the adventures the two of us had there years before. But not today. Malaysia was a world away and my mind simply couldn't go there.

Shay knew I was annoyed, she always did.

"How was your visit with your dad last week? You never told me," she said, getting right to the heart of the matter.

"Typical," I replied. "As expected."

"He didn't go with you to visit your mom?"

*"I didn't go either," I said. "That was the whole point … to go with him."
I paused, knowing that it was time to voice my doubt. "We'll get the time
later, I guess."*

"What do you mean?" she asked, her voice serious.

I was silent.

"Chad?"

*I couldn't hold it in any longer. Throughout the time of entertaining
the fantasy of missions work, I kept a positive attitude around Shay. But I
couldn't keep that front anymore, and if I couldn't be honest with my own
wife, who could I be honest with?*

*"Are we making the right call? Leaving, I mean." There. I said it. I had
finally voiced my waning courage to follow this dream. This stupid, senseless
dream.*

*The TV cut off. "It seems like this is something you're really intent on." She
paused. "Did your dad say something?"*

I didn't have to confirm it. It was obvious.

*I sat next to her, recounting the things my dad had said while I was with
him.*

"Since when do you ever listen to what your dad says?" she reminded me.

*"Well, maybe I should start," I insisted, but she seemed confused. I tried
to grasp for an example. "Look, it's like when I asked my dad about playing football, he told me that he wasn't sure about it, that I might not have
the skill or strength to do it. And of course, when I didn't make the team,
I thought he was right." I stood up, knowing she didn't understand and
returned to staring out the window. I didn't want to see the disappointment
in her eyes.*

*Her soft tone followed me. "Yeah, I get it. Plant here. Get an office job.
Make some money. Settle. It works for a lot of people. But I don't think you'd*

be happy doing that. I knew when I married you that our life wasn't going to be conventional." I could feel her smile.

She continued on, but I wasn't listening anymore. I was too distracted. My eyes had caught sight of a black police vehicle slowly creeping toward the house. Something was wrong; I could feel it.

"Chad?" Shay asked, joining me at the window.

We watched as the vehicle parked in front of our house and two officers exited, walking toward the door.

The knock was deafening. And then another.

I opened the door.

"Are you Mr. Daniel?" one of the officers asked, his expression making it clear that this wasn't a social call. Yes, something was really wrong.

"Yes," I spoke without thinking.

"Is your father, Gene Daniel?"

My heart dropped. Dad? A police officer was asking about Dad!? I flashed to the memory of him sitting on his porch, cigarette in hand, our argument now the last thing in my mind. What happened? "Yes, Gene's my dad, is he okay?"

The officer gave a dutiful look to his partner, then lowered his eyes to his feet. "May we come in, sir?"

THREE

THE SILENT COUNTS OF EXPECTANCY

You are going to die here as well.

The words haunted my restless sleep. That same sinister voice from my dream, it festered like an open wound.

March 11th.

Barely following sunrise, my eyes flew open and I reached for the curtains I had pulled closed the night before. I had hoped they would block out the lingering shadows and the mysterious images Miku and I had seen out in the forest. Whether they were real or not, I did not yet know. The curtains, however, proved worthless and gave little sanctuary. In addition, the paper-thin walls failed to dampen the hours of Miku's cries and Asuka's consoling. Had sleep eluded them as well?

What exactly were those shadowy, phantom-like figures moving through the forest?

I scanned the bare room for the slightest clues that could offer answers, or at least some peace of mind. Unfortunately, the Ryokan in the light of day did not bring any more clarity to the situation at hand. Nor did it relieve the new burdens that last night's viewing unceremoniously dumped into my mind. At best, the morning's dim light merely muted last night's haunted darkness. I could accept that; I would have to.

Beyond my window, overcast clouds had climbed atop the forest, creating an encompassing fog that spread and clung to every tree, limb, and twig. Despite my hopes, daylight had not brought any clarity to the forest either. Instead, the grey fog drifted through the branches, hugging them closely and further shrouding the Aokigahara in uncertainty. But that uncertainty would have to wait. The muffled sound of Miku and Asuka arguing was the more immediate issue.

I found Miku frantically packing her bags while Paul and Asuka were trying to calm her down. Miku was extremely disturbed and disheveled. Her hair was done up in a hurried ponytail, her clothes mismatched and wrinkled.

"I told you!" Miku said, breathing heavily, her eyes panicked. "I am not staying here another minute!"

"Miku, please! Calm down," Asuka said.

Paul shook his head and remarked, "This is ridiculous."

"There is something *very* wrong with this place!" Miku insisted.

"Miku," Asuka said gently, "you were exhausted."

"And you were freaked out by that story the driver told us," Paul said.

"You know how these things get under your skin," Asuka added.

"I know what I saw!"

"You can't be sure –" Paul said.

"They were moving!" Miku insisted. "Giant shadows, blinking in and out …"

"Shhh!" Asuka looked around, on guard for any appearance of our housemother, and whispered, "Miku, it was just your imagination." Auska took a few steps hoping to close the gap between her and her friend.

"I heard them!" Miku pronounced as if that would make all the difference. "And they were laughing and playing in the forest!"

"You couldn't have," Paul stated matter-of-factly.

"Yes, yes, they were laughing!"

"And playing?" Asuka asked.

"Yes!" Miku turned to Asuka but realized that Asuka's question was not admission or acceptance. "I am not crazy!" Then, the distraught girl noticed me and pointed her finger. "He saw it, too!"

I looked over to Paul and Asuka. "We don't know *what* we saw last night, Miku," I said, feeling Miku's furious glare. I glanced empathetically at Miku.

After a moment, she sighed, defeated. "Okay," she said, dropping her gaze. "If that is what you think, then you can stay. But I am leaving!" She grabbed her half-packed bag and stormed out of the room, accessories haphazardly falling out as she left.

I looked over at Paul and cued him to go and try to convince her to stay. Paul understood my request without me having to say a word. He trailed after Miku, who was scurrying toward the stairway leading downstairs. I could hear Paul's remarkable ability of persuasion kick into gear.

"Come on Miku," Paul started.

Miku snapped over her shoulder, "Stop!"

He pleaded, "Don't be like this. We need you here."

"Not enough to put my life at risk!" Miku blurted. "There is something *very* wrong with this place!"

"That's not true," he tried to reason.

She spun around, her eyes glowing with anger. "Not true? Not true?! I know what I saw!" She paused. "I'm … not … crazy!"

"No one is saying you're crazy." He took a step closer and added softly, "It was late, you were tired and—"

"Enough!" Miku snapped away.

Paul glanced back at me, uncertain. But, quickly, his eyes widened with a sudden revelation. "But you have to stay! Because … you're going to be our *actress* in the film!"

The man was brilliant!

Miku halted. I could feel her mind turning over his proposition. Finally, her curiosity spun her around. "What did you say?"

"Yes, Miku! You see, that's why … um … that's why Asuka let you come. It was going to be a surprise! umm… for your birthday!"

Miku's cautious eyes blinked. "My birthday is November the eleventh. That's eight months from now."

Paul's face didn't break. "It's a very late birthday present. For a very, very talented actress!"

Miku's eyes widened, dropping her bag. "A *talented* actress?"

"Of course, Miku," Paul nodded. "In fact, I have a script …" I couldn't help chuckling to myself, knowing full well that Paul had no script for her. "Would you like to read it?"

Miku stood silent as her eyes roamed around the still unsettling Ryokan. She looked out at the forest through the very window where she saw the ghostly images last night. She shook her head just the tiniest bit and blinked her eyes again.

Paul closed in smoothly, placing his hand on her shoulder. "This is a big opportunity, Miku," he said gently. "This piece could be shown around the world—and to *millions* of people." Well, that was a blatant exaggeration, but perhaps, a necessary one. I knew he was desperately, yet tactfully, trying to sell Miku on this, but the way she looked out of the window had me worried.

Miku looked at Paul, hesitant trust in her eyes. "You said ... you have a script?"

"Yes," he answered, backing up a little. "Would you like to have a look?"

Miku picked up her bag again and inched toward him.

"I'll bring it to your room after you unpack," he said smiling and extending his hand.

I knew something neither Miku nor Asuka yet knew about Paul. "Convincing" was what he lived for. Yes, he loved to produce, but more than that, on a primal level, Paul relished in swaying people's emotions to get them to acquiesce to his vision, especially when he knew it would be a win for everyone. I had on occasion, advised Paul not to do this because it could be misconstrued as manipulative; however, it was a very handy tactic when needed. Like right now.

Miku slunk back down the hall, nervously sold on her new role. She stopped as she reached Asuka and I, looking steadily at her friend. "If there are any more strange things," she started, shaking her finger, her other hand fiddling with her necklace, "I am leaving."

Asuka nodded, grabbing Miku's free hand. "Kishi Kaisei, Miku-Chan," she whispered.

Whatever the phrase was, Miku's eyes filled with tears, dropping her head and nodding. After a quiet moment, she turned to go back upstairs.

Pitch closed.

Paul, following Miku, paused at me. "I have to go write a script," he muttered with frustration, and I had to work hard not to laugh out loud.

"Thank you," Asuka whispered to Paul.

Having lost both of our companions as they left to prepare for today's events, Asuka and I made our way into the dining room of the Ryokan for breakfast. The room was beautiful. Paper walls against light, wooden, low-set tables were paired with white high-backed cushions. The open sliding doors let in a lovely view of the surrounding gardens and ponds that reflected the greens, pinks, reds, and golds of the autumn tapestry, as well as the blaring white haze of fog that encased the garden in a haunting stillness.

Asuka and I sat, and to ease the uncomfortable silence between us, I considered telling her more about what Miku and I saw, or what we thought we saw, last night. But I just couldn't bring myself to say anything. The words simply wouldn't form, nor would my mouth give utterance because, unlike Miku, I just didn't know what I saw.

Sometimes, you just don't know. And sometimes, you have to be okay with that.

I smelled the mellow scent of hot tea. Holding a Japanese-style tea tray, the housemother entered the room. Dressed once again in a traditional yukata, the folds of her gown were graceful and charming, even cheerful, if cheer could be found in this place. Little white flowers were sprinkled here and there within the pleats, but not too many. It was simple even in its extravagant quality and design.

Did she dress this way because it was what was expected from hosting such a traditional inn? Or rather, did she find personal importance in it? Perhaps she liked the style and was happy for an excuse to be able to wear it daily. Whatever her motivation, she wore it well.

She silently placed the cups on the table and poured the tea in a manner suited for a perfectionist. Not one drop spilled, and the cups were equally filled.

There will always be one thing a person is meticulous about.

But perhaps our housemother's graceful preparation fell on a man who, unfortunately, had little understanding or appreciation for her respectful rituals; I had no idea the hours of training she had probably spent learning to prepare and serve this tea. Even with my inexperience, however, I could never disrespect the heart behind her efforts. They were genuine and appreciated, if not a little disconcerting.

I gave her a polite nod, "Thank you."

She repaid my courtesy with a stern stare and the slightest bow of her head before retreating from the dining room.

Asuka and I sipped our hot tea in silence and looked out at the white blanket of nothingness. The thick and dreary fog added to the already dark mood that beset our first day. The thing about fog, though, is that you cannot just shake it off, just as you cannot always shake off a melancholy mood. When it surrounds you, it encroaches on your view, and fills your being with its grey rolling vagueness. Fog has a way of seeping into your mind and clouding your already muddled thoughts.

"There's something comforting about a hot cup of tea before a day of, well, uncertainty," Asuka mused.

I sighed, "That sounds like a loaded statement."

She grinned and said, "Perhaps." Her fingers hugged the little teacup, soothed by its warmth. She contemplated into the fog.

Taking advantage of her waning attention, I pulled my phone out only to find there was still no service.

"I gave up trying last night."

"What about WiFi?" I asked, but the slight shake of her head solidified that I would have no signal of any kind for the time being. None of us would.

"Traditional inn," she reminded me.

I stashed my phone, resigned to the fact I was cut off out here until we made our way back to the station tomorrow.

Asuka and I stared into the grey nothingness of the outside world in which we would soon find ourselves. But I couldn't stand the stillness another second. I reached into my bag and retrieved the suicide manual. Asuka snapped her attention back to me.

"What are you doing?" she asked, controlled panic in her voice.

"I wanna know what the heck we've gotten ourselves into," I said, thumbing through the stiff pages. "Would you mind translating some of this for me?"

She stared at the book with reluctance, then looked around the hall, searching to make sure we were free from the housemother's judgmental eyes.

"I believe I can." She exchanged the comfort of her cup of tea for the heaviness of the book. "After all, this is the purpose of your trip, isn't it?"

She took the book with both hands, trying to contain her nervousness.

Opening the book, she scanned through its pages from top to bottom. "What exactly would you like translated?"

"Which chapter talks about the Aokigahara Jukai?" I asked.

Asuka checked through the index and responded matter-of-factly, "Chapter Ten. 'Asphyxiation.' "

She turned to the appropriate page, silently reading the Japanese text. After a few moments she translated its text into short and somewhat broken sentences.

"Well, from here, what its telling you is, you know," her head shook slightly, her hands roamed over the book, feeling its cover as if to find answers, "just the general history of the Aokigahara." Her hands animatedly joined the conversation. They alternated between pointing at the pages, gesturing to emphasize key points, and grasping the book. "This is telling about how you get inside … and the three different landmark points that you can look at in order for you to get to the place where you can … kill yourself and not be found …" She read in silence for a moment, then continued, her sentences now ending on even higher notes than usual, "Okay, so there's a bus stop called Momeshedi … the entrance. It says if you keep going on the path for one kilometer, it's going to come to a point where there are just trees. And then it's talking about … the X-Zone—*here*. The X-Zone is a place where your body will not be found. So if you go just 100 meters into the X-Zone, even though you try to remember where you came from, you won't remember. And it says here if you have a compass, this is the place where you can throw it away. And you will never be able to go back. You will be eternally forgotten by others …" Her voice had lost its sing-song nervousness characterized by high notes. It was low, sad, and heavy.

I tried to picture it: the bus stop, the trees, losing your way in just a few steps, then continuing to walk until being eternally forgotten. Broken compasses. Lost souls. Deep in the forest—in Aokigahara Jukai. "We'll need to get there, the X-Zone. Whatever answers are in that forest, the X-Zone might have some of them."

Asuka began to answer but stopped suddenly, her cheeks flushed instantly, and her eyes widened. I followed her gaze to find our housemother standing beside us, holding the breakfast tray. I had no idea how long she had been there, and her scornful stare at Asuka sent chills through me. Asuka stiffened and subtly closed the book, bringing it into her lap and removing it from sight.

After a moment, the housemother silently set the breakfast on the table. She sternly spoke to Asuka in Japanese.

Silence.

Asuka answered back—clearly repentant.

The woman left us again. Asuka looked around our now vacant room and then back out into the fog.

"I think … the rest of this can be read while en route …" I could tell that the innkeeper's words had an even more sobering effect on her than the text she had read.

"This does not make sense!" Miku's irritated voice cut through our uneasy quiet. "What is the motivation of this character?"

"It's fine, Miku," Paul's voice quickly followed. The two entered the room, arguing back and forth about the script Miku now held in her hand. It was two hand-scribbled pages, clearly thrown together in the last ten minutes. But this fact seemed to remain unknown to Miku.

"This says that she has black hair … my hair is DARK BROWN!"

"It doesn't matter what color hair she has," he said, agitated while trying to wrestle with the camera gear.

Miku looked down at the script analytically. "Why would she be walking through the forest by herself?"

Paul looked at me helplessly and announced, "Hey! The taxi's here."

"There is NO WAY she would be walking through the forest alone!" Miku continued on. "Is she crazy?"

Paul shook his head and headed outside, Miku at his heels.

Asuka and I gathered our things and rose to leave the dining room. Following her as she disappeared around the doorway, the housemother rounded the edge of the threshold, blocking my way.

I stopped.

The elderly woman's gaze fixed on Asuka as she strode down the hall. As Asuka's footsteps grew more distant, I prepared myself for another awkward interaction with the elderly woman. Soon, Asuka's voice joined the chatter of Miku and Paul outside. Inevitably, the housemother's cold glare turned on me.

"Leaving so soon?" The sides of her mouth nudged upward.

I swallowed a lump, along with a healthy slice of intimidation. "Just for the day, Ma'am. We'll be back before nightfall." I forced a smile.

The woman raised an eyebrow, letting my tension simmer.

"And … then we'll be checking out first thing tomorrow morning!" I added, hoping to keep her sights set on our imminent departure.

The woman gave a slow nod in agreement, then scanned the ceiling above us. "It appears that my guests didn't rest well last night. Were my rooms not to your *American* standards of comfort?"

"No, no! The rooms are fine!" I assured her in the most optimistic tone I could muster.

" 'Fine'?" she echoed, head cocking, fingers rhythmically tapping on the wooden archway, marking each quiet second in straining beats. "Or perhaps it was something else that kept you from sleep?" She took a step closer. "*Someone* else?" she whispered.

My mind raced to the Ryokan's late night guest. But I refused to let the subject of that mysterious girl escape my mouth. Instead, I rummaged through last night's events, desperately looking for a different *someone* to allude to. "Miku!" I said.

The housemother's glaring eyes narrowed.

"Ha! Yeah, umm, one of my colleagues, she's … uhh, afraid of ghosts." I strained a humorous smile. "She, uhh … she thinks the forest is haunted." I gave a contrived laugh.

Nothing.

My attempt to break the tension with the housemother once again fell void.

Or did it?

A small smile, crept over the woman's mouth. "I see, ghosts!" But the fire in her eyes betrayed her smirk. "And is *that* why you are here, Mr. Daniel? To capture a ghost on your video recorder?" She took another step closer. "Maybe take your little movie back home? Broadcast it on television to lazy, plump Americans in big recliners?" Another step. "Show your country how troubled we Easterners are? Help those obnoxious piggies feel less disgusted by their miserable lives?" Her eyes poured over me with disdain.

Concrete closed my throat as my own fury matched the blazing glint in her eyes. But as I loaded my own vile retort, Asuka's words on the train echoed in my mind: *Please be respectful, the residents there never asked for this publicity and they don't want it.*

Of course, though the housemother's hostility was obviously uncalled for, maybe a healthy dose of empathy might help. "I'm not here to ghost hunt, Ma'am. I'm just here to understand this place."

But my words did nothing to suppress the housemother's animosity; it only fueled it. "I see." Another indulgent agreement. "And you believe that the secrets of the Aokigahara really lay within that suicide manual?"

The book in my bag hit my heart with a thud.

"That is all you came to the Aokigahara with, isn't it, Mr. Daniel? Some articles on your computer and a book penned by a no-name writer a mere twenty years ago?" She paused, letting the weight of my naïveté fully sink in. "That is exactly what I thought. You know nothing of this place! No matter how much you search, you will not find any answers in that book. It is merely an echo of a much older darkness, welcoming us to all of our ... unavoidable end."

Silence filled the inches between us. It was a quiet that reflected an embarrassing image of my own foolishness. "And what end is that?" The words escaped from me before I could arrest them.

The woman gave a demented nod. "That we are all destined for death, Mr. Daniel. No one, no friends, no god, can stop that. The love and trust we think we share with others is just a fleeting diversion, and a burdensome one at that. Eventually ..." the elderly woman released me from her gaze, shifting it down the hall, out to my waiting friends and seethed, "everyone will forsake our trust, our love." Then her gaze shot beyond them to the misty forest above. "There is a power here that has existed long before ancient time. It holds us in its knotted strands." Her eyes pierced my pounding heart. "If you go there, into the X-Zone, it will hold you, too."

Her eyes narrowed once more, locking with mine. But I was shocked to realize the fiery eyes of the hostile woman now reflected a different person entirely. My dad. I would never be able to forget those eyes; they were eyes filled with years of bitter contempt. The housemother's expression contained the same bitterness that had darkened my father's countenance since I was a child. A flood of tired memories overflowed in me; anger, enmity and my *own* heavy baggage of contempt. I began to sink under the weight of it and my only defense from being swallowed up in it was to respond. I tossed aside Asuka's little voice in my head reminding me to honor our local hosts, breaking its hold on my tongue. An avalanche of offense bubbled up from within me. "Well, at least *I'll* have company. Unlike you."

A dagger-like glare stabbed at me. "Get out!" she hissed.

I stormed passed the housemother, leaving the woman to the isolation she demanded. I was all too happy to oblige.

Leaving the confines of the Ryokan, still steaming from the fight, I found Paul loading his equipment into the back of the taxi.

"You look terrible!" Paul looked me up and down. "You alright?"

"Yeah, let's just get out of here," I muttered.

The team loaded the taxi and sped away, leaving the Ryokan, along with the housemother, to disappear into the thick blanket of fog.

The ride in the car had an aura of quiet, except for the taxi's radio, which softly played a Japanese talk show. The volume was so low that I could hardly hear the voices at all. The hum of the engine and sound of the wheels grinding on the highway added a rhythmic background ambiance.

I gazed out the window and into the passing forest still nestled in the fog. The small bits of trees and foliage were barely able to peek into view as we sped down the wet highway.

I caught the sight of figures in the forest, this time real human beings, two dozen or so forest workers wearing reflective vests and holding long black poles. They methodically poked and prodded at the forest floor as they walked in unity side by side.

"What are they doing out there?" I asked.

The driver looked over at the group of people and answered, "Forest staff."

"Forest staff?"

"They are looking for bodies, sir. They do this two times a year."

It made the occurrences in the forest more real. Everything up to this point had been rumor and conjecture, internet media hype, or just content in a book. But seeing those workers, scouring the forest for the tragic remains of life ... of hope .... It felt too tangible.

Miku fiddled with her cross necklace. I could hear her muttering a quiet, repetitious prayer in Japanese. Her murmuring was soothing, and I felt a slight calm, though not relief. More like the eye of the storm.

As the car rolled on through the forest, Asuka, in the front seat, continued to look through the manual of suicide. She spoke with the driver, seemingly discussing which way to get where we needed to go. He didn't seem as bothered by the book as our housemother.

Our housemother.

My blood boiled at the thought of her.

So harsh, combative, and hateful. But her words: were they true? Or were they simply the deranged thoughts of a person who had spent too many years in solitude?

"Okay, Asuka. I'm sorry, but I have to ask, what's up with that house-mother? Do you know her?" I asked.

"I do ..." Asuka paused for a moment, again, hiding her face from my view.

"Soooo ... has she always been a heinous nutjob? Or is that just a recent development?" I couldn't help but say it.

Asuka's fiery eyes lasered back at me. "Excuse me!?"

Then again, Asuka hadn't heard the housemother say what I had. No, Asuka had no context and I slumped, "Sorry, sorry! That wasn't what I meant."

Asuka held her stare, then resigned it to a sigh. "I had a feeling that's why you took so long to meet me outside. You talked to her, didn't you? I really wish you hadn't done that, Chad." Her eyes fell. "Did she say anything about ... me?"

"Okay, wait," I asserted. "To be fair, *she* mainly talked to *me!*"

Asuka whipped around, burying herself in the suicide manual once more.

Silence.

"And for your information ..." I casually added, trying to lighten the heavy mood, "you didn't come up. So ... do you wanna talk about it?"

Another frustrated sigh filled the front seat.

Quiet again. This time, I couldn't accept the silence. No, there were too many unanswerable questions on this trip without Asuka's secretive background adding to the pile. Besides, she was cornered, trapped in this car with us now. She had to know she had to spill the beans sooner or later, right?

I rhythmically slapped at my cramped knees, letting Asuka know I was counting the fleeting moments of her not supplying me with an appropriate reply.

"I'm just saying it's all kinda weird," I commented nonchalantly.

But Asuka wasn't taken off guard. She seemed to have perceived my easygoing tactic before I had. "It's not that weird," she retorted.

"It's weird!"

"Not weird at all, Chad!" Her voice rose to an exaggerated level.

"Pretty weird, Asuka!"

"YOU'RE the one making it weird!" Annoyance rang in her voice.

I rolled my eyes, vocally musing over the evidence against her. "You bring us all the way out to that backend Ryokan, no beds, no internet, and you *just ... so ... happen ...* to know the housemother personally? And *you* don't think that needs an explanation?" I animatedly brought my finger to my mouth. "I'd say that's actually *beyond* 'pretty weird.' I'd say that's downright odd!" My body shifted to Paul in a proper detective manner. "Wouldn't you agree, Mr. Black?"

"Nope, leave me out of this," Paul deflected.

I turned, "Odd, Miku?"

Miku's quiet prayer ceased as the girl opened her eyes wide. She looked around at us, disoriented. "Hmm? What are you two talking about again?"

"Alright! Alright!" Asuka yelled. She slammed the suicide manual shut, throwing it to her feet. "Yes, I know Miss Ritsuko personally! And yes, I booked us at the Ryokan because I knew her!" Asuka stared straight ahead, spinning her hands in circles, seeming to hope that they would help get her through the explanation quicker. "Mizushima Ritsuko was my mother's best friend before she died, okay? She was the person we would come stay with when I visited the Aokigahara as a teenager."

There it was! Everything made a little more sense now—Asuka's extreme subservience, and the woman's judgmental eyes. It not only explained Asuka's behavior, but it also clarified why the elderly woman allowed us to stay at the Ryokan, despite her contempt of us.

Asuka released a confessing sigh. "Ever since I started spending my summers in the Aokigahara, Miss Ritsuko was like a second mother to me."

"Her?" I didn't mean it to be an insult, but Asuka's sulk confirmed it did.

"She wasn't always like that, okay? When I was younger, she was kind, and adventurous. We used to go swimming in the ponds in her garden, put on plays for the Ryokan's guests, and sit on top of the roof at night, counting the stars, that last one Miss Ritsuko's husband didn't approve of."

"She's married?" I asked, perplexed.

"She *was* … he died." Asuka's voice went low. "Mizushima Fuyuki. He owned the Ryokan. He met Miss Ritsuko while he was on a business trip to Tokyo. I think my mom was actually a third wheel on their first date." She gave a melancholy smile. "They got married. Miss Ritsuko went to live in the Aokigahara, and my mom moved to America for school. But they kept in touch almost every day. Then they reconnected when my mom moved back." Asuka let out another long sigh. "And … umm, yeah!"

A thought escaped my mouth before I could stop it. "How did Ritsuko's husband die?" I asked, forgetting myself.

Asuka gave a nod of agreement. "Yeah, I thought you'd ask that." She paused, eyes dancing over the passing forest. "He, umm, he … killed himself." A defensive, matter-of-fact tone grounded her words. "Just walked into the forest one night with a bag of pills and never came out." Another flustered sigh filled the car. "After the funeral, my mom reached out to Miss Ritsuko too many times to count. Sometimes, she would call back, but mostly she wouldn't. So … when my mom died too …" Her voice grew louder, stronger, seeming to fight against tears of frustration. "That was pretty much the last straw for Miss Ritsuko. She stopped seeing *anyone* after that, just walled herself up in the Ryokan. Now keep in mind, I was a first year university student at the time, and pretty much all I could handle was dealing with the death of my own mom and trying to stay in school. I was so wrapped up in my own pain, I pretty much forgot that Miss Ritsuko was alone in the world now, living in the solitude of the Ryokan. Unfortunately, it wasn't until a few years later that those pieces started to fall into place for me. And by then, it was too late." Asuka shrugged. "When I finally did reach out to Miss Ritsuko, she didn't want to see anyone. Not even me."

"Wow!" An inappropriate reaction, I knew, but the only one I could summon. The story she just shared was a lot to take in. "Wow, okay. I am SO sorry, Asuka!"

She shook her head. "Don't be. It is what it is. I just thought with university finished and an excuse to come out here for work, I'd give it a shot, maybe try to reconnect with her. I didn't think it would be such a … *thing* with you, okay? Besides, Miss Ritsuko is just as closed off as I feared she would be. I don't think there will be any fences mended between us now." She gave another shrug, but the strength in her face remained undefeated.

Now it was only the random bumps in the road and the jolts of the taxi that counted the silent moments between us. "Let's just forget about it, okay?" Asuka said, retrieving the suicide manual once more. "We have a job to do."

I closed my eyes, letting another picture become clear.

What becomes of us when the love of others is snatched away in a moment's time?

Asuka caught sight of one of the landmarks from the book; a tree along the road with a black squared piece of wood attached by nails. The white symbols contained a cryptic message assumingly meant for those who wished to be lost in the forest. "I think we're getting close."

She was right. The forest had become even thicker as tree after tree reached skyward from the dark, damp earth. Branches overlapped each other, creating a patchwork canopy.

What was I doing? Here I was, leading the four of us into the depths of a forest guaranteed to make you lose your way. Was there the possibility that we, too, would soon be counted among the forgotten?

What if we lose our way?

No! I was sure we would be okay. Paul had precautions. We came here intending to come out again. Argument closed. Only, deep down, I knew it was just opening.

I felt the car slow to a stop and heard our driver's voice announce we had arrived. With the work at hand, my insanely industrious imagination would have to cease. We all stepped out of the taxi to take in our new surroundings.

"Where are the birds?" Miku quivered once the sound of the taxi could no longer be heard.

We all stopped and listened. There was no singing, no chirping, no scuttling along the branches. There were no scurrying little footsteps on the ground either. The silence was a tangible, breathing entity, as enticing as it was foreboding. It marked this place with a finality, its distinct punctuation.

Asuka stepped toward a big wooden sign at the start of the path ahead of us, and she read it aloud:

> *"Your life is a precious gift from your parents.*
> *Please think about your parents, siblings, and children.*
> *Don't keep it to yourself.*
> *Please get help.*
> *Don't go through this alone."*

Paul stood with his arms crossed, looking down the pathway. I wondered what he was planning but I knew better than to ask. This was his forte; he would visualize and let the sights and sounds (or lack thereof) inspire his next step.

After serious contemplation, he nodded. "Okay. We can do an opening right here."

Both Asuka and Miku stayed quiet during the process of setting up the shot. They seemed to instinctively know better than to try to offer their help.

Once the camera was set up, Paul guided me to stand at my mark.

But the haze of the housemother's malice and the tragic story Auksa had shared clouded my mind even more than the fog clouded the depths of the forest behind me.

So many questions. Not enough answers.

The red tally light flashed on, Paul gave me my cue, … and I was speechless. Seconds passed. I opened my mouth. Nothing. I felt my heart beating and my mouth dry. Frustrated, I took a deep breath and readied myself again. I looked past the camera to Paul and then to Asuka and Miku. They all stood looking at me, expecting … all three of them … expecting ….

* * *

I stood in my living room. All three of them looking at me. Shay and the two officers. All three of them … looking … expecting …

"Y'all wanna sit?"

We sat.

Uncomfortable silence.

"Sir, I have some bad news. I hate to have to tell you this, but your father is deceased."

Deceased. That word. The word I feared since I watched their police car pull up to my house. But … my father? What? What was he saying?

"We don't have much information. He was found dead in his kitchen, a neighbor discovered him this morning." The officer shifted in his seat. He looked through his small black notebook as my brain scrambled. Deceased? Dead … my father was … dead? This was a mistake, right?

"Wait, what?" I asked.

Only silent nods returned to me. The officer looked down to the floor, then back at his notebook. No, there were no more details. No answers. Just an empty fact.

"You are the only family member we could get a hold of. This is obviously a shock, we know. We are very sorry, sir. We hope to have more details once an autopsy is done."

Autopsy ... no, this isn't right. An autopsy on my dad?

Numbness.

Silence.

A scribbled number on a page torn from the notebook.

It was hot in my hand.

"You can call this number," the officer continued. "They will be able to provide the details once the autopsy is done. They will also tell you what to do next."

They stood.

Sympathy extended.

Shay shut the door.

My God ... what?

My hand latched onto Shay's.

"Chad...?" *I could hardly hear her.*

"This doesn't make any sense." *Finally words came.*

Shay's eyes were wet.

"I didn't notice anything wrong."

Deceased ... how? Did he have an accident? A neighbor found him ... he was at home ... his home ... the one I was just with him in. Dad ... sitting in that tattered chair ... his chair ... talking, breathing ... and now .... deceased.

Deceased. The word defiled the memories.

No, this can't be right! What happened to him?

I had to know, I had to have the answers. If the officers didn't have them ... I needed to find them myself.

Oh, Dad ... How long was he there in that house? Alone, dying ... scared.

I stood in a fog and grabbed my keys. "I've got to get over there!"

* * *

I felt Paul's hand grip my shoulder. "You okay? Looks like you spaced out there for a moment." He smiled, pulling me away from the memories.

"Yeah, sorry." I hesitated. "I just …" I looked back to the pathway. The Aokigahara, this place of tragedy, a tragedy that felt all too intimate to me. "What if you're right, Paul?"

"Right about what?"

"What you said last night. What will be provoked if I do this?"

"It's cause and effect. It could provoke everything. It's Pandora's box, man. Always is. Once we open it, everything changes, and there's no going back. I don't know what this will provoke. But, neither do you. But like you have always told me, if what we make can help one person, isn't that worth the risk?"

Of course, he was right. And if it did help just one person, it was worth every risk. "Okay," I said, "so what's the angle here?"

Paul shook his head. "There isn't any angle on this one. We just … don't know yet."

How could we know where to go with this one? No script. No path. Just like this forest, it would be so easy to get lost in this project. But I tried to remind myself in that moment of all the times someone *greater* than me has stepped in when I had nothing in my hand or my head.

"You got this?" he asked.

"Yeah. I got it."

Paul returned to his camera. Once again, the red light flashed on.

I looked intently at the camera before turning slightly to look behind me into the darkness of the forest. I pondered the many ghosts of this place, both past and present. Considering them and the hopes of preventing just one person from joining them, I turned back to the rolling camera and took a starting breath, hoping that if my words couldn't come, *His* would.

FOUR

THE THINGS WE
LEAVE BEHIND

The mind is devious by nature, isn't it? It can create lurking shadows in the corner of our eyes, whispering vicious deceptions and counterfeit truths.

As I took my first steps into the Suicide Forest, I wish I could tell you that I had the courage to rebuke that corrupt voice in my mind, but that, too, would be a lie. To my own demise, my doubt allowed that voice to take root in my heart, concealing its wicked existence from Paul, Miku and Asuka. My anxiety of the Aokigahara fueled that little voice into a roar, repeating one evil "truth" in a paralyzing tedium: *Don't trust them.*

The depths of the Suicide Forest were just as chilling as I had imagined. After an hour of standing outside its entrance, recording the opening of our piece, we began to slowly make our way deeper into the forest—deeper towards the X-Zone. Paul and Asuka led the group with Miku right behind them. Not in the mood to talk to any of them, I brought up the rear. It seemed that this forest had sucked out all my would-be thoughts and replaced them with a heavy dose of apprehension.

The hour we had just spent laying down our 3-minute open left me exhausted. As long as I had been in this industry, I still found it astonishing how only 3 minutes of film could take so long. And this particular project, well … it was already taking everything out of me, wringing out my mind. And this was just the beginning.

I couldn't worry about it now, though. For the moment, I just needed to gather my thoughts and take this place in. Since it was my job to verbally convey the secrets of the Aokigahara, I would have to find the words that now escaped me. Those lost words seemed to drift through the leaves and through the sideways tree trunks like the fog that never seemed to disappear.

I pondered why so many of the trees grew sideways. They literally crisscrossed everywhere without rhyme or reason. Some even lay on the forest floor, and our footsteps crunched the twigs and leaves as we stepped over and around them. The sky was still a glowing white blanket, barely visible through the thickness of the upright branches and leaves. Beautiful, yet terrifying, green branches created a mass of tangled webs, reaching out in finger-like mazes. These labyrinths were designed to make you a memory. Or in this case, not even a memory—just lost, just gone.

Trinkets from bygone visitors littered the forest floor, or perhaps, not visitors … victims. Victims who never made it out. Did some of them stop and go back, changing their minds? Massive bottles of sake and other alcohol lay smashed against boulders of all sizes, creating a sparkling glitter of broken glass along the trail. This hardly cheerful glitter indicated that certainly, at least some did continue, their feet crunching through the twigs toward their unknown destination. But what really gripped my heart were the school bags that were carelessly dropped and unceremoniously left behind by young people.

How long had they lain in the dirt, covered by fallen leaves and twigs? Then there were the shoes. So many shoes left behind! This seemed to be the greatest mystery to me. Why would they take them off and leave them? Wouldn't the forest floor hurt their bare feet? Was it in reverence, like when they would have entered their homes? Were they "coming home?" It wasn't a thought that I relished, and I tried to push it aside. By now, we had seen dozens of pairs on the forest floor. Shoes of all different types: work boots, school shoes, slip-ons, and even dress shoes.

Dress shoes. I remembered the immaculately clean pair of dress shoes worn by the disheveled man at the train station. It seemed so long ago, though, in reality, it had been less than twenty-four hours since I noticed him wiping the imaginary dust off his immaculate shoes. They were perfect shoes—perfect for carrying him to an important destination, perfect for leaving at the "front door" as he entered his home.

Then a similar pair of dress shoes caught my eye, and I caught my breath. Dread filled me as I knelt down to examine them, not noticing as my group continued ahead. No, these not-so-perfect dress shoes were much larger and more worn out than the pair I had seen yesterday.

Relieved that they were not the cherished shoes of the disheveled man, I couldn't help but notice the details. They had yellow stitching on the soles and were scuffed beyond repair. Each shoe had a hole where the big toe would have worn it out, one a little bigger than the other, and the laces hung open, morbidly untied. I stared at the shoes, and my thoughts drifted as I wondered who the possible owner could have been. Or rather, who the probable *person* could have been. It was a *person* who wore those shoes. A *person* who took them off. A *person*. Were these, indeed, the last pair of shoes that this person ever wore?

My eyes then caught sight of an anomaly that loomed over the countless others; a beige nylon shoulder bag. It was inarguably aged beyond the rest of the abandoned effects. As I examined the bag, the only object inside was an old weather-worn journal. The book's pages remained intact, preserved from the full onslaught of the elements.

I slowly removed the book from its protective confines. Soil and dead leaves fell from its leather-bound cover. The cover no longer had its outer spine but was just barely held together by the failing inner binding. Ragged pages, brown and tattered, lay uneven and unkempt.

Who wrote in these pages? What was their story? Was this their last attempt to *not* be forgotten? My fingers trembled as I opened the book and carefully thumbed through the fragile paper. As expected, the words were in Japanese, unreadable to me. The handwriting was neat and calm, but other entries were erratic. The dilapidated book became a weight that I could not, *should not* carry. I went to place the journal back where I had found it.

But as my hand reached out, I felt a nauseating ache in the pit of my stomach. A darkness swelled in my mind and dizziness ensued, like stepping off a high speed roller coaster.

I looked up and down the path, thinking that the sight of my group on the trail would make me feel better.

But they weren't there!

Panic!

There was no way I could have knelt in the leaves and brush long enough to lose track of them entirely, right? And they wouldn't just leave me behind. Would they?

Wouldn't they?

Alarmed, I pushed the appalling thought away and looked in the opposite direction. Perhaps I was turned around? Still no one.

Then, I spotted *someone*. Only it wasn't Paul or anyone else in my group.

Off the trail, deep in the forest, and barely visible through the fog and trees, stood a lone figure, staring back at me.

Who was it?

From such a far distance I could barely make out the man's features. He made no movements, gave no greeting, a long dark shadow amongst the trees. I closed my eyes, refocusing them in the hopes that they were playing tricks on me. Perhaps I was mistaking him for a tree stump in the fog and shadows.

But upon opening my eyes once more, there was no mistaking it, no mistaking *him*. He was as real as the discarded objects that laid between us. Nausea again overpowered me. Could I marshal the courage to approach him? The obscure visage provoked a volley of disheartening emotions.

Don't trust them. The words echoed in my mind again, seeming to belong to that ghostly figure. *Rest in me.*

Dread enveloped me as if standing at the edge of a precipice, gazing into an abyss, beckoning me to retreat from my sanity and fall into its black expanse of chaos.

A strong hand grabbed my shoulder and I nearly jumped out of my skin. My eyes snapped up at my three companions who stood right beside me. Where had they been? Where had they come from without making a sound?

"You okay? You're acting weird," Asuka said. I whipped back around to the ominous man. He was gone.

"I know. Sorry." I scrambled to my feet. "I'm okay," I reassured her. However, I couldn't rid myself of the image of the figure I saw. He was seared into my mind.

Miku searched me, her eyes troubled. I pulled myself together and tried, for her sake, to play off the moment as casually as possible. The poor girl wouldn't take well to experiencing any other strange incidents today. I smiled and sighed as though relaxed.

"Let's keep going just a bit longer," Paul suggested. "Then we can take a break, alright?"

"Sure, whatever you wanna do!" I forced a smile. A small shrug finished the act and ... success.

Miku's eyes lowered. She bought it.

They all bought it.

We continued on the path, and as the group began to walk ahead of me again, I glanced back into the forest once more. There was something so familiar about that figure, something I couldn't quite pin down.

Minutes later, we arrived at the end of the pathway. Only woods and unmarked forest floors lay ahead. The trees grew even thicker, covering the view of the sky in patterns I knew I would never forget. Like the figure, they engraved themselves into my mind. I could only assume that the rest of the forest would continue the trend.

No wonder people got lost in here. What were we thinking, about to step off this path? From this point on, it would surely grow more and more difficult to find our way. The question was—would we be able to make our way back?

This was crazy, but we had no choice, right? In order to bring this story to light, to help even one person, it was a risk we had to take.

"How close do you think we are to the X-Zone?" I asked Asuka.

Asuka looked through the book and shook her head, "We still have a way to go."

I glanced back down the pathway and my mind blanked, trying to place the image of that shadowy figure once more.

Did I know that man?

Paul rummaged through his bag and pulled out a role of red tape. He tore a piece and fastened it to one of the trees. As he stepped back, our eyes fixed on that red strip of tape as it stared blankly back at us. We all felt its importance, knowing it would be our best chance, maybe our *only* chance, of making our way out of the X-Zone. That red tape was our trail of breadcrumbs we could follow back to the pathway, back to safety, back to our exit point.

"Okay," Paul nodded, his eyes still focused on the tape, "I think this will work. We place a strip of tape every 60 seconds. That way, upon returning, we'll know that our next marker is roughly a minute away."

"Like the suicide manual says," Asuka added, "'compasses don't work either. So it would be best to just throw them away at this point.'"

"Who owns a compass in this day and age?" Paul smirked.

"Good point," Asuka nodded.

We all hesitated, contemplating the next moves.

"Alright," Paul said. "Let's take this slow." He lifted his foot and took the first step off the pathway as we all held our breaths. There was nothing left to do but follow him as the darkness of the forest swallowed us whole.

We trudged through the rough forest bed, placing tape every 60 seconds, only stopping now and then for Paul to collect some short landscape shots or photograph poignant pieces of discarded possessions. These were the habits of production work that we had perfected over years of working together, and they helped bring a sense of normalcy to our journey. Asuka and Miku walked closely together, softly whispering to each other.

"Chad," Paul called out to me, "can you grab me the 24-70 lens from your bag, please?"

I reached into my bag. But instead of the lens, I was shocked to feel a dirty, unexpected object. I pulled out my hand and it was soiled.

What? I turned to Paul, but he was too distracted to notice my confusion. Taking advantage of his preoccupation, I reached back in again and felt ...

My heart stopped. My fingers distinguished the dirty and unmistakable rectangular edges of the worn out journal I had been looking through back on the pathway! *Impossible.* Unless? Did I thoughtlessly tuck it away in the fog of the moment? How else could it have gotten into my bag? I tried to remember if I had stowed it away, but I couldn't. Still, here it was, so I must have, right? I pulled out the book, no longer caring that my hands were now filthy from its dirty cover. A small etching on the lower left-hand corner read in English, "Dreams."

Dreams. What dreams did this book's author have? What did he or she hope for? What did they lose? What brought them here? It was heart-wrenching to think that they had given up on all those dreams. Instead, they had come here, to the Aokigahara. They had intentionally tucked their dreams away, no longer able to believe in them. How could I have taken this book?

"What's that?" Paul's words startled me.

"What's what?" I froze, responding instantly, as a child caught with their hand in the cookie jar, stalling the inevitable. He was on to me! I stashed the book into my pack and turned to Paul, only to find that he wasn't staring at me or the book. Relieved that it was now snugly put away, I followed his upward gaze. Confused, I looked back at Paul but he wasn't looking intently at any one thing. More like he was *listening* in a certain direction.

"Do you hear that?" he asked, frowning.

Until now, all I had heard was my pounding heart, but as it settled into a steady rhythm, I held my breath and kept silent. After a moment, I thought I could hear something. "Yeah …. Is that music?" The sound was faint but undeniable. Music was being broadcast from somewhere in the forest.

"Do you hear that?" Miku asked as she hurried over.

♫ *A new morning has come. A morning of hope. Open your heart and fill it with happiness.* ♫

The music, though faint, undeniably chimed forth, filling the foggy sky. Happy, child-like, with a catchy and cheerful tune, it was a juxtaposition that implied a balance between calm and creepy. Uneasy, unable to speak, we all looked at each other and around the forest, listening to the faint melody.

"Where is it coming from?" Miku broke our silence, fiddling with her necklace.

Asuka shrugged. "It could be coming from anywhere." She was right. It was impossible to determine its direction.

Another moment passed as our ears attempted to search for the source.

"Let's keep going," Paul said. "Just a bit longer."

"Yeah. Sounds good," I agreed nervously.

Miku shook her head slightly, her eyes filled with fear.

"Come on," I encouraged her, and she opened her mouth as if to speak, then pressed her lips together.

"Come on, Miku," Asuka said with empathy, taking her friend's hand.

"It's okay," Paul reached out and laid his hand on her shoulder. "How about we go a bit farther?" Seeing her eyes flicker, he coaxed her more, "Just a little more."

Miku stared at each of us incredulously before taking a deep breath and uttering something under her breath. Asuka pressed closer to her side, and we continued on.

♫ *The sky is big and blue. The wind is full of fragrance.* ♫

I tried and failed to shove that melody out of my head. As we headed farther into the forest, I figured it would fade away eventually, but it only seemed to grow louder.

♫ *Open your heart and let it in. It's as easy as one…* ♫

♫ *…two! …* ♫

♫ *…THREE!* ♫

The louder the music grew, the more miserable poor Miku appeared. There was no doubt we were heading closer to its source. Minutes later, we were proven correct as we discovered the tune's origin in a small treeless expanse populated solely by an ominous watchtower.

The wooden tower stood square and three stories tall, the top of which (from our ground-level perspective) housed a wide veranda, giving an unobstructed view above the forest line. It was crowned with a traditional sloped Japanese rooftop, supported by angled beams at each corner.

A long, wooden staircase flocked the structure, turning again and again as it wound its way up from the forest floor to the top of the watchtower, and leading into a simple outdoor deck with wooden chairs that sat in and between the shadows and light that filtered across them.

Yes, it was just as we suspected; the tower was the source of the music. Four large, heavy-duty speakers were mounted under the roof's overhangs, each facing a different direction and blaring that music, beckoning anyone within earshot to come.

♫ *Let's spread our wings and marathon across the sky! It's our destiny and it suits us well.* ♫

♫ *It's as easy as one...* ♫

♫ *...two! ...* ♫

♫ *...THREE!* ♫

Having no clue what to do with this new situation, Miku and Asuka turned back to me, seeking guidance for their next move. As I studied the tower, I could see something moving on the third floor ... a person, waving furiously at us.

I looked around quickly to make sure that we were *all* seeing him, not just me. Paul, Asuka, and Miku all timidly waved back. From his uniform and baseball-like cap, I deduced he was a park ranger, like the ones we had seen before. Only instead of sweeping the forest for bodies, he was up a tower blasting music across the Aokigahara.

Smiling at us through his goatee, he waved us to join him. With a friendly tone, he yelled out something in Japanese.

"What did he say?" I asked Asuka.

"He said to come upstairs," she shrugged.

It wouldn't be wise to decline this official's invitation, right? I looked back at Paul. He looked up at the man, then glanced back into the forest toward the tantalizing mysteries of the X-Zone, and finally met my eyes. This was the next step on our journey, whether we wanted it to be or not.

"What do we have to lose?" I shrugged.

Asuka and Miku nodded in agreement, and though none of us could be certain of what to expect at the top of that tower, I led our way to the foot of the wooden stairs. Gripping the handrail and looking up to see the park ranger wave again, I took the first step up the long stairway.

The red patch on the ranger's uniform shirt made me think of the red tape we were leaving behind every 60 seconds to mark our journey. Funny how an innocuous roll of colored tape can mark a situation of life or death. Like the yellow tape you find at a crime scene. The forest disappeared as my feet climbed upward on their own accord.

* * *

My father's house was marked with yellow caution tape. Do not enter.
10:00 pm. It had taken me hours to gather the courage to go there.
Police officials: long gone.

I could now do my own investigation. What answers would I find? Did I
want to know the truth? This house that held so many precious memories for
me now had morphed into a crime scene. And like a crime scene, I had to go
in secretly with only a small flashlight. Through the front door? No, locked
I'm sure. He had taken the key from me long ago.

I circled the house, and passed the deck. His ashtray still held the cigarette
butts next to the chair where I saw him a week ago. Where I last spoke to
him. I pressed against each window. Most were all locked up tight. Symbolic,
I suppose. Finally, I found an opening, a small, unlocked window. His bath-
room window. Putting my hands on the wooden sill, I hoisted myself into the
opening and crawled through.

The faint street lights illuminated the otherwise lifeless home. Orange
light. Heavy shadows. The distinct smell of mothballs and cedar lined closets.
I looked around the house. The empty house.

My heart ached.

Oh, Dad …

Flashlight in hand, I navigated to the kitchen. The place where they had
found him, in front of the refrigerator. I opened it, careful not to step where…

Inside the refrigerator the tiny light blared white and bare. A couple of
apples, an old carton of milk, eggs.

And there it was, the anomaly: a metal cookie sheet filled with a number of used syringes. There had to be something, some evidence of his death, and there it was. Used syringes, more than two dozen of them. An overdose? Did Dad …? I couldn't ask the question, but I didn't have to, the syringes … that cookie sheet screamed the answer.

I shut the door, and the little light gave way to shadows.

Nothing made sense!

Next, to the living room. I silently searched through his paperwork and unopened mail. Stacks of magazines. Stacks of books.

Neatly tucked away in the catalogues next to the TV, a green spiral notebook.

I thumbed through the pages filled with his writings. An unadulterated glimpse into his heart—raw, and unfiltered.

Resumes. A list of money owed. Never enough money. No future. No friends. All those lists wrote his story. The story of a lost man. The story of lost hope. The story of my father's desperate search for something more. Lists that solidified that he would never make it through.

I continued to look through the notebook. There had to be something. Anything.

And there it was. An entry written unlike the others, addressed to his children. My heart sank. Clearly, his final words. No, my father's death was no accident; that fear had been hovering over me all night, and this was the proof …

"Dear kids. After the death of your mother, life didn't have much meaning to me anymore. I've tried to reenter the workforce with no luck. This world can be very, very hard and the most important thing in this life is having money."

Then to me, "Chad, I never wanted anything to do with your holy roller Jesus. You are my greatest disappointment, a freak, a fanatic ... I don't want you to have anything to do with my funeral. There are a few life insurance policies that are available, but Chad, I've taken you out of them. I've left you nothing, Kid."

The floor fell out from under me. I was free-falling. The notebook fell from my hands and disappeared into the blackness.

Oh, Dad ...

FIVE

WHISPERS IN THE DARK

Each step up the wooden stairs of the watchtower, my mind raced faster and faster.

Was this actually a forest ranger? Could he be a crazy murderer that had killed the resident ranger and had been posing as a park official to lure unsuspecting hikers into his outpost of *death*?

My overactive imagination was the result of having watched too many crime movies and not getting enough sleep. I had to get a hold of my thoughts!

However … things do happen …

As we climbed the stairs, a quiet nervousness washed over all of us. The staircase was still wet from the morning mist that insisted on hanging low in the sky. The damp wood beneath my feet, the moisture in the air I breathed, the heavy greyness keeping out the sun … it was all too unnerving.

Miku whispered to Asuka, "Are we in trouble?"

No answer.

We reached the top and arrived at the forest outpost. The ranger greeted us casually. He stood slumping as he leaned over the guardrail. Arms folded, he wore a courteous smile on a face that wasn't far from middle-aged.

He sported a neatly kept black goatee and longish hair that curled out from beneath his cap. While his face appeared youthful, his eyes were old and weary, having seen too much heartache to bear in this life. It made sense, given his station here in the Aokigahara. How many lives had he seen slip past him to go into the other world? How many people had he tried to stop and save?

Asuka instinctively took the lead to greet the man. But as she began to speak in Japanese, he held up his hand, stopping her.

"It's okay," he said. "You have foreigners with you. Let's not be excluding. Let's speak English, yes?"

Asuka nodded.

"I'm Hiroshi." He gave another smile and a bow.

"Yoroshiku onegaishimasu," Asuka, replied, forgetting herself. "I mean, it's nice to meet you."

"It's nice to meet you, too," he grinned. "I apologize for stopping you on your …" He hesitated and looked over at the camera in Paul's hand. "… your hike. But I don't get many people … many foreigners … up this way. I want to make sure you know where you're going."

Do we tell him where we're going? Do we know ourselves? Sure, the X-Zone. But was that enough to go on?

No one answered, and I wondered if the rest of my party was mulling over the same thoughts ping-ponging around my own mind.

Hiroshi smirked, "I can see that your journey is a complicated one. Please, come inside for something warm to drink."

Hiroshi ushered us into the bright and airy one-room watchtower. It gleamed with polished cherry wood, and the most notable features were the wall-to-wall windows encircling the room. Framing the windows, long shelves housed food supplies such as dried and canned goods. From the inside, the windows gave anyone in this room a bird's eye view of the forest. On one panel of wood between windows, hung a guitar, on another panel hung a lantern and a clock.

Every surface was cluttered with lanterns, batteries, food, and bottles of wine. Boxes on the floors were stacked against the walls, and even more boxes were shoved under a makeshift desk that held a huge green Apple desktop.

As we gathered around the little table, the aroma of freshly brewed coffee filled the air. Paul, Miku, and I sat quietly, not sure what to expect or what to do. Asuka, however, seemed perfectly at home as she helped the ranger serve us.

"You know your way around a kitchen, I see," Hiroshi smiled to Asuka.

Asuka nodded, pouring the coffee. "I've had a lot of practice, sir. When I was younger, I would help serve guests breakfast in a Ryokan nearby." Her voice trailed off, clearly lost in more childhood memories.

"Hmm?" Hiroshi's bushy eyebrows raised. "I thought I knew the face of every resident in Aokigahara. But I don't know yours."

Asuka nodded, standing beside Miku's empty cup. "I've been away for a long time."

Hiroshi began to pour coffee into Paul's mug. "Is that right? And what family's Ryokan did you work at before you left? As I said, I know all of them."

Asuka set the kettle down on a wooden coaster and wiped her hands from the residue with a dingy rag. "Mizushima," she said solemnly, clearly aware of the Ryokan's daunting reputation.

Hiroshi froze, waves of the steaming brew overflowing onto the tablecloth and into Paul's lap. Paul snapped from his seat in an instant, violently brushing off the blazing liquid. Hiroshi broke from his trance, recognizing his blunder in a moment. Asuka flung her towel at Hiroshi who caught it in mid-air and attended to the mess.

"Mizushima, uhh …" he stuttered as he dabbed at the spill on the table. "Ritsuko … she is … I mean, she's a little … uhh …"

"I know," Asuka gave a short reply of admission.

Hiroshi finished cleaning the mess, tossing the soiled rag back to Asuka. "And you *chose* to stay at--"

"Yes," Asuka interrupted, catching the rag.

Hiroshi glanced to me in bewilderment. "With an *American*!?"

"Yep!" I spoke for Asuka, feeling her stare in the corner of my eye.

Hiroshi let out a sigh of bafflement, resigning himself to one of the chairs. "I am very sorry, sir." He chuckled with confoundment, then paused in thought. "I didn't even know Ritsuko's doors were open to guests anymore. I mean, it's not like she needs the money."

Asuka found the last of the makeshift seats beside me. "They usually aren't."

The ranger crossed his arms tightly, narrowing his eyes at Asuka. "Except for you." He tipped his chair back, rocking it as his thoughts raced. "Very odd …"

"Thank you!" I glowed as I slammed my hands onto the table and shot a victorious gloat at Asuka.

"Shut up, Chad," Asuka said, rolling her eyes.

Hiroshi's foot rested against the edge of the table as he continued to sway his chair. More thoughts. "Is it true that Ritsuko hasn't left her home for years?"

Asuka's eyes dropped to the table. "I don't know," she shrugged.

"And you haven't seen her for, how long has it been?"

Asuka's eyes rose to the oak ceiling above us. "Five years?"

Hiroshi's eyes danced in recollection, then grew dim once the simple math was solved. "Oh … yes, I see." He nodded, "That makes sense now."

A sober moment of reverence fell between Asuka and the ranger. Hiroshi let his chair slam back on all four legs and lifted his iron mug in the air. "To lost friends!"

We all rose our cups in varying degrees of apprehension and echoed the words. We brought our mugs to our mouths, tasting the bitter refreshment, save for Hiroshi. The ranger held his cup raised for another moment, then acknowledged Asuka with a sparkle in his eye. "And to the prodigal daughter! Though Ritsuko's heart is long closed, you will always be welcomed in the Aokigahara." A warm smile crept over the ranger's mouth.

Asuka's eyes scanned over the view of the forest around us, then lifted the little cup to her quivering lips.

"So," Hiroshi said, slapping his knees, bringing a formal meeting to order. "I can see what brings this one here," gesturing to Asuka, "but that still leaves you others." His hand indicated over to Paul, Miku and me, seeming to mystically sense the de facto mastermind of our group. His waving hand and searching eyes both settled on me. "What brings *you* to Aokigahara Jukai, sir?"

I blinked. "Well," I hesitated, "I am a television host. I've come here to document the suicides taking place in this forest." As awkward as it was, sometimes the best explanation is the most straightforward one, right?

Silence once again. Hiroshi looked down, deep into his mug. "I see."

"We're not here to capitalize on the deaths of these people," I added, hoping he would understand. "We just want to understand this place. We want to communicate the value of life to people around the world."

"Yes, yes." Hiroshi brushed off my response. "Please understand that you are not up here because you have done something wrong. I asked you out of curiosity, that's all."

The last of the tension visibly fell from us.

The ranger continued, "I grew up here. When I was a child, this place was my backyard. I used to run through the forest barefoot, and swing on the trees like Tarzan." He laughed to himself.

"Then that book came, and with the book, came people who were sad, people who had no hope. At first, there were no bodies found, only visitors coming to drink. Maybe they, like you, were just curious. But then, after some time, people actually started ... doing it."

He looked over at Paul, who by this time, had subtly turned on his camera to document the ranger's words. Hiroshi paused. After a moment, he nodded, "The forest has never been the same. I took this job because I wanted to watch over this place and maybe help anyone that I could."

"So it was you who was playing that music?" I asked.

The ranger walked over to a small radio control station. He flipped a switch and music once again filled the surrounding forest.

♪ *The sky is big and blue. The wind is full of fragrance.* ♪

Hiroshi looked out the large window into the vast expanse of trees. "I play music because I think that it will make visitors feel happy. Music warms hearts."

Hiroshi's sincerity could not be denied.

After a moment, he asked, "You're going to the X-Zone, aren't you?" Hiroshi seemed to have been one step ahead us of.

"That was the plan. Is that ... not a good idea?" I asked.

He folded his arms, "It depends on what you have heard about that place." He searched me, waiting for an answer.

What had I heard about the X-Zone? I didn't even know it existed until Asuka brought it up at breakfast this morning. That and Ritsuko's warning, that there was 'a power' in there. But 'a power' was a pretty blanket description. "I haven't heard much, sir. Just that the X-zone might have some answers to our questions."

"Questions like ..." he prompted me.

I thought for a moment, "Why does *The Complete Manual of Suicide* tell people to go there? What's so special about that place? And ..." I didn't want to ask, but the question came anyway, "Is there really something evil in there?"

Apparently, the question didn't come as a surprise to Hiroshi. "As I said, I have lived here my entire life. I have seen many sad things in Aokigahara. Whether there are really demons here or just broken people, I can't say. What I *can* say is that this forest is older than we could possibly understand. There are remnants here of a religion that dates far beyond our collective memory. Who that tribe of people were, I don't know. What, or *who* they worshiped, forgotten. However, the answers *might* be found in the X-Zone; that area was the center of their holy place. But, the real question is, will you be able to face whatever you find in there?"

I looked over to my companions with trepidation. Were we really prepared to uncover what truths were hidden in the X-Zone? "I don't think we have a choice at this point, sir. We've come this far."

Hiroshi nodded. "Then, please. Here," he gestured for me to join him at the window and pointed to a large patch of dark trees roughly half a mile away. "That's where you want to go."

The rest of the crew were by my side in an instant. We all stared intently at the darkest area of the woods.

"If you need anything today," he nearly whispered, "please come find me. And do not stay after nightfall. The forest can play tricks on your mind, especially in the dark."

This was a clear sign that the ranger was releasing us to continue on our journey. We collected our things and headed out the door.

Only, Miku remained, though I didn't realize it until I was outside on the balcony. Miku slowly closed the door, keeping her hand on the knob.

"What is she doing?" Asuka asked.

"I think she needs a private word with Hiroshi," Paul added.

Although we couldn't hear Miku, we could see her clearly, as the large glass pane windows assured nothing could be hidden. Her face was filled with concern as she pointed out to the X-Zone then back at the three of us. The ranger stood before her, his hands folded in front of him, shoulders slumped, and nodded empathetically. Was she asking him about what we saw (or *thought* we saw) last night?

I began to piece it all together. Here was a perfect opportunity for Miku to find an outside party to confide in, someone who knew the forest, someone who could give her the assurance she needed to prove that she wasn't crazy. But at what cost? If she wasn't crazy, then we did see *something*! And what we saw couldn't be explained, which was scary. But if she was crazy, then she was crazy. It was a no-win situation.

The ranger reached into a cabinet and retrieved a small black fabric bag. After speaking a few inaudible words to her, she bowed and quickly stashed the bag into her purse. What did he give her? Miku nodded and bowed, continuing to exchange apprehensive gestures with the ranger.

I sighed, patience growing thin. "I'm going to head down."

"You alright?" Paul shot me a cautious look.

"Yeah, I'm fine, we're just losing daylight. We've stayed here long enough." I spun around, taking the first steps down the winding staircase.

"We'll be right down, man," Paul assured.

As my feet thudded on each slippery step, I breathed in the fresh air of the forest once more, hoping it would aid in the clarity I desperately needed. My hand brushed over the flaking white paint on the guardrail as my eyes took in the blanket whiteness covering the horizon. No, even the height of the watchtower couldn't break past the elevation of fog. It was endless! And the presence of its gloom, even at midday, assured me that it would linger with us. I took more melancholy steps down the stairs. Paul, Asuka, Miku and the ranger, out of sight and mind. And with the veiling fog, my colleagues might as well have been a mile away. I was alone, alone with my thoughts, both for good and for bad.

But, was I *really* alone on that staircase?

A playful humming emitted from below my feet. The cheerful sound of soft, childish singing filled the pale, damp air along with slow, small footsteps.

I peered below me to find the source as the song grew louder.

♫ *A new morning has come. A morning of hope. Open your heart and fill it with happiness.* ♫

The voice grew closer, though still unseen. Nervously, I strained my neck around the bend of the stairs before me. A dark shadow moved around the curve. My mind raced to the memory of the man I spotted hours ago. Was it him? Had that mysterious figure followed me here? But as the figure continued to sing, taking one deliberate step after another, the form became more vivid. No, it wasn't the man I had seen in the forest earlier.

It was someone much worse.

"We meet again," a familiar archaic accent greeted me. The Ryokan's late night guest! She still adorned that same bizarre black dress and shoes as she had the night before. An eerily cheerful smile filled her pale face.

My head swam. She *was* a local adolescent, right? Did she *really* think it was worthwhile to continue her ludicrous prank? "What? Are you following us now?" I glared, taking a couple of defiant steps down the stairs towards her.

She smiled, taking her own steps up the slippery flight. "I don't follow anyone," she gracefully replied in a seriousness that disturbed me. "Maybe *you* are following *me*," she beamed, her ribbons seeming to dance in a breeze absent to my senses.

I took more steps down the stairs. "I have more important things to do with my time today than follow you."

She matched the distance. "Good," she blissfully agreed. "No sense in wasting your time worrying about the inevitable!" Her pale hands firmly gripped the dilapidated rail and glanced over the white nothingness of the Aokigahara.

I rolled my eyes as my hulking steps slammed onto the stair above the strange girl. "Oh, okay, what would *that* inevitable be?"

Her gaze returned in a crazed euphoria. In an eternal moment, she rose to my stair, her black ribbons seeming to twist around the banister and out of my view. I could almost feel their fabric edges grazing the back of my neck. "*That you are marked for death,*" she whispered with a chilling absolution.

The *The Complete Manual of Suicide* in my bag pulsed against me like a pounding heart.

My eyes went wide as my mind blanked. Every hint of practicality, every trace of wisdom instantly surrendered to panic and despair. It took every fiber of my determination to deny the overwhelming urge to shove the menacing girl off the edge of the stairs, letting her dark visage disappear into the foggy nothingness below.

I leaned in closer to her, eyes dancing with my *own* controlled fury. "You're crazy." I calmly delivered the statement like a professor teaching a student a crucial lesson. I viciously shot a finger at her and seethed, "Get the hell away from me, psycho!"

The girl remained unaffected. She blinked. Then a gleeful smile spread across her mouth as she climbed another stair above mine, now fixated on the watchtower above.

"And leave my friends alone, too!" I shouted as the distance between us grew wider.

She froze, " 'Friends'? " Her words nearly vanishing into the fog. She turned her head back to me. "Haven't you already realized, Mr. Daniel?" Wicked eyes of pity furrowed her brow. "You don't have any friends here." She turned, ascending to the top of the flight and gazing up at the rest of the twisting staircase. "Those who venture into the Aokigahara do so alone."

I rolled my eyes and spun around, earnestly finished with our pointless banter. There was so much more to do than stand idly by, wasting my breath on this lunatic. I marched down the rest of the flight, planting myself at the rickety base. "I don't want to see you again today!" I demanded, returning my gaze to the girl.

Her eyes didn't meet mine. Her petite frame expanded, taking in a deep, serious breath. Exhaling, she whispered, "That's not my decision. It's yours." The words fell from her mouth and flowed down each weatherworn step before hitting my feet. Pensively, the girl began to ascend the next flight, disappearing into the fog.

As my feet dug into the soil at the watchtower's base, my lungs heaved in shallow breaths. Even with my decent physical shape, I felt like I had just ran a marathon. But it wasn't the stairs that caused my exertion; it was that blasted girl! Why did she continue to harass me?

I wiped the chilling sweat from my brow, peering up to the top of the watchtower once more. Was that strange girl speaking with the others now? Or, hopefully, Hiroshi was chastising the juvenile for her obviously distasteful joke. The thought made me smirk. Kids can't get away with that kind of behavior for long! Thankfully, Hiroshi was stationed in the Aokigahara to handle this type of stuff, despite the oddity of the girl's prank.

Moments later, I caught sight of Asuka, Paul and Miku, rounding one of the many flights of wooden stairs. Being too high to call out to, I waited anxiously as they descended the tower. My hands fidgeted with the zipper on my bag as a hundred questions I wanted to ask them filled my mind, creating an imaginative dialogue that craved satisfying answers.

What did that freaky girl say to you guys? Why do you think she was dressed in that black, eerie costume? What about Hiroshi, is he going to detain her up there and call her parents? She was weird, right? Like, I'm not sure she is playing with a full deck. Did she try to scare you guys, too, with all that 'death is inevitable' nonsense?

Miku, I bet she really got under your skin … but don't let that little brat scare you for a second. Paul, I should probably go up there and help Hiroshi deal with her, don't you think? I've had a ton of experience with off-the-wall people and I bet he could use my help and expertise. He'll probably be so happy I came back up to save the day. "It's the least I could do!" I announced.

I gave a grandiose bow, and started back up the stairs.

"Do about what?" Asuka's voice emitted behind me.

I froze, mid-step. My eyes strained sideways to find my three companions, not only on ground level, but right beside me! How long had they been there watching (and apparently listening to) my little internal drama?

"What are you doing? You're being weird!" Asuka said, looking me up and down.

I composed myself, shaking off the awkward moment my imagination had abandoned me in. There was no time for embarrassment, however; Asuka, Paul and Miku had the answers I was dying to hear. My eyes went wide, crazy even. "So??"

Asuka stood on guard. "Sooo …. what?" She shrugged.

Why was Asuka playing games? Surely her interaction with the girl was too juicy to hold back. "What did she say?"

Miku gestured to herself. "Me?" she stuttered. "I am too embarrassed to say." Miku's shame-filled eyes dropped to the dirt as she clutched her bag tightly.

"Oh, no, no! I don't care about you, Miku! What did the creepy young girl—"

"Excuse me?!" Asuka fired, grabbing Miku's arm, pulling her close. "Chad! That was rude!"

"Ok, yes! I'm sorry! I didn't mean that! I mean, it's not that I don't care about you, Miku, what I meant to say was that I wasn't talking about Miku! I was talking about the freaky little girl with the snaky black ribbons in her hair, the one talking about how we were all marked for death!"

They just stared at me, confused and unexcited.

"W-what? Marked for death …" Miku whined. "We are??"

Asuka scoffed, laying Miku's frightened face on her neck. "Chad Daniel! Why would you say that?!!?"

"I didn't say it, SHE said it!" I argued.

Silence and three cautious stares returned to me. What was going on?

My mind drifted into terrible suspicion as I asked, "She … didn't … say anything?"

More silence.

"Who are you talking about, Chad?" Paul was trying to help me out.

"You didn't see her?" A thud hit my heart.

They couldn't have missed her. It's a ONE WAY staircase! Impossible, right?

"The only thing I see is the weirdo in front of me!" Asuka shouted. "And you're scaring Miku!"

Miku whined.

My hands of excitement fell to my sides in humble, but horrifying, realization. I tried to get myself out of this embarrassing spot. "I am... SO sorry, you guys!" I turned to Paul. If anyone would understand, it would be him, right?

Paul addressed me with a thoughtful look. He was trying to decide if this expedition into the Suicide Forest was worth it. Worth risking our well-being, maybe even our sanity.

"Are you alright to keep going, man? We could head back now if you'd prefer," Paul said, as Asuka and Miku slowly moved behind him.

They all stood as one united front and waited, waited on me, the *outsider*. I worked hard not to glare at my old friend as a wicked thought laid siege in my mind: either the others *really* didn't see the girl (which was impossible unless it was me who was going crazy) or ... *they're all in on it too!* And if that was the case, I couldn't trust any of them! Even more than that, I couldn't let them know I was playing into their hand. I had a split second to decide if I was delusional or if my friends were secretly against me. I *know* I saw that girl, so that only left one choice, and I certainly wasn't going to act like I was ruffled by their plot.

I guarded myself, retrieving a pleasant smile. "Hey, let's just move forward. I'm totally good! Let's get going."

Paul examined me with his eyes for a moment. Was that concern ... or betrayal? I didn't want to face either, so I strode ahead, leading the group back into the forest.

Several minutes into the trees, Asuka stopped and looked over the new markings on the map Hiroshi gave us, forcing us all to pause. Silence. A silence that I didn't want; not with that dark turning in my stomach. There was something pressing against my mind. An agitation. Agitation at all of my 'friends.'

Were they all in on this plot with the archaic girl? Were they just trying to scare me? Are they really all against me?

How could I not have seen the pieces of the puzzle right in front of me?

Did they *really* not trust me?

Miku: did she really feel she needed to confide in a stranger to settle her fears? I had told her over and over again that there was nothing to be scared of! Why wouldn't she listen to me?

An anger flared in me and I couldn't help but think that this trip would have been a lot easier without Miku, particularly. She was slowing this whole thing down. Why did Asuka ever allow her to come? The invitation was for Asuka only, not her drama queen friend. Asuka should have warned me that I was going to be playing babysitter on this trip, on top of everything else I had to do today!

Asuka should have also told me that she was bringing her *own* emotional baggage with her. This trip to Aokigahara—an excuse to check in on a distant friend. It was all so inconvenient for me! So frustrating, so maddening. And every step further into this place, made it that much longer I had to deal with them.

I shook my head, trying to get myself out of this depressive funk.

What was this? Why was I being so inflexible? My aggravation came out of nowhere, but stuck with me like black tar. No, worse than tar, like scalding hot magma! The frustration washed over me and seared every thought about our two guides, the Ryokan, the housemother, even this trip itself. I found myself sinking into those foreboding thoughts, those agitations. Maybe all this was by design? Maybe the distractions Miku and Asuka were causing were intentional to keep me from doing what I needed to do here?

But that was not realistic, right?

That couldn't all be real, could it?

My mind desperately tried to decipher the fact from the fiction: the girl, my thoughts, whether my team was for me, or against me ...

"Let's settle here for a while and start taking care of the dramatic sequence of this thing," Paul's voice cut through my thoughts.

"You want to do this *now?*" I asked, surprised. There was never a good time to produce—we both knew it. Production was never convenient, especially when trudging through a damp forest. But this hardly seemed the time or place.

"Yeah, let's get this part over with," Paul said. "I don't want to be caught running out of daylight."

I looked down at my watch and saw why Paul wanted to speed things up. The hour was later than I thought. It was already well past 2:30 pm. Where had the time gone? I agreed, nodding absentmindedly.

"Ok, so ..." Paul clapped his hands together, his way of clearing his mind and getting laser-focused on what needed to be done. "Here's what I would like to see happen." He looked at Miku. "I want to start collecting some footage of you, Miku, walking through the forest alone."

Miku nodded and retrieved the script from her purse, that mysterious black bag peeking back at me.

What did Hiroshi give her? Why was she being so secretive with me?

She looked over the hastily written words of the folded paper.

"So just to clarify," I said, not having read Paul's impromptu script, "what's the premise here?"

He nodded. "Yes, well, what I was thinking was ... during this documentary, I want to illustrate someone who has come to the forest to end their life. That's where we'll use this footage with Miku."

"Wait," I asked pensively. "Are you really going to stage Miku ... dying here?"

A blank expression from Paul. His silence confirmed everything.

Miku was horrified. "What? No. No, no, no, no, no." She began to nervously pace the forest.

"Miku, come on ..." Paul started.

"No, no, NO!" Miku stammered, abruptly cutting Paul off. "You didn't say ANYTHING about this!"

Here we go again. I sighed.

"What were you expecting, Miku?" Paul asked.

"I thought I was just playing someone on a hike in the forest! Like ... a pretty celebrity who was on a vacation after a movie shoot ... in Paris!"

Miku's assumption was naïve and ridiculous! But none of us wanted to explain that to her, not while she was in such a frantic state.

"Sadisutikku," Miku muttered.

Paul approached her. "Miku, Miku, come on. We don't even have to *think* about how we'll do that right now. All I need is for you to walk, just to walk through the forest. That's all. We'll take it slow. And if you're uncomfortable, we'll stop. Can you do that, Miku? Can you just walk through the forest?"

Miku thought for a moment, looked at us and sighed exasperatedly. "Ugh!!! Ok. Just a walk."

"Just a walk ... for now," Paul added in the simplest way he could.

Miku disappeared into a patch of forest with Asuka to prepare for her role. Paul began to set up the shot. He meticulously plotted a course in his head that would follow Miku through the forest.

Once again, waiting. Waiting on Miku. Burning daylight, waiting for Miku. This was a waste of time. Miku shouldn't be here! And her melodramatic attitude landed her a last-minute role in the film, in hopes that she would calm down. This was her plan all along, wasn't it? To come with us and throw a fit until Paul and I acquiesced to her. She was like a spoiled child. I was frustrated. And now, frustrated at *Paul* for going along with it-- letting Miku's anxiety call the shots. My nausea flared again.

"You sure this is the best use of our time?" I said bluntly to Paul as he adjusted his camera.

"It's fine."

It's fine. Paul always said that. But it wasn't fine. "Is this really what we came to do? Film Miku in the forest?"

"Well," Paul set the camera down and gave me the attention I required. "I wasn't planning on it. But sometimes a better plan comes along, you know?"

A better plan? Better than what? Better than the rushed direction we threw together on the plane? Or was it bigger than that? Was Paul referring that he needed a better plan than *me?* Better than the TV personality who couldn't formulate a single cohesive thought today?

It all made so much sense in its own wicked way.

I could picture it clearly now, the three of them, secretly meeting last night while I slept. Paul telling Asuka and Miku that I was useless, that they would have to subtly push me to the side. Asuka telling Paul that Miku could throw a fit tomorrow morning until I finally gave up and let them do whatever they want.

Still, no! This wasn't real. This was just paranoia, right? Lack of sleep — that *had* to be it. We're all on the same team here. Paul's been with me for years. I can trust him, right?

We're fine.

It's fine.

The uncomfortable silence ended when Miku and Asuka reappeared. Miku now sported her hair thoroughly disheveled. Her makeup had been mostly wiped away to reveal a more ordinary face. What's more, she had removed her shoes and applied a generous amount of dirt to her feet and legs. I had to admit, she did a thorough job of fitting the role. Despite the fact that I barely knew the girl, Miku had disappeared and then reappeared, transformed into another person altogether.

"Ok, great," Paul said. "But you should probably put your shoes back on."

"There's no glass," Miku protested, lifelessly.

Was she getting into character or just embarrassed by the way she looked?

"Alright then, fair enough." His eyes examined Miku the way a sculptor would inspect a block of marble. "Can we have you take off your necklace?"

Miku's pale face shot a look up at him with wide eyes, her hand familiarly grasping the cross.

"I have had this since I was a child. I do not often remove it," she said, pain in her eyes.

Silence from Paul.

"I can hold it for you," Asuka offered her hand.

Miku hesitated. Then, closing her eyes, reached behind her neck and unclasped the chain. She ceremoniously coiled the necklace in her palm until it diminished in size. "Please take care of it."

"I will," Asuka slipped the necklace into her pocket.

Paul let a moment pass. "There's just one more thing before we start." Miku lifted her eyes from the forest ground and met Paul's.

"I'd like you to hold the suicide book."

Miku pulled in a breath, about to protest, but then let it out in defeat and nodded.

Paul looked over at me, cueing me to give her the book from my bag. No way. I'm not giving up that book. It's *my* book.

Even though a part of me was surprised at the wave of childishness that just washed over me, the rest of me dove right into its waters.

This is my production and I'm supposed to be the point guy. Why is Paul all of a sudden calling all the shots? Does he think, just because I've been off my game a little bit today, that this is now *his* deal? Have they been in cahoots this whole time to edge me out of the project? First, they didn't admit to seeing the girl in the black dress, and now they are wishing I wasn't even here. Fine. I don't need them either. Let them have the damn book.

I reached into my bag for the suicide manual, pulled it out and looked over its immaculate white cover with red and black symbology. The ugliness inside this book seemed to match the ugliness in my heart at the moment.

"Just be careful with it. We only have one of these." I held the book out to Paul, but he didn't make any move to take it. "Paul, here. It's fine, just don't lose it!"

Still, Paul didn't make a move.

"What's wrong with you? Just take the damn thing!" I looked down and realized why the others were confused.

There I stood, arm outstretched, holding the tattered journal I had found earlier, not the suicide manual at all! Instead of the pristine feel of a new book, I could now feel the torn, filthy cover of the weathered journal in my hands. How could I have mistaken it for the manual?

"Chad, are you okay?" Paul asked, taking a step toward me. Miku and Asuka both looked a little scared.

I was at a loss.

"What … is that, Chad?" Asuka asked.

I couldn't tear my eyes from the book. "I …" my head was racing, stomach spinning. "Something I found this morning. I'm sorry, I must have gotten confused." I knew what they were all thinking. They wanted to ask why I took it. But I couldn't answer that even if they did ask.

"Can I see it, Chad?" Asuka said cautiously, as if she was talking to a crazy person. I found myself glaring back at her. A familiar scenario. Asuka made her way toward me and slowly reached out her hand to take the book. I hesitated before releasing it. Letting go of it was like losing my only vindication.

I shoved my bag, which still held the suicide manual and a few lenses, into Paul's hands. "I need a minute."

"Do you need to talk?" he asked.

"No, I'm just tired. I'm ready to get out of here!" This seemed to relieve the rest of the group. I could blame my behavior on exhaustion, at least for the time. "I'm going to go on ahead."

"We should probably stay together," Paul suggested.

"Paul!" I snapped back. "I'll be a hundred feet in front of you! Just get your damn shots and let's get going! Okay?!" I stalked away. But even as I left, I could hear Miku and Asuka whispering to each other in Japanese. Of course, they were talking about me. But even as their foreign words drifted throughout the gnarled branches between us, a sting of warning pricked at my heart, a caution that I just couldn't heed. Still, that small internal voice whispered rationalities to me. But as I took the first of many steps away from my group, those rationalities were thrown off in lieu of the quiet comfort of disdain.

SIX

THE QUESTION

Ritsuko was right, wasn't she? I couldn't trust anyone. They took my book. They took the journal. And now they are whispering plots behind my back.

I just needed time—time to feel the nothingness that seemed more comforting than it probably should.

As I walked through the forest, the sickening pain in the pit of my stomach only grew stronger.

I'll get through this.

I went deeper, keeping the position of Paul and the others firmly in the back of my mind. I wasn't foolish. I knew better than to wander off and get lost here.

Ring!

Was that my phone?

I could feel its vibration in my pocket, and when I looked at the screen, the caller ID read: "Shay"

It was impossible, right? No service for miles and a call was able to make its way all the way out here? But the cell signal icon gave some hope: one bar. I swiped the phone open.

"Hello?"

"Hey Chaddy!" The voice on the other end had a familiar southern drawl to it and a tone that reflected someone sitting in a warm and comfortable house. "How are you? I haven't heard from you in days!"

"Yeah, I know, baby, I haven't had any service out here."

"How's Japan? How's the project going?"

I tried to keep my voice as high-spirited as I could muster. "The project? It's going fine. Lots of good progress."

"And how's Paul doing?" she asked.

Paul and the others are sabotaging this trip, Shay. I should just leave them here. Make them pay.

"He's doing well," I answered, fighting myself. "Everyone's good."

I should burn this place to the ground.

Changing the subject, I asked, "How are you? Everything alright?"

Shay was hesitant on the other end. I couldn't tell if it was poor reception or just silence.

"You there?" I persisted.

"Yeah, sorry. Must be terrible service out there, ay Chaddy?" Her voice sounded different. It had lost its soothing tones.

"Yeah," I hesitated. "I'm surprised that you got through at all."

"I'll always track you down, Chad. You can't get away from me." Her voice changed even more, deeper, distant.

The words sent chills down my spine. "What?"

"You're right about the others, too, Chad. About everyone. They really are against you. You can't rely on anyone but yourself, kid." Her voice was now unrecognizable, unnatural.

"What are you talking about?" Shay would never talk that way!

The words continued in a strange, loud, and now malicious voice. "You're never leaving this place."

"Shay, I …"

"See you soon, son!"

A loud static hit my ear. I dropped the phone. Something was wrong. Was it all in my head?

Confused, I turned around to try and spot Paul and the others—but to no avail.

"Paul!" I yelled out. "Asuka! Miku! Where are you?" My voice drifted through the woods like the tripping, tumbling fog. No answer. Where were they? I had stayed right in front of them! Where did they go? My heart beat wildly, and my breath came in gasps. The sickness swelled in my mind as my stomach began to lurch.

And yet … as the darkness deepened and felt more confusing, at the same time it felt comfortable and strangely inviting. After considering the invitation for a few moments, my heart stopped racing, the panic subsided and I could breathe easily again. I looked around but still no Paul, no Asuka, and no Miku. How could they have left me?

I didn't see them anywhere.

But then I spotted someone. It was the presence I had been feeling—the same shadowy figure from before. He was now much closer, his back to me. I found myself moving toward him without thought.

Who could it be, stranded out here in the forest?

Another step closer. I could now make out his details. An older man, well dressed, white hair.

Another step, my nausea swelling.

"Hello?" I said.

I *knew* that person.

He turned.

"... Dad?"

It couldn't be right! This isn't real. I'm sick. I'm seeing things. *The forest can play tricks on your mind.*

But ...

"Dad?" I asked again.

The figure smiled in recognition.

I didn't want to believe it but he was dressed in the very suit my dad was buried in.

"Dad!"

"Let's take a walk, son," the figure said. "There's a lot we need to talk about."

Confusion washed over me as the image of my father rushed through my mind—this was all in my head, right? Was I having a breakdown? But it was all too clear. If I wanted to, I could have reached out and touched his black funeral suit. I glanced away, shook my head, and then squinted back to him. His face was nothing more than a fleeting shadow.

Riddled by a volley of visuals, violent and aggressive images of my father flashed before me. They wouldn't hold still ... hundreds of figures, hundreds of voices, yet all were uniquely his. I closed my eyes again, trying to get a handle on it. But it was growing more severe with each passing second.

Take deep breaths. Head … be still! Separate the real from what is not real.

"Oh God, please …" I whispered. It was all I could say. Safe thoughts, safe thoughts only.

But when I opened my eyes, still the same figure was there dressed in the same black suit that my dad wore in his casket, fifteen years ago.

"Dad?"

Nothing.

"Dad?!"

Still nothing. I moved toward the figure, but every step I took, pushed him farther away. With each step, my senses continued to dull. I glared at him and murmured under my breath, "Why are you here?"

A ghostly reply came from everywhere and nowhere at the same time. "Why are *you* here, son?"

I remained silent, my mind following the shadow's question. Why *am* I here? What brought me to the Aokigahara? No, not just the forest, but here, in my life. What started all this?

"Yes, that's what it is, isn't it?" the voice asked. "You're here to ask a Question. It's been one you've wanted to ask for years. Ever since that night."

One question? There were a *thousand* questions flooding my mind: What is this? Why am I feeling this way about my life? Is there a point to any of it? But, with every possible inquiry, nothing satisfied the void in my mind. Somehow I innately knew none of these was the question he was referring to. I searched within, looking for the question. What is my question?

"The Question, Chad."

I glanced behind me trying to spot the others. Emptiness engulfed me.

"They're not there, they never were, Chad."

I returned my gaze to the figure; time felt irrelevant. How far away was I?

"Where are we going?" I asked.

"We're going home, son," the figure replied.

My mind was foggy. There was simply no sense to be made of any of this.

"There it is again. That Question."

I didn't ask a question. What was he talking about?

The figure stopped and turned, the face of my father, so vivid! "All the lives that have ended in this place. Lives filled with a vast sea of hopelessness suddenly silenced with the taut of a rope or the pull of a trigger. Do you know why they all came here, son?"

My vision became tunneled. My head spun. A deafening sound of motion surrounded me from all sides. From every which way, red-hot magma coursed through the forest. Bubbling, consuming everything in its path. It was so real. I felt the heat on my face. Magma erupted from the forest floor! More of it spewed from hills and rock faces.

Terrified, my eyes scoured the forest. There had to be a way out! But no. All I saw were the trees, the smoke, and … no!

The same sparkling figures from last night! Only now, there was no mistaking them. No more telling Miku that we can't be sure of what we are seeing. The human-shaped spirits danced through the trees. They spun and turned, flipped and moved, in and out through each other until they began to simultaneously turn into particles, diffusing into the fire.

"I don't want to see this!" I panicked, falling to my knees and covering my face with my dirty hands. "Stop it. Stop it!"

"Isn't this why you came? To see this? To understand this?"

"No. Not this. I'm not ready for this."

"You've been running from *this* for years. But it's followed you. *I've* followed you. I've been with you in every country, invading every thought. That dark corner of your mind. Always looming, with that Question."

The Question.

I tried to still myself.

I lost my breath as a boulder sank into the depths of my soul.

There it was.

The Question.

"Was it my fault?"

The words echoed loudly. They drowned out the chaos of the fiery visions. I opened my eyes. The forest was normal again, but the figure of my father remained.

"That's right, son. That is the Question."

A scream!

Miku.

I snapped back to reality in a cold sweat. The rest of the group was now a stone's throw behind me and from the cautious look in Paul's eyes, I felt my face grow cold, and no doubt, pale white. Where had they emerged from?

I spun to the source of Miku's terror.

My reality was challenged again. What I saw was, in fact, exactly in the same place that the shadowy figure had been. Instead of the visage of my father, there hung the withered remains of a body. It dangled from a filthy yellow rope. I could not process what I was seeing, surely it could not be real? But no, as much as I wished it were an illusion, the corpse was, in fact, as real as the trembling breaths escaping my lungs.

A full-grown man hung suspended from a branch. His body had decomposed to a length of only about four feet and dehydrated to nearly nothing. His clothes were simple, a white-now-yellowed shirt draped over his bony shoulders and a pair of brown pants hung loosely around his decaying frame. Of course, his feet were bare. The top of his head was bald, with light brown wisps of medium length hair curled on the sides of his head.

The corpse's face had ... melted away.

His eye sockets, hollow, revealed two vacant holes, exposing the emptiness of his now blackened skull. His nose was gone. His cheeks had fallen, settling his jaw into the remains of what was once his chest.

It was real—there was no denying that.

Paul rubbed the back of his neck and nodded to himself, taking refuge behind his lens. The camera began to fervently click.

The smell from the corpse was overwhelming—and all too familiar. It permeated my soul with one absolute truth: man is mortal. Was there life beyond the veil of the flesh? It wasn't the first time I had contemplated this mortal coil. It bombarded me, shook me, and took me—once again—from the present moment.

* * *

I stood in my dad's living room, his notebook at my feet. His suicide note. I had reread it a dozen times. I couldn't escape its reality as it stared deep into my soul. His short, handwritten letter: a tragic epilogue of a life that had been marred with pain. There was no one that could bear this with me.

I was alone.

Dad, what must this have been like for you? Alone ... more than alone. Isolated. Isolated in a world that you hated.

I wandered the darkened halls of his home and found myself in his bedroom. A small, simple room adorned with mementos from his life, a life that was now over. Nothing left in his story. The final page of his book, closed forever! We never appreciate where we are in our story until it comes to an end. Always looking to our future, waiting for our lives to start, when in reality, it's been off and running without us.

I sat on his bed inside the deafening quiet. What I wouldn't give for a Bible. The stillness of God's Word would have been a place of solace from the torment raging in my heart. My father was gone. And what hurt even more, was the fact that, based on his suicide note, he never loved me.

Then something wicked began to stir in me. Anger. A twisting blackness. It swirled in my chest. I crossed my arms, uncrossed my arms, buried my head in my hands, pressed the palms of my hands so hard into my eyeballs that I saw stars.

Tangible pain.

Escape.

Any feeling, even physical pain, was better than the one pythoning around my heart. Was this really what the world had to offer? Everyone, running from an inevitable pain that each of us was bound to experience or inflict.

Was there nothing more?

* * *

The flash from Paul's camera broke into the memories.

Who was this man?

What could his life have been like?

What drove him here?

Miku and Asuka hugged each other, shocked and terrified. Paul remained quiet as he documented the gruesome sight. He approached the corpse and instinctively, though tentatively, I followed suit.

As we took the first steps toward the body, I heard the inevitable breakdown from Miku behind me. Heaving agonized moans and stifled words poured from her broken spirit. This wasn't part of our plan, but how could we have been so naïve?

Miku held the sides of her head, trying to deal with this new unforeseen discovery. Amidst her sobbing, Asuka grabbed her, turning her away from the sight.

Asuka pressed her head against Miku's cheek.

"Kishi Kaisei, Miku," Asuka whispered to her.

My heart felt Miku's pain. Tears streamed from her eyes. She jerked away from Asuka's comfort, moving backwards, aimlessly into the forest.

"I have to leave!" Miku wailed.

"Miku, you can't leave," Asuka commanded.

"I can't …" Miku stormed away, bolting back into the forest.

"I have to stay with her!" Asuka exclaimed, concern drenching her voice.

"Please keep her close by," I said.

"I will," Asuka promised, hurrying after Miku, calling her name.

After Asuka disappeared into the branches and fog, I turned my attention back to the horrific sight. I moved closer, my heart racing in rhythm with the fervent clicking of Paul's shutter. This was Paul's job, and that job had to be done.

Is this how it really ends? Our bodies are so fragile, our lives, so frail. This man had once been alive and breathing. What was his name? Did he have a family? Was there anyone in his life that could have helped him? Had they failed to see the signs?

The Question.

Was it my fault? Had there been anyone in my dad's life when he needed help? Had I failed to see the clear signs? Did I knowingly choose to ignore them? Was that why I was seeing him today? Was this revenant of my father haunting me now because of my inaction, my rejection of him for so many years? Was he the manifestation of a guilt I tried to bury along with him? Would the life of this unknown man do the same, daily haunt his family, riddling their hearts with guilt, shame and countless unanswerable questions?

Or were the visions of my father something else entirely? Was the Aokigahara playing host to something more sinister? The entire encounter with my father's ghost clung to me like the stench from the dead corpse before me. There was no escaping it ... nor those words that the wicked creature spoke:

"See you soon, son."

"What do you want to do about ... this?" Paul gestured to the body.

What to do? The best thing seemed to be to simply call the authorities and let them know what we found here. But we couldn't make calls. Not *real* ones, anyway. "Let's make our way back to the watchtower. Hiroshi could help us."

"Yeah, good call," Paul soberly agreed.

The sound of running footsteps approaching from behind, panicked, erratic footsteps. Asuka appeared from the trees. She was out of breath, sweaty, dirty and alone!

"Asuka?" I asked.

Her face, white with terror, she gasped, "Chad … I can't find her!"

SEVEN

THE SHADOW OF
THE MARKED

Asuka, Paul, and I called out Miku's name over and over as we ran through the slowly dimming forest. I tried to bury the fear; she could be anywhere by now, alone and scared. And who could blame her?

The image of the body hanging from the tree, although half a mile back by now, still felt as though it was right behind me. The image of his empty eye sockets was burned into my mind. All of this felt so wrong, so out of control! What were we thinking? Did we really believe we were smarter than the thousands who had come before us? Were we going to share their same fate, lost in the Aokigahara? Alone with the darkness in our minds? A darkness that, at least for me, continued to creep into my reality. Were the others experiencing something similar? Or was I alone with these torrid visions?

"Miku!" As Asuka's panicked voice called out again, my heart felt stale and heavy. This was real. This was serious. This was dangerous. What made it worse was that the sun had begun its descent toward the horizon. Long shadows quickly stretched even longer. Red and orange hues were beginning to tint the evening sky. We didn't have much daylight left. My watch determined that we had about an hour before the place would be enveloped by night and a darkness that ensued.

"What about Hiroshi?" Paul asked. "He could help find her. I mean, that's what forest rangers do—find people."

I looked at him. This would require a lot of time, time that the setting sun was reminding me that we *did not* have. "Well, it's a good idea. But that would mean doubling back the way we came, finding our trail of red tape and following it back to the tower."

"I'll go," Paul said.

"No. That's crazy. We can't split up and risk losing someone else."

"I won't get lost! I can do this." He stopped behind me.

I stopped too, Asuka frantically pressed on, calling Miku's name. A silent moment passed. Paul began to step backwards. "I'm going to go, Chad," he raised his hand, stopping me from following. "We'll work this out. Go catch up with Asuka!"

I sighed. "Just …"

"I will." He wrapped the strap of his camera over his shoulder and disappeared back the way we came.

Vastness of time passed as Asuka and I continued our search. Asuka's sweaty hand held her phone, frantically calling Miku's number over and over again. Each time, as expected, no service.

I didn't have to remind Asuka that the forest was a dead zone; she knew that more than *I* did. Still, if that was her way of feeling like she was covering all her bases, best to let her keep trying. After another failed call, she stared blankly at her phone, displaying Miku's name.

"I'm really worried, Chad."

"Me, too," I said.

"She could be anywhere by now."

I stopped, taking a real moment to assess our situation. "We're going about this all wrong," I said, looking up at the darkening sky.

"What do you mean?" Asuka asked.

"We're trying to find a needle in a haystack here, one person in an immense forest!"

"Well, this is a person," Asuka said softly, "after all."

"Right! And we'll never find her if we search only *this place*. We need to search through *Miku*!"

"You're not making any sense."

"Okay. You know her. Where would she go if she was scared?"

"What do you want me to say?" she stammered. "Where would she go in a forest she's terrified of? How about NOT THE FOREST?" Her eyes filled with angry, hot tears.

Not the forest.

"Right …" I mused. "So Miku would try and get out of the forest, obviously. But what if she *couldn't* get out? What then?"

"I don't know, Chad."

"Come on, Asuka. Where would she go in this place to find solace and safety?"

"There *is* no solace or safety here …" but Asuka's wheels were starting to turn. "But maybe …"

We both said at the same time, "Where would she go to clear her head?"

Clear her head.

"That's it!" I said.

"What's it?" For the first time, her eyes were hopeful.

"A clearing!"

"A what?"

"Miku would go to a clearing!"

"A clearing? A clearing …" Asuka frantically whispered to herself as she pulled out Hiroshi's map. She knelt down on the ground, spreading the map over the soil. "Ima dokoni iruno." She traced her finger over the map.

Four will go into the Aokigahara, but only three will return.

The foreboding words that strange young girl told me last night echoed in my mind. Who was she? Her warning turned my stomach upside down. No, it couldn't be true!

Asuka's eyes flashed back and forth between the map and her surroundings while her finger moved slowly, honing in on one area, until it rested on a yellow spot.

"Here, it's west of us," she said.

Asuka's words sparked a remembrance of vivid visions and words from that terrifying dream I had days ago vividly returned: *West of us, towards the setting sun. The clearing: that is where it all started … and where all of this will end.*

What could it all mean?

God, please!

"What do you think?" Asuka asked, looking in the direction we had to go, towards the setting sun. There wasn't a defined path, not even a level forest floor, only volcanic rock jutting out from the ground, creating straining highs and dangerous lows. It was climbable. It was maneuverable, but only *just*.

This could end in disaster!

"Let's do it. It's our best shot," I assured Asuka.

She stood and folded the map, stashing it into her bag. We looked ahead to the terrain in front of us before she said, "Yes, let's go."

We gripped the rock and navigated the steep climb. The setting sun filled the sky with wispy oranges and bright reds. It cast long, deep shadows in our direction as the fog finally began to lift. The rocks were sharp and cut at our hands with each grasp.

Finally, we made it to the top. However, the rest of the imposing terrain would prove to be as strenuous as the cliff side, if not more so. This part of the forest felt ancient, almost as if the Aokigahara Jukai was birthed in this very area thousands of years ago. A seemingly endless maze of massive boulders and petrified trees stood before us, like countless armed guards, intent on protecting their timeless secrets.

"We keep going," Asuka directed as she stood to her feet and took the lead. Ducking under fallen trees, and climbing over boulders, we continued to navigate the uneven ground. Asuka's determination was a powerful force, reigniting my own resolve. Despite her exhaustion, and the odds stacked against her, Asuka pressed on without hesitation to find Miku and to pull her out of this dark place.

But this place would become darker still as we came upon another obstacle. In front of us, moss-covered boulders created an uneven and slippery path. Beside it was a plunging ravine with a ten-foot drop.

My feet slipped on the rocks. I caught myself before any damage was done, but Asuka's feet slithered as they too slipped and scuttled.

"Do you think we can make it across?" she asked.

"Let's just take this slow. Watch your footing. There isn't much to grab onto here."

Asuka nodded, and I took the lead, stepping slowly onto the rocky overpass. The slimy moss shifted underneath my feet.

Careful, now. I peered down into the ravine. Wow. Do not fall down there! I gave Asuka the go-ahead only to find that she was already making her way onto the rocky surface. She instinctively stretched her arms out to help her balance.

I continued on, keeping focused on the darker areas of moss, knowing those would be more saturated with water. Every inch of the path was a new battle of time and pressure. My foot slipped again and my stomach dropped.

"Are you okay?" I called back to Asuka.

She stayed silent, trying to focus on her footsteps. "More than halfway there," I said, gauging the distance.

"Mmm-hmm," she replied.

I ought to stop distracting her. But the distraction was helping *me*. Nearly halfway there. Silence filled the forest. Silence, save for the rapid beating of my heart and the one thought that kept me sane: We're nearly there.

A foreign ringing hit my ears. A ringtone! Asuka's phone was *ringing!*

I turned, and Asuka was just as stunned. Her eyes were wide and her face flushed. We froze, perched on the dangerous rock as the phone continued to ring on.

Asuka's hand darted into her pocket.

"Don't!" I protested. But my warning fell on deaf ears. She raised the phone to her face, reading the screen.

"It's Miku!"

"Watch your footing!" I said, now inching back toward her.

She brought the phone to her ear. Her face twisted as she listened to the voice on the other end. In the quietness of the forest, I could almost make out the sounds emanating from the phone. It sounded like crying. No, wailing!

"Daijōbudesuka?" Asuka stuttered.

The voice continued to emit that weeping voice, speaking back to her. My mind flashed back to the *single* phone call I received today. Had it been real or was it all in my mind? Or, is it possible that the same *thing* that had spoken to me earlier, was now trying to contact Asuka?

Asuka's eyes filled with tears and she covered her mouth. "Miku…"

I took another few steps toward her, holding out my hand. "Asuka, give me the phone!"

She turned away and started to cry. Whatever the voice on the phone was saying, it was obviously breaking Asuka's heart.

"Give me the phone!" I repeated to no avail. She quickly grew frantic, stepping away from me, yelling back into the phone in Japanese. My eyes dropped to her feet as they began to slip on the moss covered rock.

"Asuka, this is way too dangerous!" I reasoned, trying to keep my *own* feet stable.

I closed in and grabbed the phone from her. She pulled away, in fury. Her other hand came up, fist clenched, and punched me hard in the jaw! Our eyes locked, both of us shocked. She had thrown all of her 110 pounds into that punch. I staggered backwards, dropping the phone into the black crevice below. In an instant, my feet slid out from under me! I flailed through the air before landing hard on the floor of the ravine: a ten-foot drop.

"Oh my gosh!" Asuka yelled down. "I'm so sorry! Chad! Are you alright?" she shouted while attempting to stabilize herself.

I couldn't find my voice … or my breath. My lungs were empty, my head throbbing. Stars flew across my vision. Everything hurt!

"Chad!" her voice called out again.

I had to let her know I was okay but there was no air for my voice. *Am* I okay? I closed my eyes, squeezed them hard, and tried to maneuver my fingers and toes. All of them were there, and all of them moved. I painfully raised my hand and gave a sarcastic thumbs up. I still had a sense of humor, that was a promising sign.

"Oh, thank God!" she shouted. "I'm coming down."

"No!" I said breathlessly. "Don't! Just … give me a minute."

I slowly sat up, afraid to stand. Surely something was broken. My entire body ached. How easily we take a fall when we're kids, and how quickly adults get used to staying on their feet.

"Can you walk?" Asuka asked.

"We're fixing to find out," I panted as I brought myself to my feet. Bathed in nausea, I almost threw up, but everything seemed to be working. "That's quite a punch you have, Asuka."

Asuka broke into a childish smile. "Judo lessons since I was ten."

I rolled my eyes. "Yeah, remind me to get the school's number after all this is over." I took a step and hollered as pain shot through my body. There it was. Something *was* hurt. Broken though?

"Chad?" Asuka nervously called again. "What is it?"

I put careful pressure on my ankle, and the pain returned. It wasn't a break. I knew what a break felt like. "I think I sprained my ankle."

"I'm coming down!"

"No, don't come down. I got it. Just …" I looked around aimlessly. Just what?

I glanced in the direction we were supposed to be heading. Perhaps the forest floor and the rock face would connect down the line. It was the best option at this point, and we had wasted enough time. By now, the sky had turned pink and golden, its final beautiful cry before the darkness came. "I'm gonna keep going the way we came. Just follow along from up there."

"That doesn't seem like a good idea," she shook her head.

"We're probably getting close."

She disappeared for a moment, and I heard the familiar crinkling of the paper map. She popped her head into sight again. "Yes, I think we're close!"

Every step I took throbbed with pain as I followed Asuka above me. My head felt like a cinder block had been smashed onto it. Inspecting the blackening sky, the sun had finally set, and the brilliant pinks, golds, and yellows had been replaced with a creeping blue and purple hue.

Miku, please be there.

I didn't know what we were going to do if she wasn't. Would it have been better for us to have gone with Paul to find Hiroshi? How far could we be from the tower by now? There was no way of knowing.

Alone in this forest again.

At this very moment, each one of us was alone in a different way.

Ironically, I longed for the uneasy stillness of the Ryokan miles away. I wanted to get in a soft bed, or at least my mat on the floor, and pretend this day never happened. What if we missed the mark on this one? What if all this was a waste? What if we came out here just to put ourselves in this much danger for nothing?

"That wasn't Miku on the phone, was it?" Asuka's voice interrupted my thoughts. Her voice: lifeless and stoic. I couldn't see her feet, but I could tell that she had cleared the dangerous moss.

"I don't know." I didn't know what to believe anymore.

"Yes, you do, Chad," my father's voice rang in my head, pulverizing what was left of my broken mind. It was him again, my father.

Sitting on a boulder, just a stone's throw in the direction I was walking, he wore that perfectly clean suit as he tossed rocks to the ground.

"Shut up," I muttered as I passed him.

"Did you really think you could make it out of here? People don't leave this place," the voice, now behind me, spoke with an unnervingly calm tone.

"You're not going to find her." The figure was in front of me again, his arms folded, leaning against a tree. "Did you forget? She has the suicide book with her," he smirked.

I froze. He was right, I *had* forgotten. Miku had, in fact run off with the suicide manual.

Oh God, no!

The figure of my father nodded in satisfaction. "That's right. And the book is cursed, you know it! It marks the possessor of it for death. So you might as well just give up; she's long dead by now, either by accident or by her own hand. Either way, she will be devoured."

Marked for death. The same words from my dream, the same words that strange girl told me on the watchtower! Did *The Complete Manual of Suicide* mark its keeper? Like a beacon giving off a signal that its owner had come to the Aokigahara with the intention to die? If that was true, *who* was the book signaling to? Was it the same spirit that spoke to me now? Was this spirit consuming those who entered the X-Zone?

"She's out there. We'll find her," I said, passing the figure, avoiding eye contact. But to no avail; he was in front of me ... again.

"The sun is nearly gone now, Chad. And you're exhausted, lost, and hurt."

The pain in my ankle seared. Everything in me screamed to stop this search. To drop everything and disappear into the night. Maybe it was time to just give up.

"Why don't you just rest here? We have so much more to discuss."

Hearing those words and the reality of my own thoughts ignited the fight within me. "I don't want to hear *anything* from you!" I shot back.

"Chad!" Asuka's voice called out from ahead. "I think I found a way for you to climb up!"

My spirits rose. At least I could finish this journey with a little more sanity. I followed Asuka's voice, which led to a joining path. Only a small ledge stood in my way. I could do it! I could get up there and get away from this man ... this *thing*. Asuka extended her hand, her feet inches away from my face.

"Come on, I'll help you up," she said.

I glanced down at my own feet, steadying myself for the push. I looked back to Asuka, and jumped at the sight of the figure now standing directly behind her! Only now, his face had changed. He was snarling, furious. I froze, terrified—glued to his image. My heart beat wildly.

Asuka looked puzzled. "What are you waiting for? Come on!"

I closed my eyes, shaking my head. When I opened my eyes and looked again, as before, he was gone! I took Asuka's hand and painfully lifted myself up.

The sky grew darker with each passing step through the forest. I couldn't help looking over my shoulder for that figure to reappear. But it didn't, and I knew in my heart why. It was because I wasn't alone now, isolated with my thoughts.

How vulnerable we are to the darkness inside our hearts when we're not with others, and how quickly that darkness dissipates with friends. What about the poor souls who walked into this place alone with hopelessness their only form of companionship. How often did people come into the forest *together* with the intent to end their lives in unity? The odds were probably low. No, this place demanded isolation.

"Do you need to rest?" Asuka asked, slowing her pace.

My body, racked in pain, begged for me to not only slow down but to stop altogether. "No, let's keep going," I said, my determination winning out. "Are we getting close?"

Asuka retrieved the map, her eyes straining to see the print in the diminishing light. Again, she traced the lines on the map with her finger. "Yes, we must be very close now!"

"Good," I said. "Not much longer to go."

"Yes, we will get to that clearing and ..." her doubts swallowed the rest of her words.

"And let's see what happens from there," I finished gently.

She quickened her pace as we winded through the branches.

"Auska, do you want to talk about it?" I asked, sensing her fear.

She remained quiet. After a moment, "There's ... *something* ... inside this place, isn't there?"

I regarded Asuka, unsure if I should tell her about the spirit that had plagued me ever since we started this journey into the X-Zone.

"I can feel it," she continued, "see it in the corner of my eye—creeping around. Like someone is standing behind me." Her arms folded, shoulders went tight as she shivered. "I think those stories might be right. Something wants to do us harm in here."

Should I tell her what I've seen and heard or would that just frighten her more?

Asuka closed her eyes. I could see tears running down the sides of her face. "I believe in God, yes. But I wouldn't say that I'm a spiritualist. I don't know if there are really demons or ghosts or spirits." She turned to face me, her eyes red with tears. "But I've never felt the things I've felt today." She looked up, as did I, into the night sky. Our returning gaze revealed nothing but shadowy outlines of each other.

"This place, it brings out bad things in me, a darkness," Asuka confessed.

She was right. I wanted to tell myself that I wasn't certain of what was happening. But I had seen too much today. It was time to face the truth.

"Yes, Asuka." I stepped closer. "You're right."

"But, what's happening to us?" Her eyes met mine, desperate for answers.

This was all too familiar; I had fought in this supernatural arena many times before. It was always a battle to the death. My mind composed hundreds of defensive scenarios, strategic words to be spoken, compromises, each to no avail. There were no trite answers to give, no easy explanations, and she knew it.

Asuka collapsed onto the ground, broken, sobbing.

I could feel a presence encircling her. It was a predator rapidly approaching a vulnerable prey.

It was that *thing* again, that dark presence, looming over her, blacker than the night itself. It closed in, set on enveloping her completely.

Asuka's sobs echoed into the darkness. She cradled her knees as her wails of despair filled the trees around us. I couldn't help her; I couldn't even help myself! I couldn't keep fighting. I couldn't go on, not for me, not for Asuka, not even for Miku. On and on, Asuka cried into the darkness the Aokigahara. Then blood chilling words fell from her mouth. "M-mom? Is … that … you?"

I buried my face in my hands. Yes, that same force *was* after Asuka! But its seduction on the poor girl held an overwhelming power to silence my tongue. I buckled under the weight of the onslaught as the darkness forced me to the ground. Never had the desperation to quit been so real, so seductive. I was emotionally exhausted, weary from a battle that had been raging in my soul for too many years. The scars from past skirmishes now scratched at me, reminding me of earlier pains inflicted. I could feel that all-too-familiar presence behind *me* now! Holding me, embracing me, inviting me to surrender.

Rest in me, I felt it saying.

It seemed so *right*, so oddly comforting. I exhaled softly and closed my eyes, yielding to *it*. Stillness and silence surrounded me. I felt nothing. No pain, hunger, warmth nor chill. Like a waking sleep— or was it death?

Was this how my father felt? Was this how his embattled soul dealt with those final moments of life?

The nothingness left me with only my thoughts, only my memories. Memories of that same darkness that beset me years ago, in my father's bedroom.

* * *

How long had I sat in my father's room? It felt like hours. Hours sitting here with this grief. A grim realization confirmed what I feared. My father's words, written in that notebook was confirmation of what I had suspected my whole life. He didn't love me, and his note made that abundantly clear.

I lifted my head and my vision began to slowly return. I caught sight of my reflection in the mirror placed on top of his dresser. There I was, sitting on his bed, eyes swollen from tears, my countenance as broken as my heart. I looked like a distraught child, a mess. Was this the image my father had of me? A crying child, desperate for love and attention? Both of which he was unable to give. Without that love, there was only the emptiness. That sickening emptiness. I was alone with only my crying face staring back at me.

But there was another face in that reflection. A small one, a familiar one. A face in a photo that hung over my father's bed.

Where had I seen that photo before?

I turned to find it and my heart stopped. It was me! A jolly baby, not even two years old in what was unmistakably an Olan Mills portrait. I was smiling, looking up beyond the camera, as babies often do … looking up at my parents …. at my father. Did he hate me then?

If so, then why would he have kept this picture of me over his bed?

My body collapsed onto the floor. I buried my face in the bed as a fresh wave of sobs heaved from my gut.

It hurt to cry, but the hurt of the crying was far better than the pain without it. Amidst the tears and the drool and the agony, there was nothing for me to do but call out to Jesus.

I whispered and yelled and screamed His name for who knows how long, gripping and hitting the bed.

In the otherwise stillness of that horrible room, I sought God with a wretchedness like never before. I remembered the scripture about Jesus collapsing in the garden of Gethsemane, pleading to His father to take the burden of mankind's sin away from him.

There, Jesus wept, yearning to have the pain lifted from his destiny. Still, God did nothing to remove that burden off of His own son. Now here I was, crippled from heartbreak—crying out to God to remove this pain from my heart. Would He do nothing? Why didn't God take Jesus' pain away that night? Was it because Jesus had a destiny to bring salvation to the world? Was that the same for me? Could I do something with this tragedy? Or was I damned to live as a victim of this heartbreak for the rest of my life?

Could I use this tragedy for... good?

Could I take this experience to deliver a message of hope to others?

Could God turn this mess into a message to ensure that even one less person walks into the veil of eternity through suicide?

Oh, Jesus!

As I continued to scream out His name, an inexplicable peace slowly settled in me. My thoughts became clear and linear.

I knew this feeling: a peace that surpassed all understanding. I was taught about it at tedium in Sunday school, but ... how much we take for granted such clichés until life gets real, until peace is severely needed. At this moment, I needed it.

Standing to my feet, I closed my burning eyes and lifted my hands to heaven.

The words didn't come - there were none to speak. What was I to say? No. This wasn't the time for words - only stillness.

What did I want? No, what did I need?

I could not let this break me! I would not let this destroy me!

But how could it not? Was there anything beyond this? Beyond this tragedy?

A question.

The Question.

One that would take time to answer.

No, now wasn't the time for questions or answers or anything. Only stillness. Only waiting. And maybe ... in that stillness, the answers would come.

* * *

"Let's pray, Chad!" Asuka's crying voice pierced through the nothingness like a pin pricking a black sheet of paper. The sound of it transported me from the den of my father's suicide to this forest of suicide. When I opened my eyes, I couldn't see her. The night had fully manifested. But a tiny glimmer caught my eye — the sparkle of Miku's beautiful necklace as it glinted off of the pale moonlight. I heard the sound of the tiny necklace clink around Asuka's neck, the cross dangling over her heart. "I wouldn't normally ask, but can we? Please?"

With those words, that small pin turned into a dagger. Just the suggestion of prayer ripped through the blackness and escorted hope into our presence. I smirked when I realized what had just happened. The

darkness didn't want prayer, did it? I could feel its anguish as it reluctantly recoiled. It wasn't gone, but it had released its suffocating grasp
enough for me to think clearly.

"Yes!" I quickly dropped to my knees and grabbed Asuka's hands.

"Jesus." It was the only Name I could utter—coming not from a place
of defeat, but from distress, hoping that He would do what He had
done before, what He had done since the beginning of time: destroy
darkness and bring a peace that surpasses understanding!

"Jesus." I felt my spirit grow. "We need you," I continued. "Help us!"

The command in my voice was not an accurate reflection of the exhaustion I felt. Rather, something *within* me arose and spoke with power, surprising even me. This was much greater than me. But the dark
oppression matched my intensity, gripping me tightly, impeding my
ability to reason.

You're going to die here, the darkness whispered.

I responded to the voice with the only answer a servant of God could
give, "I'm already dead. It is no longer I who live, but Christ in me."

The darkness shuddered violently as if sucking the power source from
a massive hydraulic pump. Slowly, the massive shadow around us re-
treated, reluctantly releasing its grasp on both Asuka and me.

A silent moment passed again, and my heart steadied.

Asuka wiped the tears from her eyes. We stood to our feet, both with
newfound strength, and Asuka declared, "Let's finish this."

I pulled out my phone and turned on its flashlight to provide slight
illumination, even though every couple minutes its battery slowly ticked
down a percent. The fading battery was a serious reminder that time was
short. Once the phone was dead, the last of the light would be gone. We
would be stuck here in darkness until morning.

Asuka remained quiet. There were no more words to speak, the only action now: find Miku.

After some time, we arrived at a spot where a wall of dense vegetation covered our path to the extent that we were forced to stop.

"I think we're here," Asuka said, and held the map in front of my light. This could be it. Just beyond could be the clearing.

I went to pull apart the overgrowth, but Asuka jumped in front of me. Without hesitation, she grabbed the branches and pulled fervently. I stood, feeling useless as the small girl ripped at the wall, her hands lacerating in the process. Blood oozed down her wrists.

"Let me help!"

"I've got it," Asuka said deliberately. "Just hold the light still!"

With a final pull, our way was clear. Asuka wiped her bloodied hands on her shirt and disappeared through the gap.

The clearing was just where the map said it would be. An empty field, save for two stone lanterns mysteriously illuminating the base of a massive camphor tree. The tree was *ancient*, as was the stone pathway that led into its hollowed out trunk.

What could be inside that cavernous recess? The tree was unmistakably a shrine of some sort, Japanese in design, but far too old to reflect the places of worship designed by Shinto or Buddhists. No, it was from a time seemingly older than that. The top of the tree swayed maliciously. Its mammoth canopy, gnarled branches, and thick leaves reflected the moonlight in a variegated design.

You shouldn't be here, a wicked voice inside my head warned.

From every side, the darkness of Aokigahara's thick trees framed the clearing and the sanctum within. I looked nervously at the surrounding forest, knowing that there could be anything just beyond the rim of those trees.

The sight of the shrine made my blood run cold; I had seen this place before, hadn't I? Those lanterns, and that cursed tree … just like in the haunting dream I had as Paul and I stood on the train platform to come here. The tree stood like an unyielding sentinel. That dream at the train station felt like a lifetime ago. Had it only been yesterday morning?!

Asuka dashed in front of me. "Miku! Are you here?"

Silence. The only sounds were the creaking of the tree and the flickering of the two torches' flames. Were those ancient torches burning with eternal flames?

"Miku!" she called again, framing her mouth with her hands.

Still nothing.

We strained to hear even the slightest reply but only the haunting echo of Asuka's voice returned.

She froze.

Was Miku truly lost?

Asuka closed her eyes, defeated. This was our shot, our only chance, and that stale truth immobilized my body as well. Asuka opened her eyes and sharply scanned the clearing. Nothing. No one.

Then, a sound fluttered into the clearing: soft, subtle, and most of all, weak.

♫ *A new morning has come. A morning of hope. Open your heart and fill it with happiness.* ♫

Singing—like a faint whisper. Oh, God, could it be Miku? Or was it that … *thing?*

A small soft voice murmured the familiar song, not at us, but up into the night's sky. It was a song we both recognized, that eerie melody that Hiroshi played earlier today from atop his watchtower. It was his song to bring happiness, a song to bring hope, a song to be *found*.

Asuka's eyes flew wide and carefully scanned the clearing, frantic to find the source. "There!" She pointed to a dark, lanky figure curled at the base of the tree and the entrance of the darkened shrine. The figure's face was slightly illuminated by the light of the lanterns. We crept closer, half cautious, half excited. The figure finished its vacant song and silence filled the clearing once more. The figure had long straight hair and a soft beautiful face.

It was Miku!

Gasping her name, Asuka lunged, crying as she collided into her friend. Asuka wrapped her arms around her, squeezing tightly.

Asuka pulled back from the embrace and held Miku's face, speaking precious words in Japanese. But my excitement was brief. I had seen this all before, I just *knew* I had. That dream ... from days ago ... it revealed a sobering truth in my heart: this was far from over.

Drums. A slow rhythmic beating emanated from deep within the shrine behind Miku.

It was coming.

Asuka paused as she looked closer at Miku's vacant expression.

Miku was blank, like she'd never been lost but had just been found in another part of a house. Or rather, like she wasn't even found yet. Miku's hands tightly clutched the suicide manual, holding it firmly against her chest.

"Miku?" Asuka said.

No response.

"Miku!" She grabbed Miku's shoulders, shaking her.

Still nothing.

The drums beat louder. Couldn't the others hear them?

Slowly, Miku's gaze rose beyond Asuka, beyond the clearing, to the darkened rim of the forest. Terror instantly replaced the emptiness in Miku's eyes.

"They're here ..." she whispered.

My heart stopped at the familiar sight. There they were, those same twinkling figures in the forest, the ones from last night. Two dozen ghosts cast shadows throughout the trees.

The dread that chased me all day had now leaped up like an approaching tsunami.

"Chad." An ethereal voice called my name. I whirled to face it, but it sounded from the same place as the pounding drums, from inside the hollowed trunk of the tree. *"We have much more to discuss."*

The tree seemed to breathe, its presence as dark and foreboding as the dread that shrouded my being.

I pressed past Asuka and Miku, past the dancing flames of the stone lanterns, and slunk towards the darkened threshold.

"Chad, where are you going?!" Asuka's voice called after me.

But I couldn't answer her.

"Yes ... closer ..." the voice within the tree whispered. *"You have come here with many questions, and the answers you are looking for lie within."* These same words that my father proclaimed to me earlier today possessed the same dread, and it washed over me. Relentless and driven by an insatiable hunger as unyielding as the grave, the force was so real, so tangible. And with it, it brought the fear and doubt of a battered and exhausted mind.

This wasn't right, was it? Should I follow this voice into that tree? Into the realm of the unknown, alone? But, was I really alone? Wasn't there Someone with me? Someone who expelled the darkness before?

A new strength began to boil in me. It did not, by any means, replace the fear. Rather, it existed in contrast to it. Somehow, I hoped this strength could challenge the darkness before me, the darkness lying in wait within that ancient tree.

I took another step.

"*Closer ...*" the voice from inside the darkness of the tree persisted.

Was it ignorant of The One who walked with me? I paused at the entrance, seeing only shadows beyond the threshold.

"There is no need to fear that which is already defeated," said another Voice, a voice from within my very spirit. I closed my eyes, searching for the courage.

"Alright, let's finish this. Once and for all," I prophesied as I pressed forward, stepping out of the clearing, through the doorway, and into the unknown regions of this ancient battleground.

EIGHT

THE ANSWER

The moonlight illuminated the hollowed expanse of the tree, revealing an interior no larger than a prison cell. Humid and heavy, the air reeked with the smell of rotting bark and damp soil. Dark porous mold covered the oddly shaped stones which made up the inner walls. Above me an organic canopy of vines and branches created a vaulted, netlike ceiling. Multiple stout vines reached down to the floor erecting a bulwark of misshapen columns, now bearing the weight of the archaic sanctum. Bits of paper, prayers perhaps, wove themselves within the sinewy vegetation. Layers of black soot, residue of sacrifices long forgotten, hung like brittle stalactites from the shallow ceiling.

My eyes strained to focus on an object in the far corner, scarcely discerning a rough- hewn stone altar. This primitive object, a meter high, resembled a lectern, though much more robust. Fragments of desiccated wax drippings littered the dusty floor at the altar's base. There, upon and around the altar, countless copies of the suicide manual lay in disarray, some old, and some fairly newer, almost pristine. It appeared that nearly every copy of the manual was accompanied by a pair of shoes, much like the ones we found at the beginning of our journey this morning. Had someone gathered both the shoes and the manuals, and collected them here? Were they, themselves, a symbol of sacrifice, an offering of some sort?

A black skulking shape caught my eye. I was not alone. Something loomed in the darkness.

"Who do you think you are?" that familiar voice scathed, sinking into the deepest recess of my mind. My father, the same figure who had followed me through the Aokigahara seethed, "Really, who the hell do you think you are?" He shot the question again with fierce inflections. I couldn't ignore him as I had in the ravine. There was no escaping his wicked words this time. No, it was time to end this, to confront this *thing*. Play his game, and hopefully, win.

"I am a child of God," I said.

"Shut up!" His words jumped over mine. "You're nothing more than a collection of carbon, water and protein!"

"No! I'm more than that," defiance inflamed in my voice, filling the shadows of the shrine.

"Oh, you really think so?" he taunted. "I'd like to hear why."

I searched myself, "Because I have a spirit."

"Delusions!" he shrieked with a laugh. "Mental constructs of a chemical reaction in your limbic system." His eyes went wide and his breath quickened as he began to maniacally pace back and forth. "No, no, no, no, no! You don't really believe that, do you? No, no, no. I'll tell you what you really are, son ... You are a vacant host with a false sense of self!" He seemed to be reveling in his mania. "You are a mistake!"

His rage was contagious. Soon, my words matched his intensity. "I am not a mistake!" I yelled, exasperated.

"You're just like everyone else. A living, self-absorbed being, just pretending to have a higher purpose than you actually do."

"How would you know? You don't even know what my purpose is!" He was wrong, spewing lies ... wasn't he?

"YOU DON'T HAVE ONE!!!" The *violence* of his words reverberated through the tree. "You're driven by a false hope that you will live forever, even when time after time, generation after generation, you've been proven wrong. And like every other human being, you're so foolish, so DELUSIONAL to keep believing otherwise!"

His torrent of nihilistic propaganda wasn't the ammunition I expected him to use against me. These words didn't even sound like my father, but there he stood, right in front of me. What was I to believe? But all the same, the spirit behind these hopeless words seeped, unchecked, into my heart. All those years of questioning myself started to close in on me. All of those secret moments, wondering if I *was* a mistake, if my life had just been one big, terrible error choked my heart. Was I *truly* fearfully and wonderfully made? Or just a pile of carbon, like this thing was accusing?

"Wake up! When are you going to realize that you're not leaving? None of you are. And if you were honest with yourself you would admit that you knew that the moment you stepped foot in this forest." He pushed closer, kicking shoes and books out of his way as he approached.

An eeriness prowled into my veins as his words dug into my ears; I could silence neither.

"You're wrong!" I held my ground, "We *are* getting out, all of us. Together!" The boldness of my retort sparked the courage to ask the nagging question that had been plaguing me, "Now you tell me: who are you ... really?"

The demented face of my father shot a smile that spread like melting wax and the moonlit skin of his cheeks began to tear.

"Do you really need it all spelled out for you, Chad? I am the father who has lingered in your mind, you 'child of God'!" he smirked and cackled, tearing more of his waxy flesh. "You want to know who I really am? There is only one god in this world: the god of ruin! AND I AM HE!" Opening his grizzly arms wide, he presented himself in crazed supremacy. "The pains you carry in your heart are the only thing that matters. They are chains, enslaving you in *my* service. By them, you are beholden unto me! ME!"

This couldn't be right! There had to be more to me than the wounds of my past. Had that pain really followed me throughout my life? *Defined* my destiny? Was that really the only thing of any substance in my existence? No. The Truth from within me fought back, "I left that pain in the past!"

"You didn't leave it and let it go; you buried it, just as you buried your father," he sneered. "Remember, what you plant in soil always grows." The words were caustic and precise. "Now your wound has grown, daily festering, and it has followed you into every country, every relationship, and every thought—unresolved and relentless." A capricious grin arose on his face, aware his assault was ceaseless. "You're nothing without your hurt, your rejection. They've justified you, identified you, and because of this, you have allowed *me* to define *you*! Now it's time for you to complete your surrender and rest in it. Aren't you weary, Chad? Don't you finally want some peace from all of this? Rest in me!"

The figure extended his arm, a cruelly victorious smile on his face.

The full volley of his mental attack had been brought to completion. He, as well as the feverish nausea within me, knew that a mortal blow had been dealt, and the broken pieces of my fortitude, inevitably began to crumble.

"Yes," he whispered again in a now familiar manner. "You're finished."

In that wayward moment, all I wanted was to submit to his malicious lies once and for all. There was an unexpected gravitational pull to his demonic weavings. A seduction to give up, embrace my pain, and follow those appalling words into the dark void of defeat. I felt as though I could follow his words anywhere.

But ... hadn't I already been doing that for years? Hadn't I already given in to the seduction of those words by means of allowing that mentality of self-pity to have influence over me? Had my devotion to the morose brought me anything more than the doubt now telling me to yield? Was it time to walk away from it? *Could* I walk away from it?

I fell to my knees.

Oh, God, Please help me!

"It's okay, my child," the figure said between heavy breaths.

I felt his cold hand on the back of my neck, gentle yet lethal.

"You can join me here, now." A cruel satisfaction emanated from him. "Too long have I dwelled in this place without the ailment of rot and ruin." His grip around my neck tightened, seemingly to have found something in me that he craved. "Rest in me. Nourish me! And in return, Slave of the Son, my darkness will give you the freedom you seek! Freedom from your wound, your curse: the curse of the father!"

Was this really all there was? This pain? This gangrenous wound in my heart? This curse? Was there nothing more I could do?

"Jesus," I whispered, closing my eyes tight. "Jesus, are you with me?"

No reply.

Silence.

Nothing but stillness.

Stillness …. but one of righteousness; the same as I felt in my father's bedroom when I had cried out to God years before.

"I AM HERE, MY SON."

As this commanding voice burst into my mind, a blinding light from an unseen realm filled the inner sanctum.

The dark presence of the figure posing as my dad: now absent. But gone? I didn't know.

Time slowed to a snail's pace.

"Lord? Are you with me?" I asked, standing to my feet, squinting my eyes in the overpowering brilliance.

"I AM," He assured. The radiance of His presence flooded every corner, every crevice of the shrine, displacing every shadow.

I surveyed the sanctum, the altar, the suicide manuals and the pairs of shoes, all now bathed in the vibrant light. "That thing, what is it?" I asked, hoping a divine explanation would bring greater clarity.

But, a sobering rebuke returned as the answer.

"Do not give that which has already been defeated the time it doesn't deserve! The threat of a starving demon on the verge of demise pales in comparison to the well-being of my son, you."

I hung my head, tears filling my eyes.

"As it has been said many times today, Chad, there is much to discuss. No, not with that malevolent spirit, but with Me." His words brought with them a power of absolution that required my heart to fall in total reverence.

I looked out past the opening of the tree, to Asuka, Miku, and the mysterious glimmering lights at the rim of the clearing, all still covered by the blanket of night and all nearly frozen in place.

"There will be time for that, Chad. But first, I must attend to your wound."

My wound? The searing pain in my ankle began to dull.

"No, a wound much older than that, deeper and hidden from view."

I turned from the sight of Asuka and Miku, my gaze now fixed on His majestic light.

"There is a scar on your heart," He said, authority resonating in every word. **"An absolute fragmentation, a fracture of your being. You've had this wound since that night."**

"The night my father took his life?" I asked, already knowing the answer; the demon made the source of my wound abundantly clear. But, did my Heavenly Father have an alternative to how I was to deal with this pain? Would He have the righteous answer to the question that wicked spirit forced from my mouth?

"Was it *really* my fault, Lord?"

The words hung in the damp air before being obliterated by another surge of holy light.

"What influence has made you believe such a wicked lie?" Another question, one which made me crumble back to my knees.

"Rise, my beloved. You are not the object of my anger. My wrath falls to the source of the deceit aimed at you, that demon. Now, search yourself, tell me why you think the death of your father was done by your hand?"

It was a question that required me to look inward; a journey I had procrastinated for *decades*. "I deserted him," I said. "Long before the night he died. If I had only been there for him, *really* been there for him, maybe he would still be alive."

He let my words echo back to me, their naïve simplicity exposing their erroneous nature.

"You don't hold the power to isolate anyone. The only way a person can be truly isolated is if he, himself, wills it."

"But, the notebook! The words he wrote! All the hatred he had toward me! The hatred towards *You!* Were those words not a symptom of his isolation?"

"The way your natural father wrote about your faith told you one story, just as the picture he kept over his bed told another one. I see all things, the beginning and the end. I also see the dimensions of your heart, as I saw the deep dimensions of your father's. One of which, told of the pain of the faith you represented. He believed that it was your faith, that it was Me, who took your mother from him."

"Exactly!" I said, bitterness rising in me again. I paused, continuing respectfully. "And he pushed me out of his life because of it!"

"And that made you angry?"

"Doesn't it make you angry, Lord?" I asked, catching my words too late. I recoiled in reverence.

"I have known countless people who use my name, my power, to blame for their struggles. It comes as no surprise to me. My love remains resolute, and my forgiveness infinite. Can the same be said for you, Chad?"

"I thought so. I thought I forgave him that night in his bedroom."

"Yes, perhaps you 'forgave' him, but you never released that pain and rejection. Even now, so many years later, they are entrenched in you, and the forgiveness you extended to your father, you have yet to receive for yourself."

"But, I thought I've already dealt with all of this," I said.

"You've sought to escape it and that escape provoked a refusal to learn the second lesson I meant for you to understand that night. That you, Chad, a minister of my word, you have denied the love of your natural father the same way you deny my love."

I searched myself, "How am I denying you, Lord? I've carried your message with me, preached your mercy!"

"You have, but in tandem, you have ignored the power and grace I have to heal your wound and release you from the pain that has held you in bondage. You deny Me access to that pain. Everyone in their own way has denied Me. Many will never yield, and it's because they're afraid—just as you are."

"Afraid?" I couldn't help but release a scoff. "Wasn't I brave to move on with my life? To make something of myself despite that tragedy?"

"Brave? Yes. But you lacked the courage to reveal your wound to me, to expose it. Without that exposure, you denied Me the ability to heal it." Then He said softly, "And yes, my son. You have made a life beyond the tragedy of your father's rejection and suicide. Yes, you have preached my name and ministered to my children, and for that, I Am well pleased. But even in doing so, you have broken the promise you made to Me and yourself that night in your father's bedroom."

I closed my eyes in shame.

Yes, I remembered it now.

The promise, the one I made that night was that I would use this tragedy to help others who were at the greatest risk. In all my travels, all my ministry, I had completely forgotten about that decree. How many people had sat in my services, desperate to hear that they were valued, that their life was worth living? How many people had slipped beyond the veil of eternity because I was too stubborn to allow God to completely heal that wound in myself?

"A surgeon cannot right the medical wrongs of their patients when they, themselves, are bleeding out. Without healing your wound of suicide, you can only operate in a small fraction of what I have called you to do. There are countless people you will encounter in your future that desperately need my words of life. A desperate cry for the message of life's value has been greatly ignored. And the harvest is great! But it will take a healed person to deliver this message." Then He asked gently, **"Will you be that person, Chad?"**

All those years of running from this pain, keeping myself busy, traveling the world, all of it, led me here, to the Aokigahara, the Suicide Forest, where I had to finally confront the spirit of suicide face-to-face. "That's why I'm here, isn't it, Lord?"

A silent moment passed.

"That's why you're here, my son."

"But, does that mean that everything that happened today, that living darkness, that thing masquerading as my father was just in my mind?"

"No. You have been embattled by an ancient spirit, seeking to consume the destiny bestowed on you and the destiny of every other soul that has entered the Aokigahara in hopes that this forest will bring an end to their suffering. Like past visitors, your mind has agreed with its influence, luring you into silent accord, demanding you abdicate your throne. Did you think you were beyond the reach of such deception? You should have known better."

It was as I had feared; an enemy, an adversary, though unseen, had gone unchallenged, exploiting my weakness. I had seen first-hand the cruelty dispensed by that demonic realm today. It was not the stuff of shadows or sleight of hand, it was much more than that. A malignant entity resolute in its hatred towards me and The One I served. "But I didn't come here looking for a fight."

"No, but you came looking for the answer to a question, one that wicked spirit set out to answer with condemnation and deceit."

"But I tried to rebuke it!"

"Yes, you tried to push its influence out of your mind, but not your heart, Chad. That creature can smell that wound in you. As long as it remains open, darkness will always have a stronghold in your soul." His words stung.

Tears welled up in my eyes and blurred my vision. Shame washed over me and abated all other feelings. "Then how do I close that wound?"

"You could try to close it yourself, as you have attempted to do. However, there is another alternative."

"What is it?"

"By the flame of MY LIFE, Chad!!" His fiery retort overwhelmed me. "My power can heal every hurt, mend every pain, and close an open wound with a scar of mercy!"

I shuddered at the authority in his voice.

Silence again.

"But, is that what you want, Chad?"

I paused, "It's all I ever wanted, Father."

"Then rise to your feet, son! And finish this fight *with me*!" His voice was bathed in righteous indignation.

"Finish the fight? No! Please!!" I pleaded. "I can't face that thing again!"

"That creature of hell was already defeated by My Blood! All I'm asking you to do is to stand firm, and walk in the authority I have bestowed upon you, son. You are not alone. And you will not be devoured by that which you know has no authority!"

That familiar pang of uncertainty began gnawing at me again. "Will you stand with me, Lord? Really, I can't do this alone."

"I have never left you, Chad! I have always been with you. I Am the One who led you here, to this place, this place of ancient pagan worship, where, as unholy as this place is, it will be the stage to the final act, where an ultimate choice between life or death will be made, son. Will that choice be made for you?"

In an instant, the stillness of His presence abated. I was back in the shrine staring down that same demonic presence as before. The flow of time had returned to its swift pace, Asuka and Miku, still out at the entrance of the tree, still looking out to the ghostly lights at the rim of the clearing. How long had I been inside the tree? An hour? A moment? There was still so much for us to do tonight. But the looming figure of that *demon* posing as my father was my first priority!

The creature paced the floor of the sanctum, taunting me, waiting for my next move. I held my breath and rose to my feet like a soldier in battle.

"Haven't had enough?" It smirked, its skin tearing even more.

I grinned, dusting the soil from my knees. Had I really been given the wisdom and strength to finally rid myself of this *thing*? "We're just getting started. You are NOT my father!" My words rang through the shrine. "Get out of my mind!"

The dark figure smiled, creeping around me. "Get out? Ha, I'm just getting started with you!"

I stood my ground, eyes locked on It. "You're wrong! This is over! I don't know *who* or *what* you are, but whatever hold you thought you had on me, isn't real!"

It rushed toward me, doubling in size. "Never! You are mine! MINE!" Its voice began to distort with deep, spectral tones. I could feel its rancid breath on my face, filling the chamber with the smell of decay. My nausea returned. I felt like I'd been sucker punched in the gut. No! This was not going to happen, not again! I was brought here for a reason, and that reason wasn't to be consumed by this wicked creature!

Jesus, you've gotta help me!

"Oh, 'Jesus, Jesus!' " The creature mocked, black drool cascading from its rotting mouth. "Did you really think you could just leave?! You came to *my* forest! You brought the book of death, my book! You wanted to uncover the mysteries of the Aokigahara!" Its hand reached to me, mutating into a razor sharp claw. "The wound in your heart has marked you for death!"

What was going on? Why was this fight so hard?

"You will be the first to die." It snapped toward the opening of the shrine, its vicious eyes fixed on Asuka and Miku. "Then, they will join you, buried under this soil until the end of time, feeding me!"

"No!" I screamed, marshalling my faith. "You can't touch them!" The words echoed in my mind with sudden revelation.

It couldn't ... touch ... them.

I took a step back, it pressed closer, its body shaking in wicked fury. But ... why didn't it just lunge at me? Why didn't it finish me as it threatened it would?

"You can't touch me, can you?" I whispered. "You literally *can't* touch me, can you?" I smirked with this revelation.

The demon screamed in rage. Flame burst from its eyes, engulfing the crevices of its sockets. The blaze ignited the black tar, frothing from its mouth, transforming it into molten lava. "I don't need to touch you to end your life!"

The heat seared my face, sweat poured off of me. Oh God, please. Stay with me.

"You're right!" I yelled.

The demon jumped at the words. Its sharp toothed snarl turned into a frown. "What?!"

I advanced another step. "You *could* end my life ..."

The creature stood tall, showing the full weight of its true stature. "Yes!"

"But not without my willingness!"

"Silence!" It stumbled back, slamming against the wall of stone. Flames danced from its clawed hands.

"I've been silent long enough!" I shouted, closing in on the creature.

"You can't hurt anyone without deceiving them first, can you? This ..."
I gestured to my father's funeral suit, "*facade*! It's the only game you can
play, isn't it?!"

The creature leaped into the air, suspending itself above me, skittering
like a spider. "You are in my web; you can't leave!" Liquid fire spewed to
the ground, pools of magma flowed around my feet.

My eyes darted to the floor and a glint of fear struck my heart. No, I
can't back down now. God, if you're not with me ... this is already over!

"Yield to me!" The demon screamed from above, new appendages
twisting and growing out of its funeral suit.

I fell to my knees, streams of lava flowing around me. God, this is it
... please, let me be right on this one! In terror, I reached out my hand,
immersing it into the liquid fire. I braced for the agony that I hoped
wouldn't come.

"What are you doing?!" The creature screeched, panic filling its voice.

Nothing!

No pain, no burning.

My hand grasped at the lava, grabbing it. I brought my hand to my
face and opened it: cold ash. It was all becoming so crystal clear. "I will
not yield to that which has no power!" I said with a victorious smirk.

The rest of the creature's grotesque form erupted in a violent rage.
"NO!" The flames ruptured its grasp on the ceiling, sending it plunging
to the ground. It landed with a boom, ash and soil filling the air. The
demon pulled itself to its knees, the deformed mutations of flame and
bone, gone!

I approached.

It scurried away, finding refuge behind the altar. "Get away!" Fear
twisted its burnt face.

I knelt down, our eyes locked, my terror vanishing as quickly as the illusion of the fire in my hand.

"Don't touch me, Slave of the Son!" it hissed.

"You have already been defeated by The One who resides in me," I said.

"No!" The demon pleaded, hands clenching its face, tearing at its skin.

"You never had any real power over me! The only power you hold is the deceit you seed into people's minds. You detected an infected wound in me the moment I came here. You smelled that putrefaction, didn't you? It was you who stalked me today, watching me, *learning* me. You studied my past, that wound, that *rot*. You turned yourself into that one thing that would cause me to question the value of my life!"

The demon's eyes filled with panic. "Yes!"

"But now, through the power of The One in me, that wound is now a scar, no longer vulnerable. You can't touch it, can you? You ..." I inched closer. It recoiled. "Can't ..." Even closer. "... touch me, can you?!" I grinned, baiting the creature.

The demon's bloody face twisted in pain, "NO! I CAN'T TOUCH YOU!"

There it was, the confession I needed, THE TRUTH. "But I can touch you, can't I?" My hand thrust towards its chest. A righteous white flame began to consume the creature.

"*Stop it!*" the demon begged.

"Too long have you preyed on the hopeless, too long have you fed on their pain! IN THE NAME OF JESUS, GO!"

I felt a sudden jolt beneath me, like a freight train had slammed into the tree. I was not shaken, but the *demon* was! The creature looked at me in fear and defeat as every fiber of its being began to turn into a fiery ember.

"You can take your Jesus and get out!" The demon screamed before glowing embers burst into a vicious flame, engulfing it. In a brilliant flash, the creature's form incinerated. Wisps of smoke rose through the trunk of the tree and vanished into utter nothingness.

The creature … the demon … was gone!

My throbbing head fell into my hands. *"Oh God, thank you."*

Silence, an infinite moment of silence.

My heart slowed into its steady rhythm once more.

Alone.

Finally rid of the darkness in my mind.

But …was I really alone?

The moonlight cascading from the entrance of the shrine began to slowly diminish.

Clap … clap … clap …

NINE

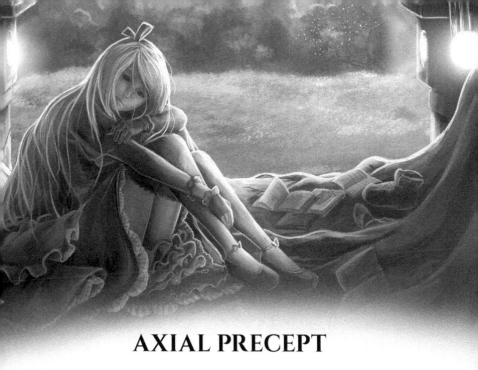

AXIAL PRECEPT

Clap ... clap ... clap ...

The muted applause echoed in the hollow shrine.

I turned and my heart dropped.

An oddly familiar petite form stood at the entrance of the tree, silhouetted in the moonlight. It was unmistakably, that strange girl! Was she *really* the mischievous teenager my mind passed her off to be? Or something else entirely?

My eyes strained to make out her shape. A demure expression contrasted a smile of indifference. Once again, her shoulder length hair fell in disheveled waves and that black tea-party dress ... those buckled shoes ... those gloves ... there was no mistaking her!

"Very good! That was fun to watch!" she said playfully, her voice soft and ethereal. Finishing her applause, her hands grasped each other in timid modesty.

"It's you!" I gasped, shock filling my heart.

The strange girl nodded. "Me." Her voice nearly squealed with glee.

Confusion coursed with adrenaline vibrated through my body as my mind raced. Tonight's events had completely overshadowed the memory of my encounter with her today, and I hadn't given her a second thought. But the way she stood, so serene, so confident and … at home in this forest of death, it forced me to consider if I *should* have given her that second thought, and a third, and a thousandth.

She said nothing as we waited for me to piece her together. She hummed softly, occupying her time while my mind shifted into overdrive, dashing through the first conversation we had. What were those things she said to me last night?

The hour is later than I think.

What did she mean?

There is much to be done at this time of night.

What was she doing in the Aokigahara?

Shall I come in, or shall we stand here all night?

Who was she?

"Who are you?!" the words escaped me.

She tilted her head to the side, inquisitively. "I think you know who I am well enough," she said. "My nature runs deep, and is as ancient as time itself." Her black eyes snapped to the pile of ash behind me. "I've known that demon for a very long time. He was an efficient colleague to my work here. It's a shame to see him vanquished. But …" Her eyes met mine again. "I have been around long enough to know that creatures like that one aren't gone for long. His hunger will resurrect him eventually."

My mind swam. This girl, this being, she possessed a different spirit than the deranged demon I faced. She was steady, composed, confident and *patient*. "What are you?!" I demanded again.

The question wiped the smile from her face. My use of the word "what" struck a deeper resonance in her. She paused, then seating herself on the ground, she began, "Consider the one final element in your natural world, compounded by time itself, and multiplied by the suffering of billions. I have met everyone who has ever walked the earth, my blade has swept across the ages of man." Her frown dissipated back into that infuriatingly playful smile. "I've been around since the dawn of an era, an era that started with a choice. Some could even say that it was the first choice ever made. That choice birthed me into existence, and I've lingered in the world ever since. But it's only recently that the affairs of the Aokigahara has piqued my curiosity."

My mind raced. "Are you another demon?"

"Do not try to rationalize my nature through your recent experience with that evil spirit. I operate under the same laws as you do."

"What laws?"

"You already know, Mr. Daniel. They are the laws by which all of mankind and all living things must abide. Some seek me out, others run from me, but it makes no difference either way. I must obey the laws that created me. Me, the most consistent and eternal component in human existence."

I searched myself. What brought this being to Aokigahara? What element obeys the laws of nature with an absolute indifference? What facet of human existence remains indiscriminately?

"Yes," she whispered to me, seeming to audibly hear my musings. "I take no pleasure in welcoming those who seek my finality. Nor do I hold malice towards those who try to avoid me. Eventually, they will all succumb to the final requirement. There has only been One who has broken my embrace and voided my nature." Her arms crossed over her chest, a visible shiver of dread swept through her. "I sense that same One resides in you."

She held her vacant gaze to me like a child wanting a treat that was just out of reach. I could almost feel a painful yearning emanating from her being. But if she couldn't embrace the One who resided in me by her nature, why did she even reach out to me last night and at the watchtower? What was the point?

Breaking the silence, she answered my thought again, "When you've been around as long as I have, you will find yourself gravitating to anomalies, boredom perhaps, or natural curiosity."

"Or to intimidate me!" I added brashly.

She blinked, "What do you mean?"

Once more, my mind combed over our exchange last night and settled on her departing warning. "You said that when explorers of the ancient world would venture off into the unknown, only three would return. You said it was the sacrifice of revelation. You meant us, didn't you?"

She blinked again, "And?"

I paused. "And … you were wrong! I didn't lose anyone to the Aokigahara. We found Miku, and Paul, I'm sure, is safe with Hiroshi. And that demon didn't destroy me the way it set out to," I said with a lively satisfaction.

She let only a moment go by before retorting, "And what about Asuka?"

The name caught me off guard. Asuka's unwavering strength kept her off of my list.

"Chad!" As if on cue, Asuka's voice called out to me from beyond the shrine. "What are you doing?? Come out here!"

The strange girl perked her head up at Asuka's cry. She took a long stare out to the clearing, no doubt in the direction of my two companions. She then rose to her feet, and kicked at the dirt lightheartedly. "You all still have much to do tonight. Your time in the Aokigahara is not over yet. No, no more evil spirits will beset your journey. But the hour IS later than you think, Mr. Daniel. And the greatest discoveries are yet to be made."

"Chad! Stop being weird and get out here now!" Asuka's voice called out again.

The strange girl turned from me, taking in the vast expanse of the Aokigahara. "We will meet again. That can't be avoided. But, I hope your destination beyond me is a better one than the fate I will face. Until then ..."

And as if leaving a social affair, she departed, leaving me with another nagging question.

What about Asuka?

TEN

A LIGHT IN A DARK PLACE

Upon emerging from the shrine, I found Asuka still holding the terrified Miku. Had only moments had passed since I departed them? Everything was just as I had left it, the shimmering lights continued their taunting at the edge of the forest rim, Miku still couldn't tear her eyes away from them, and the manual remained in her vice-like grip. Was she aware she was holding it? Or was the book holding *her*? Her face glistened with sweat and tears. Asuka continued to comfort her while keeping an eye on those twinkling shapes at the rim of the forest. "Miku," I said, bending my knee.

Miku kept her eyes glued to the edge of the clearing.

"It's okay."

"No, it is not okay!" she shot back.

"Miku, get up."

"No, no. I cannot!" She shook her head hysterically.

"Miku, listen to me!"

"No!" Her eyes were swollen from crying.

I gripped her shoulders. "Listen to me! There's nothing in this forest that can hurt you unless you allow it!"

She didn't answer.

"Miku, please ..."

"I ... don't ... want," she gasped, "to be alone anymore!"

"Miku," I assured her. "You're *not* alone anymore. I promise, no matter what happens, it won't be as hard as it's been by yourself."

Tears welled up and fell in streams. "But, there *is* something in this place, not like the ghost stories. Something *real*. I felt it! I felt it *pull* me here!" Her eyes raised to the tree limbs above us. "The beginning of all things, the end of all things." Her gaze met mine again. "I could hear something whispering to me, telling me terrible things. I tried not to listen, but I could not stop!"

I knew that voice all too well. The battle with the demon in the shrine was the confirmation I needed; not *all* of this was in my head. Miku felt it, too. The creature tried to consume her as well, didn't it? There was now no denying that force, that menace. But I now knew the final act to this story: that demon was, in fact, subdued. But how could I communicate the truth of this revelation to Miku?

The words from my conversation with my Heavenly Father rang through my heart with relevance, but how could I explain it to Miku? What was the truth she needed to hear? I stepped into her shoes, attempting to see how her perspective of this entire journey had brought her to this place of desolation. I realized as she struggled with her fears and insecurities, amplified by the otherworldly sightings from last night and the deadly aura surrounding the Aokigahara, she had felt unsupported by all of us. While we never questioned her stability, we certainly diminished her anxiety, at times even brushed her off. Without friends who would believe and trust her, she found herself isolated with those fears, vulnerable to that demon's influence. My heart ached for her. I had to make it right.

"Miku, you are not crazy! And, yes, you were right all along! There *was* something in this place. No, not like a ghost story, something much worse. Something sinister wanted to do us harm. But understand its tactics, Miku: it can't hurt you if you know the Truth. It's the Truth that the thing wanted to silence. It wanted us to doubt each other, instill fear and to isolate us, lie to us, convince us to yield to its authority. It's only then that it could destroy us from the inside out."

I needed something tangible. Spinning to Asuka, I motioned for the cross around her neck, Miku's cross. Asuka unclasped the necklace and handed it to me.

I held the cross in front of Miku, trying to get her to focus on it rather than the lights at the rim of the clearing. Miku's eyes widened at the familiar symbol. Even so, her hands would not release the suicide manual. "You said that you've had this cross since you were a kid?"

"Yes."

"Who gave it to you?" I asked.

"My mother."

"My mother never gave me an *actual* cross," I said, "but she gave me something that this cross represents, something even greater than her: *faith*. After my mother died, her faith was a constant reminder of the price that was paid for my protection. The blood that was shed on The

Cross was a payment for my future, *our* future! Jesus' sacrifice and victory over death assures our peace with God, our salvation. It was the great exchange, Miku!" I glanced down at the suicide manual, now damp with her sweat and tears. "I'm asking you to step out in faith and make an exchange with me."

Miku's eyes followed my gaze to the book. Shock washed over her face, and her grip instantly released. Falling from her hands and tumbling into the soil, Miku scrambled away from the book as if it were a venomous snake. Asuka knelt, wrapped her arms around her, and whispered reassuringly in Japanese.

I picked up the manual; its dark mysteries no longer held any spells of intrigue. There were more important things to do than dwell on the contrived power found in its pages. I turned to face the twinkling lights and took several steps toward them. Straining to focus, I discerned that they were, in fact, real and tangible, nothing like the ethereal visions from today. What could they be?

Asuka joined me. "How's your ankle?" she asked, her eyes scanning my leg.

My ankle? I had completely forgotten about it! How odd that now as I put my weight on it, there was no more pain. "I think it's healed!"

She nodded, "Umm, thank you, by the way," her words came in her usual melodic tones, "for helping me find her, I mean."

"I should be thanking you," I shook my head. "Miku is lucky to have someone like you to rely on."

She nodded, "We're both lucky."

We stared quietly at the twinkling figures, the final riddle of a night crammed with too many mysteries.

"So ... what should we do," she asked, "... about those?"

What should we do? Should we turn back the way we came and flee from this one final great question? But, without light, the journey back through the forest would be nearly impossible. No, we were stuck here until we had proper illumination, both in the forest and in ourselves.

"I say we face whatever those are together," I suggested. "Something tells me we're going to be alright."

"Are you sure?" Her eyes searched mine.

"Hey, if I can fight off what's been plaguing me since I stepped foot in the Aokigahara, then we can certainly handle …" we both looked back into the twinkling forest, "whatever those are."

She nodded apprehensively, gripped her arm and looked away, but I couldn't do the same. The untested strength of her face had now been replaced with a nervous vulnerability. A twinge of heartache stabbed at me. Would the otherworldly girl's prophecy surely be fulfilled? Were we *still* liable to lose our fearless guide to the mysteries of the Aokigahara?

BAM!

We both jumped in fright as a sudden flash of orange pierced the blackness and a loud bang struck our ears. The orange light filled the clearing with a smooth, flowing glow. I caught sight of a blazing flare just starting to arch over my head emitting huge orange and yellow sparks as it descended back to earth. The smoke trail created a thread-like ribbon across the darkened sky. The source of the shot originated from behind us. I turned back to Miku, still collapsed at the tree with an orange flare gun cradled in her shaking hands.

This must have been what was in the bag Hiroshi gave her back at the tower, a last resort if we found ourselves in desperation.

"Miku?!" I asked.

"Let's get the hell out of here!" she said with determination, her face lit by the slowly fading orange hues. She rose to her feet, grimacing from exhaustion, and joined us.

Together, we stood, ready for whatever came next, as the sparkling lights continuing their playful taunt.

"Kishi Kaisei?" Miku whispered to Asuka.

"Kishi Kaisei," Asuka repeated.

Suddenly, another flash of light filled the clearing, bright, overpowering and artificial. We spun around to find its source.

Floodlights!

One of the forest's tower had finally spotted us!

Then, one by one, dozens of other floodlights from surrounding watchtowers flashed on, now illuminating the outer expanse of the Aokigahara. Some towers were close by, while others, mere pinpoints on the forest rim.

As the marvelous white lights filled the sky, a familiar tune filled our ears: the same music from earlier today—the music from Hiroshi's watchtower. Had Hiroshi found us? Did Paul make it back to the watchtower to get help?

We stood dumbstruck, quietly watching as the darkness of the forest systematically vanished.

"What's that?" Asuka asked.

"What?" Miku said.

"I don't hear anything," I strained to hear.

A loud, commanding voice emanated from the distance.

"There!" Asuka pointed into the forest. "Is it …?"

The familiar voice of Hiroshi rose in the distance. However, it wasn't the gentle tone he had from earlier today. Instead, he was furiously speaking, almost chastising someone.

"What is happening?" Miku asked.

Hiroshi's voice originated from the direction where the sparkling lights were, or *had been.*

In all the chaos, I hadn't realized that those twinkling lights had vanished the moment the watchtowers had turned on. Asuka and Miku were just as confused as I was.

"What's going on?" Asuka asked.

"Let's go find out," I reached my hand out to Miku. She cautiously took it, grabbing Asuka's as well. Holding her between us, we led the exhausted girl to the rim of the forest, toward Hiroshi's voice.

The smell of sulfur greeted us as we neared the edge of the clearing. There Hiroshi stood, berating a dozen or so Japanese tweens and teens. The children bowed, clearly apologetic to the ranger. And there in their hands were fireworks! Between them were all sorts of little sparklers and bottle rockets.

"Hanabi?" Miku asked. "Those flickering lights were fireworks?"

The three of us exchanged looks of puzzlement and relief. The pieces all fell together. The "child-ghosts," the flickering lights, all of it was nothing but these children playing in the forest.

Miku fell into the grass. "Children," she whispered. "Real ... live ... children ... with fireworks."

It all seemed so obvious now! But doesn't everything become clearer when a little light is shown on the matter?

There was nothing to be afraid of. Clearly by their remorseful demeanor (and how quickly they stashed the fireworks in their bags), these children were just as scared of getting in trouble as we adults had been scared of being haunted by ghosts just a few short moments ago.

"Chad!" Paul's familiar voice called out.

I grabbed his shoulders tightly. "Paul!"

He glanced at Asuka. "Did you find her?!"

"We found her," Asuka smiled, gesturing to Miku sitting in a relieved clump on the ground.

"You did good, Paul!" I said.

He shook his head. "You should thank Hiroshi, really. He was already on alert because we hadn't come out of the forest by sunset."

Hiroshi appeared by Paul's side, grabbed my hand, and gripped it tightly.

"I was beginning to think I would never find you," he smiled, holding his grip. "You have caused me a lot of nervousness tonight. Well, you and those disobedient children!" He shot a glare over to the youths, who now quietly talked amongst themselves.

"Yeah, what are they doing all the way out here?" I asked.

"Camping trip with their school. This kind of thing happens every year, though. Kids sneak out after dark to go light fireworks and tell ghost stories. I've been trying to catch them for the last couple nights. But now," giving a giant grin and yelling in their direction, "I got them! HA!"

The children jumped at his words.

"Are they in trouble?" I asked.

Hiroshi shrugged. "What am I to do? They're children. I did the same when I was their age. They will be reprimanded, but …" Another shrug.

"Can I go talk to them?" I asked.

"Yes, of course. I have to keep them here until their counselors retrieve them."

I turned back toward Miku, still collapsed in the grass.

"Are you alright?" I asked.

"I am alive, yes. But this … all of this …"

"I know," I smiled. "I went through it, too."

"You did?"

"I'll tell you about it later. But right now, can I ask you a favor?"

"What?"

"Come with me?" I asked.

"What is it?"

"It's alright," I reached out my hand, inviting her to stand.

"Oh, Chad, I don't know," she hesitated nervously, as though unable or unwilling to put herself through anything else tonight.

"Don't be afraid and just trust me. There's something that you and I *have* to do."

Her tired, dry eyes blinked for a moment. She reached up, I sprang her to her feet and then guided her through the last of the tall grass until we were in front of the children.

They all regarded us, quietly. They were surprisingly groomed after having been in the forest without adult supervision for the last few hours.

I stood speechless for a moment; my charisma had suddenly fled.

"Hello …" I stupidly muttered.

Hellos returned.

I turned to Miku, "Say something, Miku."

"Why?" She asked.

"Just … say something."

She reluctantly addressed the children, speaking in Japanese. The children replied, pointing to me. "They want to know if they can speak to you in English. They are learning it in school and want to practice."

"Yes, of course!" I said.

Miku nodded to the children. They excitedly broke out into a myriad of questions.

"Where are you from?"

"The United States."

"What are you doing here?"

"I'm making a documentary."

"What's a documentary?"

"It's a movie–"

"Are you a movie star?"

"No," I laughed. "But Miku here is!"

"You are?!"

Miku blushed as the children swarmed her and, returning to their native language, asked so many questions that she couldn't keep up.

I spoke up, "Hey! Can I ask you all a question?"

"Yes!" they all responded in clipped English, growing quiet again.

I paused for a moment, trying to find a good place to start. "Tonight has been a scary night, huh?"

A chorus of agreement rose amongst them.

"And sometimes, it's fun to be scared, especially when you're with your friends."

Again, nods and yesses.

"You get to be scared, knowing that you're *actually* safe. Like coming out here at night. It's been fun, right?"

"Oh yes!" they laughed.

"But would you come out here alone?"

"No!" they exclaimed.

"Why not?"

"*Yūrei*," they all said in unison.

"Ghosts?" I asked, incredulously.

"Yes, ghosts!"

I smiled and lowered my voice to a whisper. "You know," I leaned in, "last night, Miku and I thought we saw something very scary!"

"You did?"

"Yes! Someone told us a story about the ghost children who live here in the forest."

The children all spoke at once, "Ghost children? What ghost children? Living in the forest? Here? Living here? In *this* forest?"

"Yes!" I nodded seriously. "The story goes that these ghost children live here in this very forest. Once we heard this story, it stuck in our heads and it scared us very much. Later, we were standing in a long, dark hallway of a Ryokan and we looked out the window ..."

The children were riveted, their black eyes full of fear. They stood silently, hanging on to every word, desperate to hear what came next.

"And we saw those ghosts ... right out the window, *dancing* in the forest!"

The children gasped.

"And tonight, we saw them *again*. In this *very* part of the Aokigahara ... just a few minutes ago."

The children's eyes widened even more. They nervously looked around, their eyes searching through the woods around them.

"Where are they?" one of the older girls bravely asked. Like most of the other children, she wore a light sweater, jeans, and sneakers. She firmly held onto her Hello Kitty bag, not too old to enjoy the fun and timeless brand.

"Well," I said, "It turns out … they weren't *really* ghosts."

"They weren't?" she glanced at her friends.

I shook my head.

"Werewolves," she decided.

"No," I said.

"Vampires!" and she was certain she guessed right as the other children huddled closer.

"Nope."

"Then what?" she asked.

I smiled. "They were children playing with fireworks."

The children looked confused, still scared.

I laughed. "They were all of you!"

A moment passed. Smiles spread on their delighted faces. They broke out into raucous peals of laughter, speaking rapidly in Japanese between breaths and spasms of giggles. Their contagious laughter made me chuckle, too. Some of the children flipped on their flashlights, held them under their chins and made spooky faces. Others even put the lit end of the flashlights into their mouths, moaning like ghouls.

I turned to spot Miku smiling happily, even laughing, a sight I hadn't seen all day. She chatted in Japanese with the oldest girl and several others, hints of blush filling her cheeks. A couple of the children hugged her around her shoulders, holding her close.

One of the boys tugged at my shirt. "Were you scared, too?" he asked, pushing his bangs across his forehead.

"I was," I admitted. "But it turned out that there wasn't really anything to be scared of. There aren't really ghosts here, right?"

Most of the children shook their heads.

"But we had imagined ghosts in our minds. And so anything that we didn't understand, we thought was something scary, especially when we were alone. It's much easier to be brave when we're with our friends, right?"

"Yes!" they replied, even more excited and hugging each other.

Already knowing the answer, I asked. "What were you all doing out here tonight?"

The rambunctious kids quickly reached into their bags and presented the fireworks they had stuffed out of sight as they fervently talked a mile a minute.

"Ah! Fireworks!" I said. They nodded, smiling. "You know, I'm from the United States, right?"

"Yes!"

"Do you know what part?"

They shook their heads. "No. Where? What part?"

"The deep south. And in the deep south, we like to shoot off big, giant, huge fireworks!" I opened my arms wide.

A couple of the boys knelt down and fiddled around in one of the bags. They brought out three large fireworks with Japanese writing on it.

"These are very big!" the oldest boy said, handing it to me.

"Ah! Yes!" I agreed. They were massive—real beauties!

"We wanted to light these tonight," he looked over to the park ranger.

"Oh, I see …" I nodded, looking over at Hiroshi, who watched me intently. I raised my eyebrows and held up the firework. "What do you think, Hiroshi?"

He stood quietly for a moment then pulled his walkie-talkie and spoke into it. We waited, as he seemed to listen to the voice on the other end.

"Okay," he yelled back at us, smiling. "You have ten minutes before your counselors get here!"

The children cheered. They rallied around me as we walked into the field. Setting the fireworks down in a safe place, the children quickly wrestled over who was going to get to light them before handing the lighter over to me. I flicked it on. Instantly, the little flame lit the surrounding area. How easily the power of a single flame can illuminate a dark place.

I flicked the flame out and glanced over at the children who had moved a safe distance away. I spotted Miku. She stood nervously, her arms crossed as a couple of children draped across her shoulders. I offered the lighter to her.

"Miku! Come do the honors, please!"

Miku hesitated. "Me?" she gestured to herself, raising her brow.

I nodded.

"No! No!" She shook her head. "I cannot. I am scared of fireworks!"

I rolled my eyes and chuckled. "Miku, really? After everything you've been through tonight, you're scared of a few little fireworks?"

Miku's face froze; I clearly had a point.

"Come on, Miku. Light up this forest!"

Miku looked around as the children nodded and cheered her on. She soon surrendered, giving way to a crescendo of delight. She took the lighter from my hand, leaned down, and flicked the flame on. Her eyes locked onto the flame in a similar fashion as mine did.

"Thank you, Chad," she smiled triumphantly, lighting the wicks, one after another, as our anticipation rose. A few moments later, three large booms rocked the clearing, exploding blinding light across the black canvas of the night sky. Red, pink, green and white sparkles shot up and swarmed all around us. The display was just as spectacular as the colorful wrappings promised they would be.

The streaming sparks swathed the clearing in twinkling light. The children retrieved their *own* sparklers and one by one, began to light them, dancing, skipping, laughing, and running about. The lights filled our eyes as Hiroshi's musical watchtower filled our ears. Even Hiroshi himself could now be seen with a couple of children, a sparkler in hand.

Miku and I stood serenely watching the show as Paul and Asuka joined us. Soon the two girls began singing along with the song that had been our constant companion today.

"What is this song?" I asked.

"It's called '*A new morning has come*,' " Asuka said with a smile before returning her voice to the melody, now clumsily converting the lyrics to English. "*A new morning has come. This morning of hope. Open your heart and fill it with happiness!*" Asuka giggled with embarrassment as she spontaneously began to twirl about without inhibition. A kaleidoscope of dappled light shimmered over her face. She shot me a big, bold grin as her cheeks flushed red. I smiled back, nodding in approval, an affirmation that was abruptly interrupted by another ominous prodding in my mind.

The image of Asuka before me, so cheerful, so full of life, stood in stark contrast to the overpowering uncertainty of the forest behind her. Again, the infinite expanse of the Jukai inferred a chilling reality; its sovereignty had the power to hold us captive here if it so desired. But at that moment, I felt that the Aokigahara now had her sights fixed solely on our courageous guide.

ELEVEN

SHADOWS DON'T DIE

The day was hot—a scorcher, even by Louisiana's standards. It was my father's memorial service. Small groups of people, just a few friends and family, gathered at the old white church. The same place where my mother's service was held, so long ago.

We stepped outside the church into the open, humid air for the reception.

On my father's direct orders, I was not to be involved with his funeral. But as ironic as it was, I arranged everything. Spite? No. Rather, there was simply no one else in his life that would handle the arrangements or perform the service.

I was particularly calm that day. My spirit was rested. It had gotten easier since that initial blow, back at my father's home, when I found his note.

Then it all became routine: plans, numbness, and the burial. And gathering what distant friends and family he had.

233

I just wanted to go home, take off this suit, take off this day, and put it all behind me.

"It's hotter than Hades out here, Chad!" An authoritative voice sounded behind me. I turned to Mason, my pastor, who was viciously grabbing at his tie, pulling at the knot. He unbuttoned the top of his dirty white dress shirt. He was a large, kind man, whose loud voice and generous heart had always been there for me.

"Mason!" I gave him a firm hug.

"Hey Chaddy, sorry I couldn't be here earlier, buddy." He hadn't made it to the memorial; instead, he came directly from his morning services.

His apology required graciousness. I nodded and a wordless moment lingered.

"Why don't we take a walk, Chad."

We stepped off the grounds of the church, venturing into the edges of the wetlands of the southern woods. Mason unbuttoned more of his shirt, removed his suit jacket, and rolled up his sleeves.

"I never liked these things. Give me a t-shirt and a pair of shorts any day!" he grinned.

"You sure you don't want an orange prison jumpsuit?" I joked in an antagonistic tone, stepping forward and quickly punched him in the chest.

Mason looked up from his shirt, momentarily speechless. "Oh, you're a funny, man! Where did you learn to hit like that, preschool? It's a good thing I'm not the guy I used to be. That man's dead, but I can resurrect him anytime you want!" He raised his fists and made an exaggerated boxing pose, shooting a big, bold smile.

We laughed, but only for a moment.

"How you doing?" he said with sincerity.

"I'm okay," I matched his tone.

"And Shay?"

"We're both alright. As much as could be expected, you know?"

Mason nodded and the moment sank in.

There was more he wanted to say; it was clear. Mason had a plan; he always had a plan to help me. He was the one who originally put the bug in my ear about moving overseas as a missionary, a general dream at the time, but one that had begun to slowly evolve into a realistic scenario.

"Hey, bro, I know we've been talking about your future and where you want to be." He looked over his shoulder, back toward the church. The guests were still milling about, giving their condolences. "But, I just wanted to let you know that there's no pressure right now. This is a bump in the road, and it may be premature to move forward." He paused. "Listen," he moved in close to me. "If you've had a change of heart, I get it; there's time, and we can always make other arrangements."

A change of heart, a bump in the road? I had been pondering that since the police knocked on my door and gave me the news about Dad. Was I ready to leave all this and venture out into the world? Would my father, even in death, still control and bring doubt into my destiny? Everything was turned upside down, inside out, and chaos abounded. But still, one constant remained; my desire to go overseas was not wavering, rather, it had now been emboldened.

Everything had changed. There was no denying that. But still, that push to go overseas lingered. It was a topic that I had wrestled with more than usual over the last few weeks, since my father's death. It had been such a bone of contention between us that now I couldn't separate his doubt from my own. However, even with this ambiguity and despite the things around

me that had fallen and crumbled in the natural, there still stood that pillar in my heart away from this place and away from the mindsets that I had subjected myself to.

I looked out over the wetlands and muttered, "If I'm not able to put my past to rest, I won't have a future." I knew it was a loaded statement, but if anyone could unpack it, it would be him.

Mason remained quiet as my words hovered in the air and rested at our feet.

Finally, he asked, "So what does that future look like to you, Chad?"

What was important to me? What were the things that I wanted to let go of and what were the things that I needed to embrace? Now that both of my parents were gone, my future with my wife became solely paramount. A fresh start may be exactly what was needed, for both of us. And where would this now undetermined path take us?

"Malaysia," I said, simply.

"Malaysia?!"

"Yes." It all fell into place in my mind, piecing things together as I spoke. "I want to move to Malaysia, and use that as a base for ministry outreach to Southeast Asia and India."

"That's ... pretty big, Chad," Mason smiled, excited and cautious at the ambition expressed. "You don't want to start with something a little more local? Like ... Canada?" He raised his eyebrows, obviously joking.

I laughed, "Very funny, you know I hate the cold." Another moment went by. "I know, it's crazy, I don't know if my heart needs healing or time. But that doesn't mean that my spirit is not ready to embrace this. I'm ready. Ready or not: I'm ready."

Mason stared into me, a proud twinkle in his eye. "Yeah, Chad, it looks like you are." He reached out his hand and firmly gripped my shoulder. "I'm excited to see the beautiful places God is going to take you."

* * *

The friendly warmth of Hiroshi's watchtower was what I needed after the events of this day; it was what *we all* needed. The windows, which just hours ago had allowed in the dim, foggy daylight, now only revealed a thick blanket of blackness beyond the glass. The only light in the living area was that from the fire in the small wood burning stove. The other watchtowers had shut their searchlights off, returning the Aokigahara to its slumber.

Hiroshi sat slumped at his desk in the corner, speaking Japanese into a two-way radio, another bit of technology that was a holdover from a simpler time. After the teenage campers were safely returned to their guardians, we told Hiroshi about the body we'd found, the bleakest spot on a day saturated in darkness. I sat staring off in our host's direction and found myself wanting to be a part of his conversation, wanting to know what someone like Hiroshi would say about something like this.

Miku and Asuka huddled close together in blankets beside the dancing flames in the stove. Miku, now adorned with her silver cross necklace again, wrapped bandages around Asuka's bloodied hands. They spoke quietly to each other in their native tongue, another conversation I could not be a part of. Asuka seemed to be asking a lot of questions, the way a parent would interrogate their child. Miku solemnly nodded or shook her head, her cheeks pink with what I assumed was embarrassment.

What exactly happened to Miku after she ran from the sight of the body? She had been so frightened and was gone for *hours*. Had the same demon that had harassed me assaulted her as well? If that was the case, I couldn't imagine the terror she must have felt, to be utterly alone with no one to steady her fears. I had been petrified by that thing, and I had Asuka right up until the end, until I had to face the demon inside the tree alone.

Even as I recounted the events of the evening step-by-step, everything quickly became jumbled in my mind. What really happened? Was any of it real? I couldn't say for sure, but one thing was certain: the twisted pain and confusion that I had felt in my heart for so many years was no longer there. I could think more clearly than I had all day. Even the darkness of the night didn't seem as overpowering as it had earlier when it was creeping into the forest as the sun vanished.

I caught Paul's shape outside on the tower's balcony. An oversized ranger coat hung off his shoulders as he looked into his camera. The viewfinder lit his face and he gazed intently at the bright images. He was looking at today's footage, and I knew he was checking to see if there was something that could be salvaged, if we got anything at all today, or if it had just been a waste of our time and resources.

This was the double-edged sword of filmmaking, especially for Paul. He was constantly split between being here and being in post production. Yes, he was here with us today, and at the same time, he was behind his lens, trying to piece it all together, testing it and double and triple checking its validity.

Did it work? Did I work? I couldn't help wondering. My answer would undoubtedly be, "No." Today was a mess! But luckily, it wasn't up to me. It was up to Paul. He had the eye and the expertise to take all the footage into account and see if we had a story. And hopefully, we *did* have a story.

"Hey," Asuka sat next to me, fiddling with her newly wrapped bandages.

"How are your hands?" I asked.

"They'll be alright, they just sting a bit," she said, not meeting my eyes. "I still feel really bad about hitting you." Her cheeks flushed with embarrassment. "Are you sure your jaw is not hurt?" Her eyes darted to my ankle, "Or …"

"I'm fine, Asuka, really!" It felt good to know I was speaking the truth. "I've had worse, and besides, I don't even know if we accomplished what we came to do today. But for me, I'm pretty sure there was a more personal reason why I was brought to the Aokigahara."

After a moment, Asuka rose, retrieved her bag and returned to me. "There might have been another reason we were here, Chad."

She tenderly revealed the tattered, old journal I had found earlier. It was the one that I had unknowingly handed over to the group in place of the suicide manual, making a complete fool out of myself in the act. I had totally forgotten that Asuka had taken it.

"I've been looking through this," she then added, "an invasion of privacy, I know." Her bandaged hands delicately thumbed through the dirty pages and they quickly soiled her fresh, white wraps. She didn't seem to notice or mind. "But, something drew me in to keep reading." Her fingers found a page near the center of the journal, and she leaned in close to show me the writing.

Once again, the Japanese language was lost on me. But I was able to discern the date distinctly written with symbols I understood. *Oct 14th,*

2003. There were a lot of years between then and now, and I couldn't help musing about all the winters, the rainstorms, the earthquakes, that thick, rolling fog and all the while, this journal remained hidden in the Aokigahara just waiting to be found. Waiting to tell its story.

"There's more to it than the age of the journal, Chad. Something much more. It's unfathomable ..." She scrubbed through the text. "The owner of the journal's name was ..." she took a slow, deep, deliberate breath and barely whispered, "*Mizushima Fuyuki.*"

My heart stopped. "The name of the woman at the Ryokan. Her name is Mizushima."

"Mizushima Ritsuko, yes."

"So this is ..." Understanding washed over me. Could this journal, in fact, be the diary of Ritsuko's long-lost husband?

A moment of silent thought.

"Yes, Chad." Asuka's eyes were wet with the tears that she failed to hold back. "I really do think this was his."

I stared down at the journal, half wanting to grab it, half wanting to shove it away. While I had, of course, been transfixed by the journal when I found it, the reality that this was the final remains of one who was connected to a living person that I'd met, moved my heart deeply.

And Asuka, what must she be feeling?

Asuka continued, "I didn't read many entries before I realized. But, the parts I did read ..." she shook her head. "Ritsuko *needs* to have this. I think the journal might bring some closure in her heart."

"Yes," I agreed. "We'll give it to her. That's exactly what we'll do, Asuka. First thing in the morning, once we get out of here,"

Asuka carefully returned the book to its place in her bag. For the first time since finding it, I felt it was exactly where it needed to be.

"The things we leave behind," she stared out the window, into the blackness of the night. "I don't know if this journal will bring Ritsuko pain or comfort. But what I do know is, well, it's *something*. And something is better than the years of questions she's kept in her heart. Do you agree, Chad?" Her eyes sought mine again, looking for answers. While in theory, returning the journal to Ritsuko seemed logical—even empathetic—in reality, doubt always seemed to try and undermine the work we think to do for good.

Did I agree? I wasn't sure, for I had not been put into this position when I lost my father. I didn't get a choice of whether or not to read his final words. Whether I wanted to know or not, I learned *exactly* what tortured his mind and heart.

What would my life had been like if I had never discovered the truths behind my father's suicide? Would it have been coupled with the bliss of ignorance, or the torment of the unknown?

"This is not an easy call, Asuka," I said. "But if you think it would help for her to have it, I'll be by your side if you need the support." It was the best I could offer. After all, today's events had taught me a very important lesson: where friends stand together, bravery can always be found.

Asuka and I glanced across the room as the door creaked open. Paul found a place on the floor next to Miku.

"Thank you," Asuka whispered to me and returned to the floor as well.

"How's the footage, Paul?" I asked.

Paul stared into the fire, his mind surely racing. "It's hard to say. There's *something* there. But, I'm just not sure *what*. Was today a wash? Maybe. But we clearly had, well, a lot to deal with." He smirked.

"Is there anything that you can pull from it?" I was not sure what else to say. "Turn it into ... *something*?"

He shook his head. "I'm not sure, Chad. I won't know until I get the footage back to my office and take a look at it with a new set of eyes."

Of course, he was right. A fresh set of eyes was usually exactly what a project needed.

He looked back toward the fire. "Sometimes, you just don't know, and you have to be okay with that."

Did we have a message for others? Did we have a story to tell that could make an impact in someone's life? Wasn't that the reason I came? To learn something and to show others? But did I have a message to share?

"Paul, tomorrow morning before we leave this place, can we record one last thought? I want to get the rest of my ideas on video before this is over."

Paul's eyes narrowed, immediately back in production mode. "Yeah, of course. I'll take care of it."

A moment passed. There was too much left unsaid tonight; we all felt it. But Hiroshi broke the silence by switching off the two-way radio and joining us. He removed his yellow cap, revealing his thinning hair, and slowly ran his fingers through it.

"Today was a bad day ... and a good day," he sighed.

"I take it you let whoever needed to know about the man we found?" I asked.

"Yes." His solemn eyes reflected the orange light from the fireplace, his courteous smile now fading. "They will retrieve him in the morning, try to identify him and let his family know that he came here."

Silence.

"How many people have you found here?" I asked, my curiosity breaking reverence again.

"Even one is too many, sir."

"Yes."

"Did you film him?" he asked.

I couldn't lie. "Yes … we did."

Silence once more.

"We don't have to use the footage if you think it would be disrespectful," I added.

Hiroshi's pensive gaze still fixated on the flames. "Disrespect is hard to avoid in our world, isn't it? Everyone knows about the deaths here. But they don't often see the reality of it. If seeing that man will bring one less soul to the Aokigahara, I think it is a risk I would take. Yes, some will criticize, but someone always will." He turned to face me. "But are you up for that scrutiny? Considering that you are a public figure?"

Was I up for that scrutiny? It would not be the first time I came under fire for a controversial message. But this was another matter entirely. Suicide is not a topic many like to discuss. And like Paul asked the evening before: what would this stir up?

"Life is valuable," Hiroshi continued, "Those children tonight in the forest, so reckless, but so very much *alive,* you know? I don't like thinking that the sadness of life will bring them back here when they are older."

That's really what it comes down to, isn't it? The hardships of life will come, they always do. How we respond to those challenges and who stands beside us to face them down can sometimes mean the difference between life and death.

"How do you cope with being out here alone, Hiroshi? You must get lonely sometimes."

He motioned to the computer on his desk; it was a machine that would have been considered far obsolete in the modern world of Tokyo. "I use this to speak to my mother and sisters; they live in Osaka now." He paused. "But it's not as," he searched for the words, "not as … real?"

"Genuine?" I interjected.

"Yes, that is it, 'genuine,'" he agreed with humility. "But we live in a society that exists behind computers. Even those living in Tokyo, even those who have people all around them, they would rather keep themselves hidden. But we *need* to be with other people, touch them, hear their voices and see their faces." He turned his attention to Asuka, Miku and Paul who huddled around the fireplace. "But, you all, it seems you had a different sort of visit than you planned today, didn't you?" He searched my three companions' eyes like an inquisitive father.

The three looked at each other and then back at me, questioning how much should be said to the forest's caretaker.

Miku's voice broke through the silence with a stutter.

"When I ran from the dead man, *something* followed me." Miku fiddled with her necklace in a now all too familiar way. "It was speaking to me."

Hiroshi remained quiet, a silence that seemed to hint that Miku's words weren't anything new to the ranger. "Were you scared?" he asked.

Miku paused. "No. I didn't feel *anything*. After I heard the voice, my body started to move on its own. Like … like …"

And just like that, déjà vu washed over me again. The dream I had days ago fell into place. "Like you *knew* where you were going?" I asked.

"Yes! I was running. But not running away from the voice. Running *to* it."

"The clearing?" Asuka asked.

"*The shrine.* The voice told me I would be safe in there, that I was home." Her face grew pale. "But then, I saw something, someone, inside the tree, and I felt as if it was going to *consume* me."

"What was it?" Paul inquired.

"I do not know. It is hard to explain. Whatever *it* was, it carried with it the same feeling I had when I was younger," her eyes grew distant in a painful memory, "when other children would bully me. Familiar, like ..."

"Like it has followed you all your life?" I stated abruptly, finishing her thought.

Miku's eyes widened. "Yes!" she exclaimed, her mind clearly spinning into overdrive. "You too!?" For a moment, a hint of panic rose in her voice. "Those voices, that feeling, it was closing in on me."

That dream. I couldn't shake the memories.

"Miku?" Asuka said. "Why were you holding the book when we found you?"

Miku looked back into the fire, her eyes squinting. "I wasn't trying to hold it, I was trying to silence it. The book was *screaming*, or at least I felt like it was. It was like, the book was calling out for something to come and find me."

I reached into my bag and retrieved the suicide manual. I handed it to Miku. She reluctantly cradled it as if it were burning hot.

"Is the book calling out for that demon now?" I didn't want to ask, but I was anxious to know.

Miku looked down, staring into the book as if beholding an endless abyss. Her face became blank. Moments passed.

"Yes," she said with remorse as her eyes met mine. "Yes it is."

Asuka's and Paul's eyes darted between Miku's and mine, waiting, waiting for resolve.

"You said it was gone." Miku's words were laced with uncertainty.

"I didn't say that demon was gone. I said it couldn't hurt us unless we allowed it to, and that was exactly what we were facing today." I looked around at all of them. "At least that was what *I* was facing." I paused. "I had a long conversation with my father today."

"You found service?" Asuka asked.

I gave a forgiving smile. "He's dead."

An uncomfortable silence fell over everyone.

"I *knew* it wasn't him, that it couldn't be right. But the more I told myself not to believe what I was hearing--or *seeing*--the more those unresolved feelings over my father welled up in me. I found myself talking to him, but actually I was talking to the demon. And the things it said to me were ..."

"Terrible things," Miku finished my thought.

I nodded, growing accustomed to our synchronicity. "It wasn't until we were at the clearing that I found the strength to push it out of my mind. I knew that if we could just stay with each other, connect and help each other in a," I looked to Hiroshi, "a genuine way, that it couldn't hurt me, couldn't hurt us."

"And the suicide manual? What part does it play?" Asuka asked.

I shrugged. "I don't think you have to look into the supernatural realm to discover its role in the mystery of the Aokigahara. The damage done by this book in the physical realm confirms the author's dark intentions."

Miku looked down at the suicide manual. "Chad, may I have this book?"

Miku wanted to keep the book? Why? Why the sudden interest in that vile text? Did she want it as a memento? A souvenir? I know I certainly didn't want it anymore. However strange the request, how she chose to process this whole experience was her choice. "Yeah, Miku. You can have that."

Miku nodded but said nothing. She looked down at the book, her new possession. She contemplated the soiled cover, the black coffins and the blood red title. She glanced toward the fireplace and in one delicate motion, tossed the book into the flames. The book erupted in a burst, as a heavy pulse shook my heart.

"Burning trash is bad for the environment," Hiroshi said stoically. Miku turned to acknowledge the reprimand. "But I will let it slide this time." A slight smile played across his face.

Miku turned back toward the fire. The charred cover receding, exposing the pages of text one last time before incinerating into smoke and ash. "At least there will be one less bit of darkness in the Aokigahara."

Hiroshi nodded. "Yes." His eyes gradually shifted from the fire into the black expanse of the forest. "But shadows don't die."

TWELVE

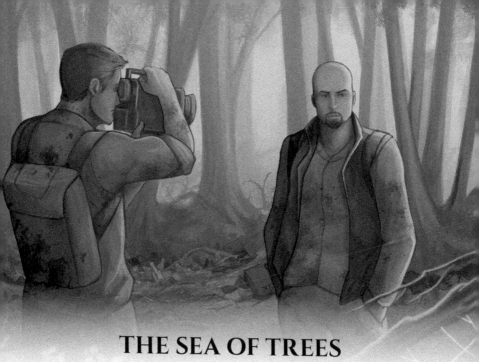

THE SEA OF TREES

March 12th.

The morning light of the Aokigahara proved to be a stark contrast to the gloom of yesterday. Not a single cloud floated through the clear, dazzling blue sky. No fog crept along and filled the forest with the dread of the unknown. It felt as if the forest itself was as renewed as I was.

Hiroshi led us down a dirt path, beaming like a child, as he carried on telling us about the different types of plant life around us. He seemed excited to be able to tell a fresh group of people the stories he'd probably spent many years sharing with visitors.

With a good night's sleep under my belt, I was perfectly content with this morning's tour, be it two hours or two minutes. For the first time, I was able to truly take in the beauty and enjoy the serenity of the trees and all the living things inside of it. Birds tweeted and critters scuttled about. Had they all been here yesterday? Had I really been so intimidated that I missed all this bustling life?

"This is where I leave you." Hiroshi stopped, gesturing beyond the trees I'd been contemplating. "Just take this path all the way until you come to a paved road. There is a bus stop and taxi service just beyond it."

I looked down the pathway, noting where it dipped up and down, wound to the side and disappeared into the distance. But this time, the curling paths leading to who-knows-where, held no intimidation over my mind. We could handle it from here. In fact, we probably could have made our way from the watchtower alone, but the company was well worth being escorted.

"Right," I said, turning to Hiroshi and putting out my hand. "Thank you."

Shoving out his hand exaggeratedly, Hiroshi's face broke into a grin. He grabbed my hand tightly, shaking it with contagious energy. "I am happy to have met you, Chad Daniel! I hope your time here was a memorable one."

"No kidding!" I added with a laugh.

He released his grip, keeping his smile intact. There wasn't much else to be said. Hiroshi turned and bowed to the others with sincere enthusiasm. He spoke in Japanese to Asuka and Miku, and they each answered back. Then he waved goodbye and began to walk away.

"Hiroshi ..." Miku's delicate voice called out in a stutter.

Hiroshi stopped, but paused before turning to meet her face.

Miku hesitated, biting her lip. "What you said last night ..." Her hand reached for her necklace.

"Shadows don't die ..."

Hiroshi gave a sober nod.

"Is that true?" Miku's question hung in the air.

Hiroshi paused, seeming to craft an appropriate reply. "Where there is light, there must be a shadow, and where there is a shadow, there must be light. Natural laws, yes?"

Miku nodded.

He nodded back. "But shadows must obey that which stands in light, yes?"

Another silent agreement.

"As long as you walk in the light, Miku, a shadow will always be your companion. But that shadow has no power of its own."

Miku's eyes dropped to the ground in quiet contemplation. A smile spread across her face. "Yes!" she said.

Hiroshi flashed a big grin, lifting his gaze skyward. "Don't let the fear of shadows keep you from living in the sun!"

And with that, the shepherd of the forest, the finder of lost visitors, departed from us.

There we stood, the four of us, alone together again for the first time since we found that body. I looked over my three companions. They were just as dirty as I was, having slept in our filthy clothes from the day before. Asuka was especially soiled with stains of blood on her shirt.

"Aren't we a sight?" I said, sensing they were as ready as I was to change out of the last remnants of a day we would never forget.

"I could use a shower," Paul agreed, taking the lead down the dirt path. We followed him in stride.

"We won't have much time for that," Asuka said, shaking her head. "Our train leaves in two hours."

"You mean ... I have to go back to Tokyo wearing this???" Miku whined, stretching her neck to examine herself in disgust.

"Don't be such a baby," Asuka fired back, but a soft smile played over her lips.

"I am *not* a baby!" Miku slouched and folded her arms but kept up the pace with the rest of us. She pouted for a moment, then rose a little taller. "After all, I faced a gang of little ghosts *and* lit *three* enormous firecrackers last night. Babies cannot do that!"

We all laughed and continued down the path, each of us falling into our own quiet meditations.

I knew that two hours wasn't very long. I began making a mental list of everything we had to do from now until we sat down on that train: Get a taxi out of the forest. Arrive at the Ryokan. Pack up. Take the taxi to the station. But the most important task: Return the journal to Ritsuko. We would have to *make* time for that—as much time as we could. Yes, returning that journal was of the utmost importance.

That and …

"Paul," I said, "let's stop off here for a minute."

Paul, Asuka, and Miku all turned.

"Yeah, man, of course." He took off his shoulder bag and dug into it to retrieve his camera.

"What's going on?" Asuka asked.

"There's just one more thing I've got to say before I leave this place."

Miku and Asuka returned curious looks.

"It will only take a minute," I assured them.

Asuka folded her arms. "Okay, we'll wait right over there," she said, pointing down the path. "But we don't have much time, Chad, really."

I agreed, appreciating her punctuality. "I won't need much time. This is what I came here to do. I don't want to blow it now."

Asuka took Miku by the hand and led her down the path.

Paul and I walked through an offshoot of the pathway and found a quiet, unassuming area of the Aokigahara.

"This will work," Paul announced as he began setting up what would be his final shot.

I held a deep breath and surveyed the area, taking in this Sea of Trees—possibly for the last time. The morning sunlight began to pierce through the green-turning-gold leaves, lighting the forest in its serene beauty.

I watched as Paul finished setting up the camera to point at me. The red light flickered on. What to say? Our little entourage had been through so much from the moment we boarded our train in Tokyo.

None of us could have known that I would be taken on a journey that spanned many years in the blink of an eye, forcing me to not only face my past and the demons therein, but to also embrace the love that I had been blind to, the love of my father for me and mine for him. It was a love that redeemed every tear and heartache. I was certain that my father now knew the mysteries of life. And I believed that in his *knowing*, if he had the chance to do it differently, he most certainly would.

The red light of the camera continued to taunt me as I considered all the people that had come to this forest in desperation. How many of them would also do it differently if given the chance? Instead, their lives were lost in the magnificent beauty and treacherous curse of the Aokigahara.

It is the dark nature of the Sea of Trees to drown you in your fears before taking what is left of you and burying it deep within its roots and caverns. It is also the beautiful nature of the Sea of Trees to be warm and welcoming. A boy-turned-man's backyard playground, where being

Tarzan was the biggest challenge and helping those who were in need was his greatest accomplishment.

Those who were in need, even if it was ONE person, that *was why I came to the Aokigahara.*

My eye caught a crafty spider's web stretching from a nearby tree trunk to a low hanging branch. I thought again of my father. What torturous threads of despair and hopelessness must have held him tightly in their embrace? What could he have been thinking and feeling those last days before he took his life? Had he even a flicker of hope for a future?

My mouth opened and the words fell out on their own accord.

"Can you imagine coming into a place like this, knowing that this was your final resting spot? You've already made all your plans. You've already made all your preparations; you've said all of your goodbyes."

I glanced around and continued, "What must your mind be thinking? Your heart has got to be racing—about to burst out of your chest, your mind is flooded, your emotions are a mess, and you know that this is where ... your life will end."

I felt my arm reach out to the trunk next to me and I leaned heavily against it, the words weighing on my heart, "Especially a place like this where it's said that your body will never, ever be found."

I looked straight into Paul's lens, but saw no lens. I saw a *person*, a person who would one day find themselves in their own forest, alone in a room someday, or somewhere else—a person with a plan to end their life. It might be one person or it might be many. But this was no longer a "project" and it was not a sensational scene in a documentary. The nature of the Aokigahara had become real to me, and I knew that if only one single person saw this film and made the choice to live, then that one person was why I had come.

I gazed at that person and continued, "Even though you may be considering suicide, in the back of your mind, you do want to be found. Maybe you're doing this out of vengeance. Maybe this is your last grand-stage exit in a life that has somehow been incredibly unfair to you. Maybe this is the way you're gonna get back at everybody. You know, that's a very selfish way to think, because when you find yourself here, all alone, it's just you, your mind, your soul, and your God. You're going to have to face Him. You're going to have to give an explanation as to why you chose to give up the greatest gift that you've ever been given. And that's your life.

"You can make all the excuses you want. You can say, 'Well, nobody ever told me.' You have been told! 'Well, I just didn't feel like it ....' It's not about the way you feel! It's about faith! It's about what you know to be true. 'Well, I was raised in a different religion.' It doesn't matter about religion. Religion's never the answer! It's always about a genuine relationship with God. There has to be a place where you humble yourself ... and you understand that what you're about to do cannot be restarted again like a cell phone that's lost its power. You can't just press the power button and it'll just somehow come back. This is an eternal act! This is a final, ultimate decision that you have thought about and premeditated."

I felt a stir as I spoke the words. I paused in repentance to God. Why had I not embraced this message years earlier? I now had a mandate and the supernatural fortitude to expose the satanic influence behind the act of suicide. "And let me tell you something else that you may not have considered—you haven't planned this on your own!"

I shook my head, knowing full well the weight of the words I would now speak.

"You've had a greater force at play with this. Those thoughts that have been tormenting you? They're not your own. Those emotions that just seem to come on you like a wet blanket? Those aren't yours, either. You've got to open your eyes and realize that we are in a war; you're in a war—you're the prize! One side is battling for you to live and the other side is battling for you to die! But as you allow yourself to give in to that negative deception, to give in to that fear, to give in to those lies … what you're saying to the side which gave everything for you is, 'I'm a hopeless case. My life is too far gone. It's too messed up.' I want that lie to be exposed, in the name of Jesus! Every one of those spirits that are lying to you, I command them to let go of your mind!

"God is not giving up on you. You may have given up on yourself, friends and family may have given up on you, but heaven is never going to give up on you. It'll keep badgering you, loving you, pulling you and encouraging you. And when you fall down, it'll keep pulling you back up. So in the name of Jesus, I speak life over you. I speak life, that darkness would flee, that the power of God would fill your heart right now. And that the spirit of death would leave. I speak life over you. If God can speak life into me, He can most assuredly speak life into you. None of us deserve what God has to offer. None of us deserve what God came to give, but He came to give it anyway.

"And for those who would believe …" I held up my fingers less than a centimeter apart, "even that much—the faith of a mustard seed can change your entire future! The Sea of Trees, a place where people come to die. But the way I see it, this is an incredible place to live. As the sun will go down on the Sea of Trees, I will be leaving. What about your life? The sun is already setting if you're considering suicide as an option.

You need to turn and walk into the light and get out of this place. I urge you, for your family, for your loved ones, for those who want to see you succeed and fulfill your God-given destiny, choose life."

I stopped. That unknown person who had replaced Paul's lens began to fade, returning my gaze to that ever-present blinking red light. The light remained on for another moment, perhaps a moment too long, long enough for me to question if all the things I just said would hold any weight at all.

Should I say one last thing? Clarify?

Finally, the red light blinked off, its taunting at long last over. Paul lowered the camera. Without a word, he knelt down and began to pack everything up.

"What do you think?" I asked, desperately looking for feedback.

"I think …" he rose to his feet, pulling the bag over his shoulder, "I think that what you came here to do, you've done, Chad." He folded his arms, looking to the canopy above us. "Let's …" he started.

I tuned my ears, ready for his next technical direction. Did he want something else? A different location?

"Let's not forget this moment, Chad."

His words caught me off guard. *Forget?* I couldn't imagine the events of yesterday being lost in my mind anytime soon.

"*This* moment," he clarified. "The two of us, standing here in the Aokigahara. This is a holy moment that we can latch onto when things are dark." He aimlessly kicked the ground. "Last night, when I was running through the forest, trying to get to Hiroshi, the only thing that kept me going was the hope that, eventually, we would be *here*, in *this* moment, a moment where we were all together again." He smiled, fixing his gaze back on the tips of the trees. "And one with the sun." He shrugged. "I know it helps me knowing that no matter what darkness comes my way, *this* moment will eventually come, too. It makes those dark times easier to endure." Without another word, he turned and headed back toward the path, knowing I would follow.

Minutes later, the four of us found ourselves at the exit point of the trail. The quiet unease of the Aokigahara was now drowned out by the sounds of the busy highway before us. I lifted my head, exhaling an earnest sigh of relief.

We made it out! The labyrinth of the forest's secrets, in the end, had failed to conquer us. The omen the ethereal girl had uttered, though foreboding, ultimately never came to pass.

Yes, at last, we were clear of any danger, free from anything (physical or spiritual) intent on keeping us, keeping Asuka, here for good. We could all go home!

"Hello again!" The familiar face of the taxi driver grinned as he came screeching to a halt beside us, dust erupting in clouds behind his vehicle. The driver leaned his head out the window, giving us understandable looks of puzzlement. "Did you stay in the forest all night??" he asked with alarm and confusion.

We quickly crammed into the car as his questions persisted.

"Did you see the ghosts I was telling you about?" he said with a snarky grin. He shot Miku a teasing look through the rearview mirror. "You know, the ones that haunt the forest?"

Miku returned the driver's stare with an unbreakable one of her own. "Perhaps," she said with a smirk.

Her reply took the driver off guard. He fumbled with his gearshift, losing the staring contest with Miku. "You did?!?!"

"Yes, we saw them!" Miku said with confidence. "The ghosts of the children, lost in the forest."

The driver was speechless. Miku let his silent tension build.

"Except," she paused, the driver now hanging on her every word, "well, not all stories are completely true."

THIRTEEN

THE UNLOCKED DOOR

"**D**o you mind waiting for us? We won't be long," I asked the driver, as we scurried out of his taxi.

"I will wait," the dumbfounded driver nodded, Miku's words still challenging his reality; they were words that had apparently taken an understandable toll on his psyche.

I closed the car door, spending one of our brief available moments to behold the Ryokan in the light of a clear day. The presence of this traditional home held new significance for me. I now knew a partial history, a glimpse into the lives of a broken husband and wife who shared this home together. Recalling Asuka's account of the tragedy, words about the now single resident of this place, was like a dark filter over my lens of objectivity. Every pillar, every window, every type of tree in Ritsuko's meticulously tended garden, every dark ripple on the pond in the center of that nursery, provoked a forlornness. It was the same emotion I had experienced the night my father died, the very same loss that galvanized my decision to relocate my life to the other side of the world. That familiar spirit had permeated every fiber of the Ryokan, its inception far beyond its wall, from a much deeper place, a fount of despair within Ritsuko's broken heart. Was this fortress insurmountable? Could Ritsuko's walls ever be scaled? Or would Asuka, now free from the icy grasp of the Aokigahara, have the courage to help Ritsuko find deliverance?

"Miku," Asuka's voice broke into my thoughts. "Would you mind grabbing my bag when you're upstairs?" she asked, her eyes fixed, not on the Ryokan, but to something, someone, *inside* it.

"Yes, okay," Miku said, hurrying off towards the entrance before stopping abruptly, spinning back to Asuka. "Wait, why? What are *you* going to do?" Her eyes narrowed inquisitively.

Asuka held her gaze, captivated by the task that lay before her. "I'll need some time to say goodbye to a dear person, as much as I can have," Asuka answered, a nervous hope drenching her words. Miku paused with introspection before nodding. She disappeared into the home, Paul trailing behind her.

Asuka took a deep breath, wrapped her arms around her bag, the journal tucked neatly inside, and gave me a decided nod. "Let's do this."

We quietly made our way through the halls of the silent house, save the ticking of clocks echoing in the halls. One of the clocks however captured my nervous attention: the very one the eerie girl gave careful attention to only nights before. The delinquent clock now kept pace with its fellow timepieces, her intervention proved successful. The accuracy of that particular clock, howbeit, brought with it a grievous reminder: *the hour was later than I thought,* and Asuka had even less time for this moment with Ritsuko than she originally planned. I cut my eyes to Asuka, whose pace had not faltered as mine had; accurate clocks and elusive moments did not deter her. She explored the rooms of the Ryokan in an ardent fashion, her steely resolve equal to that which she possessed the night before while searching for Miku in the treacherous forest. Only now, the Aokigahara's stinging branches, fatal ravines, and treacherous moss were replaced by paper walls of distant memories, closed rooms of isolation, and the reverential silence of uncertainty.

At the far end of the hall, Asuka stopped, peering through a door left slightly ajar. The courageous face she now displayed told me that the housemother was spotted. But *found?* Not yet. It would take more than searching the halls of the Ryokan for Ritsuko to truly be found in her palace of defense, whose ramparts, no doubt, loomed high and ran deep. I joined Asuka and peeked through the small crack in the paper door. The opening was like a portal to another world, one that conveyed an air of reverent elegance and relentless discipline.

The traditional dining room, the one Asuka and I occupied the morning before, now played host to its stringent proprietor: Mizushima Ritsuko. The woman seated herself at the immaculately polished table. The tableware, flower vases, and the woven straw placemats were now replaced with a simmering stone teapot and a single porcelain cup, whose design bore an uncanny resemblance to the floral pattern sewn throughout the exquisite Kimono she adorned over her aged, but still soft and pale, skin. Beyond Ritsuko, the two large doors were kept open, allowing the artistry of the room's decor to blend with the refinement of the tended garden and the falling petals from sakura trees beyond the frame.

The dutiful clocks behind us chimed a quarter hour note in unison, breaking our gaze, reminding us of the limited time we had, time that was fleeting with each subsequent tick.

"Still up for this?" I whispered.

Asuka's eyes returned to the sight of the housemother in nervous reluctance. I could only imagine the memories racing around her mind, memories of running these halls as a child, skipping along the stones in the garden's pond, or falling asleep in the lap of her loving mother as she and Ritsuko burned the night away in warm conversation. Asuka's feelings from those distant moments were more than likely dissolved by the passage of time, new friendships, education, and the tedious deliberations of a singular nagging question: where did she belong in this world? Without the gentle guide of her mother, Asuka had to bury those memories along with the premature end to her childhood, hoping that the things left unsaid could be resolved without her active presence. But as she gave one final glance to the journal in her hands, she now understood a very poignant truth: genuine connections to those you love do not come without intentional participation. And it was an intentional participation from Ritsuko that Asuka longed for as she took her first anxious step over the threshold and into the guarded palace of this widow's heart.

"Did you find what you were looking for in the X-Zone?" Ritsuko asked without giving any acknowledgement to the soiled and bloody intruder.

Asuka froze, her dirty bandages gripped her arms as her shoulders slumped, almost as if to appear smaller: a broken commodity in an otherwise idyllic setting. She turned back to the hallway, looking to me for the reassurance that I was eager to give. I gave a comforting parental nod, but kept my words restrained, knowing the presence of a big, loud personality would not be an appropriate addition to a scene that required a deft touch. But it appeared my encouraging gesture was all Asuka needed to finish her silent approach and kneel beside the stoic woman. Her dirty and disheveled form soiled the tatami mat beneath her. She matched Ritsuko's gaze out to the garden beyond, Asuka's nervousness, no doubt, simmering as violently as the water in the teapot before her. I saw Asuka's mouth begin to open, but her words would escape me: a tone and language, no doubt, used as a culturally acceptable wall, facilitating this intimate waltz of reconciliation.

Asuka's trembling hands cradled the weathered journal. Then, leaning forward, she placed it gently on the table before Ritsuko. Was the journal *truly* destined to be there? Would it elicit the resolution Asuka prayed it would? Would that journal become a bridge connecting these two estranged women? Or would it reveal itself as a blade? A razor-like sickle, severing the last remaining threads of a frayed rope connecting them to one another?

Still, no words, no communication, audible or otherwise, were exchanged in the room. The presence of the journal impeded the civil discourse between them, and a bitter respite settled over them like a dark cloud.

As the tension of the moment reached its crescendo, Asukas eyes met mine once more. She desperately sought for my reassurance and approval, yet the uneasiness of Ritsuko's silence confirmed to Asuka that I had neither to give. Without the strength of a mediator, Asuka was left with only one, bleak option: accept the stillness … and wait.

Asuka bowed her head.

An infinite moment passed. A moment that, I'm sure for Asuka, felt like an eternity. And as that endless moment pressed on in tedium, the doubt I hoped would not manifest, began to sprout like a weed in my mind.

I hung my head, beleaguered.

This was a mistake, wasn't it? How could I have been so naïve? Ritsuko was clearly a person who didn't see value in the support of others; the woman's ironclad constitution made that certain.

Suddenly, that weed-like doubt in my mind erupted into a forest of anxiety when a violent motion caught my eye. Ritsuko was on her feet now, the teacup from the table lay shattered on the floor. The long fabric of the housemother's kimono flew through the air as her arm came hurtling down at Asuka. The deep, resonating sound of a slap and a following whimper from its recipient echoed in the once silent room.

I bolted in, prepared to defend my friend and berate Ritsuko with whatever expletives came to mind first! But as my vision of the scene returned from its tint of crimson, I found the housemother absent; she had quickly made her way past the threshold and into her garden beyond, assumably in hopes that the serenity of her garden would help her regain the composure she had brazenly discarded. Asuka's eyes filled with tears, the fresh pain on her cheek, a tragic confirmation that a worst-case scenario could inevitably come to pass just as effortlessly as a good one might. Whether because of shock or boiling indignation, Asuka's hand shook violently as she pressed it against her tender flesh.

"Asuka …" I said.

Another quiet moment passed as her eyes dropped to the floor. I knew that look, an anger so great that it arrests you from any expression, commanding you to freeze, infusing you with its malignancy.

"I should never have even bothered." Asuka's words washed over her like a deluge of defeat before falling lifelessly to the floor. "Let's just go, Chad. She can rot alone here for the rest of her life for all I care!" Her harsh words rang absolute, absent of her familiar melodic tones, almost as if it wasn't Asuka speaking at all, but a primitive impulse that had swelled inside her, taking reign of the chaos in her heart.

A sense of helplessness flooded my mind and in that moment, I would have done anything to remove that weighty burden from her, and return her to the brash, energetic and commanding person I had grown to not only tolerate but to value. "Asuka? No!" But the words I wanted to say, fell muted on the hard reality that the rejection Asuka had just experienced had wounded her grievously.

"I tried," Asuka muttered, lips quivering. "But, now I'm through."

"She's just trying to keep you out!" Where was the resolve Asuka had before? Had she discarded is as quickly as Ritsuko did her self-control?

"Please, Chad. Stop. I … can't." Asuka slouched deeper toward the floor, deeper into that murky pool of sorrow and self-pity, one that I knew all too well. And it was contagious. As her shape fell beyond my view, I glanced outside, spotting Ritsuko brooding in her garden of despair, those same lethal streams of failure now began to saturate my spirit.

"Asuka?" No answer, and this time, I could feel that her silence was one of absolute abandon. Was Asuka still with me? Had the bitter embrace of despondency stifled what little hope that remained?

In the fatal silence of that moment, I became keenly aware of something else, something oddly familiar. Something, or someone, now loomed in the halls behind me, someone dominant, potent, and *ruinous*. Yes, it was that merciless entity, the same one that delighted in our distress only hours ago. This diminutive figure whose words were a harbinger of death's bittersweet appointment, had again infiltrated Ritsuko's dwelling. The monotonous ticking of the clocks throughout the Ryokan had ceased, replacing their incessant reminders of finite time with a dreadful quiet and dismaying giggles.

She was, in fact, here.

The pitter-patter of those black-buckled shoes merged with her eerie snickering as the light of the dining room began to diminish, along with my resolve.

No, please, not yet, it's too soon!

Diffused sunlight behind the paper walls of the dining room illuminated the hallway beyond them, revealing the heart-stopping visage, one I had hoped to never encounter again. The distinct silhouette of her small feminine form filled the checkerboard paper framework. The contour of her ribbon-clad hair and black tea dress were unmistakable. Her shadow-like outline paused, her hands loosely clasped behind her back as she teeter-tottered from her toes to her heels, waiting for a date she knew I understood was inevitable.

Was this appointment inevitable? Did her arrival herald certain catastrophe? Or was there still time? Was there still time to attend to the broken hearts and withered strands of intimate connection?

Oh God, please!

"I said we would meet again," the gloomy silhouette giggled, "but I didn't think it would be so soon!" A playful euphoria drenched her deadly nuance.

"Why are you here?" The question shot from my mind without the words needing to form in my throat.

The dark outline's head cocked with inquisitive intent. A disturbing smile radiated from the silhouette, defying the natural laws of light and shadow. "After all you have seen in your time here, after everything you've learned, you still carry such ignorance to the laws of the world that you are bound to." As a war horn sounds the victory over a bloody battlefield, another haunting giggle slithered from behind the paper wall once more. As the screeching giggle grew more and more triumphant, I recoiled from its rising intensity. I staggered back, widening the distance from her. Her laughter subsided, and she took a step back as well. I took a step to the side, she matched my movement. Back to my knees, again, she silently mirrored, genuflecting slowly and lowering herself into a crouch.

"I like this game!" Her radiant smile returned, sending chills through me. "Let's play another one! One of my favorites." Her hands delicately brushed at the skirt of her dress, mischievously spreading each seam into precise folds on the floor. "A game of questions, where your friends are pawns, you can be a ..." a slender finger tapped her mouth as her head rose to the ceiling, "a bishop!" The same finger shot at me like a loaded gun. "That's very pertinent, I suppose! Poetic even."

"I'm not here to play games with you!" my mind spoke as my mouth remained still.

"Oh, but I think you'll like this game very much. It will be played on a board of truth. And the spoils of victory is the life of a friend." My racing heart skipped a beat as the girl's smile reappeared. "I don't think it's a game that you want to forfeit."

A silent moment passed, one which concluded when I glanced down at Asuka, still collapsed in frozen desolation on the floor. "And what piece are *you* playing as?" I asked, feeling my heart pounding in my throat.

The silhouette gave me a condescending sigh. "You still don't understand, do you? I'm not a piece! You're not fighting against me." Her two glowing eyes blinked back at me.

"Then…" I started, mind darting as quickly as sweat ran from my face, "then you're a player, right? Something that moves the pieces?" I began to see it all so frighteningly clear.

"No," she said. "I don't carry that power."

"Then what?!"

An anxious moment passed. "I am the empty void beyond the edge of the board. Once a piece is removed from play, it comes to me."

Another vivid smile crept across her silhouetted face. "Now, let's begin, shall we?" she said gleefully. "I'll go first! A question, and you have to answer truthfully. It's no fun to lie!" The silhouette composed itself. "What did you do with the book entitled: *The Complete Manual of Suicide?*" she chimed inquisitively, craning her head sharply to the side.

The suicide manual? My foggy mind rushed back to the scene of Miku throwing it into Hiroshi's stove, the wicked token sending a seismic wave through my mind.

Did she *not* know we burned it last night? No, she knew. She was getting at something more immense than the destruction of a petty book. *"That wicked book is where it belongs,"* I spoke out in my mind, "in ashes!"

Her head shot upward again, my candor was unexpected. "Very good! I didn't think you would be so good at this game!" But soon her head was back to its tilt, ever more inquisitive. "Burning such a thing was very brave, even if you didn't directly do the burning." She broke her gaze off me, her eyes drifted to the floor above her where Miku, no doubt, was also frozen in this moment of time, in the midst of packing to go home.

"But, I'm curious," her attention returned, "what did she hope to accomplish by such an …" (another impish giggle), "… igniting act?"

My reasoning staggered. I couldn't let this thing near my friends! Not now, knowing the spirit of fatality she carried. There was so much at stake. I had to abolish her! But could I? Or did I have to cooperate with her? Resigning my will to the laws in which she abides, I telepathed, "Burning the suicide manual means that one less wounded person will be vulnerable to its lies!" Miku's earnest words echoed in my mind.

The silhouette nodded in deep understanding, or was it agreement? "Then, I'm curious," her tone shifted, slightly more sincere now. "Does 'one less' corpse for the Aokigahara to decompose, one less soul nourishing the creature within really make much difference in the expanse of time?"

Doubt welled up in me as I considered the influence the suicide manual possessed. It could be found, sitting on bookshelves, tucked away in a student's school bag or under a mattress, its hypnotizing message, though hidden from others, permeating every fiber of the possessor's psyche.

Why did the suicide manual demand such secret intimacy with its reader? The answer came with a hint of clarity: because if loved ones knew of the manual's presence, there could still be an intervention, some hope that its influence couldn't take root in the soil of their broken heart. "It matters to the people who love that person. Death is never a cursory thing when it happens to someone you know, someone you love. As long as someone has connections to those they love, their life will always be valued!"

"I see …" the girl's words rang with a sobering tone. "I know nothing of loving connections or fiery symbols of defiance." Her shadowy gaze drifted to Asuka, still collapsed on the floor beside me.

My body tensed in a panic. This wasn't about Asuka, was it?

"But if you believe that these invisible connections to loved ones keep you from a willful appointment with me, where does one turn when all those connections are severed? What respite will humans seek when their trust of others dissipates?" Her head rose beyond Asuka, slowly lifting herself up, looking beyond the room, beyond me, and fixing her sights squarely on Ritsuko. "If I were to believe that were true, that those connections to others hold you back from deliberately walking through my veil," she paused, rising to her feet, her eerie shadow now towering over me, "then unfortunately, it appears that the last of Ritsuko's connections have now been broken."

My gaze shot back to the garden behind me. Was *this* the endgame? Ritsuko? Was it Ritsuko's life that hung in the balance in this game? Had the walls she built severed her connections to those who loved her? Was the death of Ritsuko's best friend, Asuka's mother, the same as my father's loss of his wife? Was she, like my dad had been, left with only her walls of a loneliness which demanded her full attention? Were those walls actively opposing others, resisting Asuka, a seductive command to detach herself from the fear of further emotional harm?

But, what if those meticulously built barricades had, in turn, manifested into a prison? What if Ritsuko was trapped in the very palace she built to protect herself? And what would happen when death crept into that palace, circumstantially, her only companion? An urgency filled my panicked heart as the picture became clear. I shot back to the silhouetted figure, who was now reaching back into the folds of her dress, retrieving her gloves, gloves used for a special kind of work, one that she would execute with professional efficiency.

"No! You can't!" I blurted, begged almost, agonizing thoughts of my father's last days washing over my mind. How long had this spirit lurked in the darkened corners of his house before he submitted to her? Was she there the day I visited him to discuss my plans for my future? Was she there on that deck, looming behind my dad, whispering allurements in his ear? Keeping him from truly seeing the connections, however frail, between him and me?

"It's not my decision," she said as she delicately slipped the gloves onto her fingers, her words radiating with simplistic truth. "I told you, I don't seek anyone out. But everyone has an appointment with me at some time, whether they meet me at the end of all things, or before their story comes to an end, I must abide by the rules that were birthed from mankind's first choice."

No! There must be more time before Ritsuko surrenders to this end! "But ... Ritsuko ..." I started, snapping to my feet, hands drenched in the sweat of realization.

"What did I tell you when we first met, Mr. Daniel? 'The hour is later than you think.' I have watched Ritsuko's clocks with an acute accuracy. Her time is up, and an accord will be made today!"

I shot back to Ritsuko, adrenaline tunneling my vision. In my darkened haze, I could see Ritsuko standing at the shallow edge of the pond, her gaze lifelessly fixated on the fatal depths in the center.

"Ritsuko has entertained the thought of meeting me for countless years, and each time, she gets closer to unlocking her door. She grows more comfortable, more at ease with returning my cold embrace. As the sun is bound to set on the Aokigahara this evening, Ritsuko's locked door will, most assuredly, be opened today. And as I keep reminding you, Mr. Daniel, the hour is later than you think."

"But, she's so close to getting free from all this!" I tried to negotiate. "Can't you …"

"Does a flame discriminate what it burns?" she interrupted. "Does a flood choose its *own* course? No. As it is the same for me." She paused, her gloves now fully fitted around her delicate hands. She folded her fingers into fists, seeming to test their ability. "I go where I am directed, I come when I am called."

"Is there nothing more we can do?" I pleaded, mind racing to any word, any act I could employ to stop the seemingly inevitable tragedy menacing in the garden. Those imagined words, those acts were the same ones, whose implementation I refused with my father, had haunted me every day since his death. Would those words be muted once again? Would Ritsuko pass from this life without hearing those words?

"Your kind are the only ones that have access to a great gift: *choice*. Throughout my existence, I have seen this gift brandished to build empires and destroy civilizations. I would envy that gift, that authority, had I the instrumentality to do so." Her voice rose with excitement as she turned her attention down the hallway, almost as if something was calling out to her. The girl paused, her eyes locked on that inaudible sound. "But to answer your question …" her momentary attention diverted, then meeting my gaze again, "there is *always* something more you can do." She giggled as her silhouette began to skip down the hall then quickly dematerialized from view. But her haunting voice remained, permeating every crack and crevice of the Ryokan, now singing a familiar tune.

♫ *A new morning has come. This morning of hope. Open your heart and fill it with happiness.* ♫

Her eerie melody wafted through the halls. She was on the move, preparing to carry out her natural assignment. Her game was complete and she must attend to the lethal business at hand. She was right about many things; we did have a choice, didn't we? We did have the power to keep fighting for the ones we love, even when in the natural, those connections appear to be a lost cause. As long as we kept a glimmer of hope in our hearts, redemption was still within an arm's reach. Yes, that macabre entity was right about many things, but as I rushed over to Asuka, still collapsed on the floor, one truth rang above all others: the hour was later than we thought, and we had no time to lose!

"Asuka! Come with me!" I anxiously brought the girl to her feet. Her body slumped, her strength surrendering to gravity's pull. I supported her flimsy form, hoping to transfer some of my fortitude to her. "Asuka, on your feet! Hurry!"

Asuka's eyes scanned the room, disoriented, almost as if she was waking from a deep sleep. "What now?" she asked, her face contorting from drowsy confusion.

"No time, we have to finish this NOW!" I lunged to the journal on the table, propping the hopeless girl up in the process. Upon seeing the journal once again, Asuka's lethargy gave way to alertness. I gave her a split second to get her bearings before grabbing her hand, frantically pulling her out of the room and into the garden beyond. But as we crossed the threshold and the beaming sunlight hit our faces, Asuka's hand unexpectedly jerked away. Her head dropped once more, stands of her wavy black hair covering the pain in her eyes. "Asuka, please!"

"I should never have even bothered," she muttered with decisiveness.

Anger whirled inside me like a vortex, provoked by her resignation. If she only knew what I knew about the seriousness of Ritsuko's situation! "Never say that!" Pointing my finger at her, she flinched. "You've come too far! You can't just let Ritsuko go now!"

Quiet.

Asuka's vacant face was like a heartbreaking mirror, reflecting the same apathy that consumed me in the months leading up to my father's suicide. What I would have given for someone to slap me in the face and tell me the hard truth: though all connections seem lost in the natural, there are always unbreakable cords in the spiritual, waiting to be leaned on in time of need.

"Asuka," I said, taking a deep look back to Ritsuko, "I never told you about my dad, did I?"

Asuka's face rose slightly, the vulnerability of my words seeming to connect with something inside her. "You said he died."

I nodded soberly, my hands returning to her shoulders. "Yes, he's gone, both my mom and dad are. What I said on the train the other day, I meant it. Like you, Asuka, I really do know the pain of losing a loved one."

A sparkle of recognition began to twinkle in her eyes. A dim spark that could be extinguished at any moment. But if given the right fuel, could erupt into an inferno of meaning.

"But I didn't tell you the *whole* story. My father and I were never all that close. He didn't believe in God the way I did, and after the death of his wife, my mother, he abandoned all of his relationships." The words came out of me with a righteous honesty.

Asuka glanced over my shoulder at Ritsuko, the familiar picture of a person suffering a great loss, striking a familiar chord in her tearful red eyes.

"My story gets more similar with yours, Asuka. My father pushed me out of his life at every possible opportunity. It wasn't long before I matched his estrangement through my hurt. I thought that because those connections were severed, there would never be any hope of us making amends. But I didn't realize the full weight of what was at stake: *his life!*" The words sent an ache in my stomach as my own tears began to fall with abandon.

"My father was found alone in his home. His body had been left to decay there for a week before anyone started to get worried about him." Short breaths and constricting sobs stifled my voice, both of which began to echo in Asuka. "The suicide of my father has followed me ever since! I tried to run from it. I moved to the other side of the world in hopes that I could forget about it, but it just kept following me!" My eyes left hers, and I thoughtfully surveyed the vastness of the Aokigahara behind the Ryokan. Regaining my composure, I continued, "All of that running inevitably brought me here, to the Suicide Forest, Asuka. To create a film that communicates the value of Life. When I first agreed to this project, I didn't think I had the background to do it. Hurt people only hurt people, you know? How could I give away something that I did not possess? But I took a step of faith and hoped God would work through me. And as strange as it seems, He has! He brought me here to heal those hurts I've tried to run from. To once and for all silence the voices of guilt and regret. He showed me that I must forgive myself so I can begin to live again. And He also brought you into my life."

My tearful eyes locked with hers again. "I see so much of that same damage that was in me, in you. The loss of your mother, and the same estrangement to another parental figure. Please. Don't make the same mistakes I made. Don't give up on them. Don't wait countless years wishing you would have taken the time to reach out. We always think there will be more time than there actually is ..." My head dropped, heart throbbing from vulnerability. "I came here because I was asked to make a film about suicide and the value of the life we have been given. I don't know if what we did can even be turned into anything of merit, but if somehow, it can be turned into *something*, I don't know who it will reach. But what I do know is this: if *one* person's life is changed by my story, *just one*, then all of this would have been worth it!"

I turned, motioning to Ritsuko then returned to Asuka's lamenting face. "She is *your* one person, Asuka! Will everything you've gone through be for nothing? Will it all have been in vain?"

The question was birthed from the deepest recesses of my broken heart; the words fell from my lips and mixed with the damp morning air. Asuka breathed both in. She stepped back as my hands fell from her shoulders, no longer needing my strength to stay on her feet. Her widened eyes took in the scene and the monumental moment in a single, lucid flash. With a small, cautious tone, her mouth began its decisive reply. "I'm the only one left who can be that for her, aren't I?"

The question required no answer.

"Please, come with me, Chad. I can't do this alone. I need someone by my side, will you be that person?" Asuka's wet face met mine again. I had seen those tear-filled eyes too many times. Was now the time to see those eyes, wet with pain, eclipsed by a smile of hope?

Together we took our first steps towards the garden's pond, slowly approaching Ritsuko standing at the water's edge. I closed my eyes and prayed that I would see Asuka's smile of hope before it was too late.

We stepped onto the manicured grass of the Japanese garden, Ritsuko's forest of isolation. But in stark contrast to the trees populating the Aokigahara, Ritsuko had designed her forest in extravagant beauty, and drenched it in masochistic self-discipline. Once again, as we approached, the woman didn't turn to acknowledge us, but the pain she wore on her face couldn't be concealed. Her face bore an expression of agony, one that I recognized all too well, one I had seen in the mirror countless times in the wake of my father's death. The night I broke into his house, there had been no other person there to comfort me in my grief. If there had, what words would I have needed them to say? Now, here I was, assuming that position for this poor woman. But what were the right words, when she, a stranger, needed to hear them?

And would there be enough time to speak them?

♫ *A new morning has come. A morning of hope. Open your heart and fill it with happiness.* ♫

My heart sank as my ears caught the sound of Death's alluring melody. She was here with us, just as she assured me she would be, preparing herself to welcome Ritsuko into her fatal embrace. The melody filled the garden like yesterday's fog had doused every empty spot in foreboding. Only this time, the melody was coupled with the tap, tap, tap of little skipping shoes. A wicked movement beyond Ritsuko, out in the center of the pond, caught my eye. The girl stood tall over the darkened waters. Subtle ripples echoed over the glass-like surface as the girl took one gleeful hop after another toward us, toward Ritsuko! Was she walking on the water? No, her movements were more defined, precise. She gently skipped, slinking from one shallow rock face to another. And as that Angel of Death continued to creep closer to us, her melody grew louder. That song was the same one Asuka sang with such carelessness in the clearing last night. Now, that same melody returned, replacing its simple connotations of joy with morbid chords of dread as its vocalist advanced ever closer to the housemother.

♫ *The sky is big and blue. The wind is full of fragrance. Open your heart and let it in. It's as easy as one…* ♫

The girl found her footing on another rock.

♫ *… two! …* ♫

Another skip.

♫ *…THREE!* ♫

She landed again on another smooth stone, descending on one foot, holding a pirouette like an amateur ballerina, one black glove contrasting against the blue sky of hope. She had closed half the distance between us.

"Ritsuko!" I shouted, using a tone inappropriate, both culturally and from my close proximity. Ritsuko couldn't ignore my cry. She flinched, turning away from the invisible threat looming closer to her. Rituko shot daggers of offense our way. I paused and her intimidation almost overtook me, advancing as mercilessly as that wicked spirit crossing the pond. Heart racing, I closed my eyes, trying to keep calm. Words fell from me as Asuka timidly translated.

"You and I are not friends. Not like you were to Asuka's mother." Ritsuko cut her eyes at me; it must have felt like she was listening to a crazy person. My frantic heart refused to yield. "But, like you, I too know the tragedy of losing a loved one to ... *suicide*." That final word hit Ritsuko like a bullet. The outrage of her nonverbal response could not be ignored; it stung hot. But I couldn't stop! The words of my taxi driver emboldened me: *If no one ever says anything, how can anything change?*

"I lost my own father to suicide!" I blurted as Asuka continued to rattle off the translation. "When I found the letter he left, the pain I felt was overwhelming, too deep for words to define."

♫ *Let's spread our wings and marathon across the sky! It's our destiny and it suits us well.* ♫

The girl's polished black shoes reflected flashes of sunlight as they jumped to another watery platform.

Yes, the hour was much later than we thought. Was this going to help at all? Was this last effort to reach Ritsuko just going to end in unavoidable disaster?

♫ *It's very easy, see! Shall I show you?* ♫

No, as long as we have breath in our lungs, there is always a chance!

"After he died," I continued, half looking at Ritsuko, half keeping my eye on the encroaching form of that wicked girl, "all I wanted was to have just *one more* moment with him, so I could ask him all the questions I still had in my heart."

♫ *It's as easy as one...* ♫

The girl pressed close enough to reach out and touch Ritsuko. She paused for only a moment seeming to examine her black gloves one final time. The gloves erupted into darkened wisps of living fog. This was it! Ritsuko's time was up! That door the girl spoke of was about to be unlocked!

"But after being here, I now know that my father *loved* me." I urgently took the journal from Asuka, stepped closer to Ritsuko, and held it out to her. "You may not be ready now, nor may you ever be prepared to read what's written in these pages—the good and the bad. But maybe one day, you may *want* to know. And if that day comes, you'll want to have this."

♫ ... *Two...* ♫

The girl extended one of her gloved hands, pointing a single index finger toward Ritsuko's neck. The girl's finger began to glow in a blinding ghostly fire!

♫ ...*Knock Knock...* ♫

The girl sang as a devilish smile of delight beamed over her mouth.

Asuka finished the translation, falling silent once more.

♫ ...*Anyone home?..* ♫

The girl sang as the light behind Ritsuko burst into a blaze. I braced myself for the girl's third count, *her* lethal touch.

But there wasn't a third count.

No touch.

No song.

No girl.

Nothing remained in her place. The pond, as smooth as glass. Almost as if she had never been there at all.

An endless moment passed as Ritsuko seemed to process the words. Or was she considering more than that? Had she been aware of the spirit of death that had loomed so closely behind her? It wasn't my words that caused the figure to vanish, was it? It was something deeper than that. It was something deep inside the palace of Ritsuko's heart. The words that harbinger of death spoke: Ritsuko's door would be opened today. But who the woman would let in was entirely her decision, wasn't it? Did she have the courage to let Asuka into that door instead of Death?

As tears welled up in the housemother's cheeks, I hoped I knew the answer.

Ritsuko took a silent step to me, her saddened face betraying any dignity left in the woman. Her eyes met mine. After a moment, she glanced down to the journal, taking it from my nervous hands. Then she fixed her painful gaze on Asuka.

"Asuka ..." she spoke wistfully, outstretching her hand to the girl. Asuka hesitated, her cheek still baring the redness of Ritsuko's rage. Slowly, Asuka raised her hand to the woman's. In an instant, Ritsuko pulled Asuka into her, dropping the journal, embracing girl tightly. Ritsuko brought her face to Asuka's ear, whispering. Asuka, like a child, replied in short, incoherent hums. The woman distanced herself slightly, taking in the sight of Asuka for what appeared to be the first time.

FOURTEEN

FOURTEEN

KISHI KAISEI

"Where have you been?" Paul asked as we caught each other in the hallway of the Ryokan. I pensively glanced back the way I came, back toward the garden, where Ritsuko and Asuka were sharing a much needed moment together. Should I tell Paul what just happened? No, there would be time for that later. It would be one of the many things I would have to debrief him on in the days ahead. "We gotta get going. Not much time left," he said, heading down the hall and out to the waiting taxi.

Not much time left. No, there wasn't. Not much time for the four of us *here* anyway. I turned to take in the traditional entryway one last time as the Ryokan began to feel distant, alien. Like the morning you leave a vacation. A temporary home, one that you've relied on more than its relied on you. There may be other guests at the Ryokan in the future, other stories, other moments in this place, but they wouldn't involve us. But what about Ritsuko? What will she do now? Leave the Ryokan and reconnect with her loved ones in Tokyo? Or would her new revelation be a fleeting one? Would that spirit of isolation creep back into her home and her heart?

I slid a finger over the polished cherry wood support column, checking it for dust, recalling the conversation with the deathly girl two nights back, and the ominous game I played with her moments ago. Did that grim spirit really have malicious intent? Or was she simply a commentator, exposing the systems at play in our natural world, most of which are ignored or are just simply overlooked? Although unconventional, most of what the girl alluded to had indeed come to pass. Be it by predestination, or by us acting on that 'great gift' she mentioned, either way, I had a long flight back to California to pray about many of these unanswerable questions.

Sometimes you just don't know, and sometimes, you have to be okay with that.

DING!

A clock behind me chimed with ferocity. I turned to address it.

DING!

There hung that same clock the deathly girl had attended to, the same one I noticed, and upon my recent return, had been keeping time with the others perfectly.

DING!

The third chime echoed, but a fourth didn't sound, the time was clearly off again! I gently opened the glass door, the thick brass hour hand resting ever so acutely on its third number.

Three ...

Only three of us would return from the Aokigahara.

Although I usually just ignore such pointless omens, that number *three* taunted me, reminding me of its presence.

"Shut up," I muttered at the clock. "I got everyone out! Everyone's safe now."

As I reached to the hour hand to reset the timepiece, Auska's voice called out.

"Hey…" She stood behind me, framed by the entrance to the dining room. Her eyes dry, but still red. She disappeared back into the room, inviting me to follow.

Upon entering the dining room once more, Ritsuko was nowhere to be seen.

"Is there anything I can do to help?" I crossed my arms, the intimacy of Asuka's moment with the housemother still lingering in the air between us. Asuka paced the floor, nervously playing with her soiled bandages. She gave a subdued smile, inhaled, paused, then released her breath.

"Umm … maybe." Her fingers continued to fiddle with her soiled gauze. She looked out into the garden, out to the Aokigahara beyond. "I'm, uhh, I'm …"

What was going on? Did she not realize that our time was even shorter than she had previously reminded me of? Why did she hesitate?

"Asuka, what is it?"

Asuka gave me a silent nod, sealing her mouth tightly, almost as if trying to keep something from escaping her lips. But to no avail. It was clear that however much she didn't want the words to come, they possessed a battering ram, they refused to be held back.

She met my eyes, motioning with her hands, apparently hoping they would help the process. "Chad, I'm ... not going back."

My heart sank as my mouth sealed its *own* words into silence.

"I'm ... I'm going to stay here ... with Ritsuko," she nodded to herself as if that would set her bizarre resolution in stone. She then froze, anticipating my reaction to her announcement. But her deliberation was too shocking for words, too paradoxical for me to be objective. I had hid that foreboding prophecy the girl uttered deep in my heart, and replaced it with one solitary goal: Don't lose any of my companions in the Aokigahara.

But this, I never considered *this*. What if the Aokigahara was *more* than just a host to things intent on making you lose your way? What if the forest could also be a *home*?

"You're going to stay *here*, in the Suicide Forest?" I asked.

She bit her lip, anxiously pacing again. "The Aokigahara wasn't *always* known as the Suicide Forest, Chad. Maybe with a little help, one day, that name will be forgotten by people. Besides, Ritsuko needs someone to look after her. She wouldn't say it, but she doesn't have to." Asuka shrugged her shoulders. "I can't do what we just did, and then leave her all alone."

Ritsuko was really what it came down to, wasn't it? Asuka's rekindled relationship with Ritsuko, however premature, was her strongest pillar, one that she could rely on; although that pillar may require her undivided attention, at least for now.

"Don't give me that look!" Asuka said, grinning sheepishly, breaking me from my vacant stare.

"I'm sorry! I'm still trying to piece this together."

"I know... me too."

I surveyed the dining room in which we now stood, imagining how this space, as well as the rest of the Ryokan could be Asuka's new home for the unexpected time ahead of her. "But, really, what are you going to do all the way out here? No friends… no SERVICE?!"

She laughed, and I joined.

"It won't be forever, just for now," she said, matching my gaze over the room. "I've finished my studies and I have the rest of the summer to figure all of this out." She looked out into the garden. "It's just what I have to do right now. It's … right."

I had to admit, I couldn't disagree with her. As scary as the thought is of moving away from everything you know, scarier is the thought of what might have been if you would have had the courage to step out into the unknown.

"Besides," Asuka continued, still gazing out to the garden, "if what you believe about this place is true …" She glanced back at me, her face radiating in the ever ascending sunlight. "Then the Aokigahara will need all the help I can give."

She was right. The strength of Asuka's spirit could be just what both Ritsuko and the Aokigahara needed to move past this dark spot in the pages of their histories. She could help Ritsuko bring guests back to the Ryokan, reinstate the inn as a serene vacation destination, perhaps even assist Hiroshi in bringing hope to those visitors who had none. Yes, Asuka could have a passionate future here! But doing so would mean that she would have to, at least for the time being, leave some fond friends and relations back in Tokyo, one of which was the delicate heart currently packing Asuka's bags upstairs.

"Miku's going to be crushed." I didn't mean to state the obvious. I'm sure Asuka had already been trying to wrestle the heartbreaking thought out of her mind.

"I know," she replied solemnly.

"Asuka!" As if on cue, Miku's voice resonated through the Ryokan. Asuka's face paled, knowing the inevitable exchange was coming, whether she had the strength for it or not. Asuka closed her eyes tight, trying to avoid the pain she was bound to inflict.

Poor Miku dashed into the room, a naïve excitement in her tone. "What are you doing? Let's go!" Her feet danced under her, as her arms reached out to shepherd us through the door. My heart broke. There was no way Miku could have known, no way to understand what the redemption of Ritsuko meant to Asuka, and no way to understand the strength behind her best friend's new resolve, and even worse, no time to explain. But seeing the inexplicable resolution upon Asuka's face, Miku's countenance shifted as well.

"Asuka?" Miku's eyes narrowed inquisitively, taking a cautious step toward her. "What's wrong?"

Asuka remained still.

"Asuka, let's go home!" Miku said, but her tone spoke volumes; Miku's heart knew she would be going home without the company of her guardian angel. "Asuka …"

Asuka sighed, shaking her head slightly.

"Asuka …" Miku's voice broke.

"I can't go with you, Miku."

"W-What?" Miku's question stuttered as tears filled her eyes.

Tears returned to Asuka as well, "I have to stay."

"You can't stay!" Miku fired back, one hand hopelessly reaching out to her friend as if she were a mile away. "You cannot leave me!"

Asuka turned away from her friend, attempting to hide the agony on her face, beholding the Aokigahara once more. "We came here to guide these people through the Sea of Trees," she faced Miku again, a glint of strength returning in her eyes, "but something was guiding *me* too, Miku. It guided me here, to someone who needs me."

"*I* need you!" Miku whimpered, "I am *lost* without you!" Her head fell, hair concealing her face. Asuka took a few steps toward Miku. Placing her hand under Miku's chin, she raised it to meet her face.

"You are Takahashi Miku, a beautiful and talented actress!" Asuka smiled.

Miku winced.

Asuka continued, "Miku: the person who braved down child ghosts in the Aokigahara!" Asuka gave a chuckle.

Miku did the same, blushing with embarrassment.

"Miku: who despite all her superstitions, burned a suicide manual!"

"Yes, but with *you* next to me!" Miku anxiously leaped over Asuka's words.

Asuka winced again, but kept her smile intact. "It wasn't just me, Miku. There was something more." She tapped Miku's chest with a gentle finger. "There is a greatness in you that is just beginning to rise, Miku. Last night was proof of that." A quiet moment. "Now, I need that greatness in you to let me stay."

Miku collapsed into Asuka's arms, her body convulsing with deep sobs. Asuka held her friend in a firm embrace, her bandaged fingers running through her long, silky hair.

"But, I am still frightened," Miku whispered through her tears.

"Me, too," Asuka admitted, "but I won't be away forever."

A blunt honk from our taxi signaled to the girls that their time was finished for now.

Asuka pulled away, eyes wet, nose sniffling, trying ever-so-earnestly to keep the smile on her face, knowing how crucial that smile was to Miku's courage. "Now, be brave. Chin up." Asuka propped Miku's shoulders up and brought a gentle hand under her chin once more. "And go back home."

Miku tearfully straightened herself, despite her lament and nodded, "Kishi Kaisei?" she whispered.

"Kishi Kaisei, Miku-Chan," Asuka repeated with a nod, peering deep into her eyes, searching for a strength she hoped was inside her friend. And as a familiarly bold smile played over Asuka's face, it was clear that she spotted that spark of strength she had been looking for in Miku.

* * *

The noisy Kawaguchiko station greeted the three of us as we stepped out of the taxi and into the radiant sunlight. My phone began chiming relentlessly. An onslaught of stacked notifications overlapped each other in one, skipping and repeating tone. There would be time for those on the train.

"Goodbye, travelers!" the driver bid cheerfully, then looked at Miku. "One day you will have to tell me your story of what happened in the forest so I can scare the other tourists, okay?" he grinned.

Miku laughed and courteously agreed before the driver sped off.

We stood in an awkward silence for a moment, unsure of our next steps without the aggressive lead of Asuka. Asuka, what must she be doing right now? Setting up her new long-term residence with the little effects she brought with her? Walking in the garden with Ritsuko, reminiscing of their days together from her childhood?

"I think that the ticket office is …" Miku pointed in a general area of the station, "this way?" Miku didn't know. Clearly, purchasing train tickets herself was something new to her. "I will go this way," she decided, seeming to lock her feelings away for the time being. Her finger moved in the air, circling around the entrance of the station. "Wait here with the luggage, okay?" Miku took the first few steps across the street, was nearly hit by a passing bus, then cautiously continued.

Paul and I exchanged nervous glances. "I'll go help her," Paul stated.

"That's probably best," I agreed. What was Miku going to do without her guardian angel? Asuka. I was still trying to wrap my head around all of it. We arrived here, at the Kawaguchiko station two short days ago, Asuka led our ragtag group into the unknown, and now that unknown has kept her in the Aokigahara. Would she be alright? Of course she would! Like everything else on this trip: the journal, the body of the unknown man, my memories of my father, and now Asuka, all were put into their needed places. Now, it was time for me to be put back into *my* place, back home.

My musings were broken by a familiar sight: black shiny shoes. Polished black shoes. I tried to steady my anxious mind. *The Girl.* Those shoes, prancing on Ritsuko's pond. Singing, counting, waiting …

I was so caught up in my recollection that it took a moment to realize that the owner of the shoes had come up beside me. I raised my head nervously to acknowledge the figure. No, it wasn't *the girl*. It was a man. A man with polished, black shoes. THE man with the immaculate shoes! The same lanky, disheveled, young businessman whom I noticed on our train coming here, was now standing so close I could reach out and touch him.

He planted himself on the curb next to me, smoking a cigarette and appearing as though he had been through a rough couple of days. He glanced at me briefly, squinting in the sunlight. Then looking out at the train tracks, he drew a puff of his cigarette. "American?" he asked with a thick Japanese accent.

"Yes," I said, taking a seat on the curb beside him; the cigarette smoke curled around us. I held out my hand to introduce myself.

The man put the cigarette in his mouth and shook my hand. "I speak very little English." He pressed his finger and his thumb together.

"Oh," I waved him off, "that's okay. I speak very little Japanese. None actually!"

We sat in a stiff silence for a moment. Two strangers in a strange world, not knowing each other's past or where our futures would lead.

The man then gestured to Mt. Fuji. "Fuji?" he asked, indicating that's what he figured I'd come for.

"No, Aokigahara," I said.

The man nodded, trying to remain stoic, although I could see the name had struck a nerve.

"And you?" I asked.

The man's eyes focused far away, he silently took another long drag of his cigarette. "I came for something … but now … I want to go home to family." He retrieved his phone and scrolled to a picture of a woman and young daughter.

"Oh! You have a lovely family," I said.

"Yes," he replied. Again, he sat in silent thoughtfulness. "They are life." Another moment passed. He nonchalantly threw the cigarette on the street, pulled out the nearly full pack from his breast pocket, rose, and tossed the cigarettes into a nearby trash bin. "I must go," he said, bowing briefly.

"Wait!" I called out. The man stopped and turned back to me. I wanted to ask him what he was doing out here. What someone like him, a young salaryman, was doing visiting the Aokigahara. But I didn't. *I couldn't!* In any culture, it wasn't my place. But still, here he was, the very person I had been dreading we might find *inside* the Suicide Forest. He was alive, a mess, but *alive!*

"I'm sorry to keep you from your train," I hesitated, trying to find the words. "But I actually *do* know a few words of Japanese."

His eyes widened as he said, "Waa, Sugoi ne!"

No, I didn't know this phrase but I still gave the usual stupid smile and agreement that a non-speaker retorts with.

"Yes, but, could you tell me ... if you know ..." I started.

"Yes?" He waited, expectantly.

"What is ... keeshee... kayseeh?" My utterance stumbled over the complex pronunciation. It didn't sound the same coming from *me.*

"Kishi Kaisei?" he asked, the words rolling off his tongue perfectly.

I apologetically nodded with humility. "Yes, sir."

The man considered the words for a moment. He looked down at the ground, smiled, then returned his gaze to me. "Kishi kaisei: Chinese proverb. Very old!" He looked out at the forest, peeking back at us in the distance. "It means ..." he looked back at me with a smile, "wake from death and return to life!"

He disappeared into the crowd.

A Japanese voice sounded over a loudspeaker in what seemed to be an announcement of the departure of a train. Paul appeared back at my side, and together, we grabbed the bags and ran down the platform, just barely making it onto the train before it sped away.

Finding our seats with next to no problem, we settled in beside Miku.

She breathed a sigh of relief, "I am sorry I took so long! I accidentally bought tickets for *Kyoto*! I had to exchange them." She bowed her head in repentance.

"You did good, Miku. Asuka will be proud!" I assured her.

"Yes! She will!" Miku beamed. "And soon," she motioned to her phone, "I am sending her an internet machine as a present. Now we can speak to each other even while she is away!"

An internet machine? Oh, yes of course: WiFi. The same as Hiroshi had in his watch tower. The invaluable conveniences of modern technology. Like Hiroshi said, it wasn't the same as face-to-face contact, but it was better than *nothing*.

We all relaxed into the rhythm of the train, which now began to pick up speed. Paul helped Miku navigate the complexity of shopping for internet routers: a task that Miku had very little understanding or interest in doing.

Soon, Paul's phone chimed in a similar manner as mine had. He quickly excused himself.

Miku and I were left to the quiet between us, neither of us sure how to fill the air. Her eyes gazed out the window, met mine briefly, then back out at the passing scenery.

"Where will you go after Tokyo, Chad?"

I thought about it for a moment, facing the reality that this project, at least for me, was in fact finished. "I guess I'll be going back home to California, at least for the time."

Miku nodded.

"What about you, Miku? Any plans for the rest of summer?" Maybe it was bad timing for that question.

She took a breath, her mind spinning. "I think I will go to Harajuku when we get back ... high-school friends."

Of course, this world wouldn't stop when Paul and I left it. Miku would go on with her life in Tokyo. Like the Ryokan, how seldom we consider that distant places carry on long after we depart them. No, those distant places don't just freeze in time, they continue on and persevere without you.

"I wish we had a little more time. I know Paul would love to have some days off to go see Tokyo," I added.

Miku nodded but did not speak. Her delicate hand habitually reached for her necklace that was no longer there. She paused as a pensive look washed over her face. Her fingers rubbed the skin of her neck, where the weight of the necklace, no doubt, had remained. How often do we feel the remnants of a moment, good or bad, long after its departure?

Miku took in a deep breath and closed her eyes, surrendering to the soothing lull of the train whisking her back home from our adventure. In her sleepy bliss, a soft song fell from her mouth in nearly a whisper.

♫ *A new morning has come.* ♫

♫ *A morning of hope.* ♫

♫ *Open your heart and fill it with happiness.* ♫

I gazed out the window as the green countryside slowly transformed back into a palace of concrete. Would any of us forget this time together? Would the lessons we learned be quickly forgotten? Or would the struggles we experienced be pillars of strength for the rest of our lives?

♫ *It's very easy, see!* ♫

♫ *Shall I show you?* ♫

The Aokigahara felt hazy, and my memories began to slowly blur until only a few mental snapshots remained, a slight nausea of remembrance, and of course, whatever footage Paul was able to gather.

♫ *It's as easy as one…* ♫

As the train sped eastward, I took one last look at the Aokigahara, nestled in the shadow of Mt. Fuji, knowing there was a good chance I'd never step foot in the Suicide Forest ever again.

♫ *…two…* ♫

But like Miku's necklace, which now rested over Asuka's heart, I too, had left an old token in the Aokigahara, an opened wound of grief, one that I also instinctively reached for.

And for the first time in my life, I felt the absence of its weight.

… three!

EPILOGUE

EPILOGUE

THE GIFT OF THE FATHER

Welcome back.

You've made it! And none the worse for wear, I hope.

I'm sure you have more than a few questions about the story you just read. As I said in the beginning, *The Curse of the Father* would contain some dark subject matters, both physical as well as supernatural, and also metaphoric fictional characters that I have taken creative license with. Please know that the more sinister aspects of this story weren't written to glorify any sort of dark allurement to the demonic realm. Rather, my intention was just the opposite. These grim elements were designed to serve as a contrast to the power God has placed in us to overcome the enemy. Without giving those dark things a legitimate voice (i.e., those metaphoric characters), sometimes it's difficult to recognize their whispers in our minds. In addition, by creating three dimensional dark characters, and then defeating them, we are able to fully appreciate how bright the light of faith can shine! And now that this story has come to a close, I'm sure there is a ray of truth shining in your heart. Through Christ, we can conquer all things that intend to keep us in darkness. If the story you just read isn't enough proof of that, then this final chapter assuredly will be.

My goal of writing *The Curse of the Father* was not to simply tell a story, and then have you close the book and be done with the truths the adventure held. I knew that if I could just get you here, to this moment, that I could unpack the analogies woven throughout this story and do what I do best: communicate the Truth of God's word in a practical way.

Before examining the parallels between my time in the Aokigahara and the spiritual battle that rages for our hearts, let me first give a factual account of what happened after Paul and I left Japan.

Once we returned to California, Paul fervently worked on editing the footage he shot in the Suicide Forest, crafting it into a final piece. The outcome of Paul's labor resulted in one of the most captivating and powerful programs we had ever produced. Through all our doubt, the turmoil and unexpected twists and turns, we *did* have *something* to share with others about the value of all our lives. Before shipping out the documentary to TV stations, Paul charged me with one final task: give the video a fitting title. Moments later, I scribbled down the same compelling moniker for the Aokigahara that I first heard when Asuka, Miku, Paul and I boarded our train in Tokyo: *The Sea of Trees.*

And just like that, *The Sea of Trees* was sent out into the world with a small prayer echoing in my heart: *Please let this piece convey hope and life, not doubt or death.*

Weeks later, that desperate prayer was answered as *The Sea of Trees* swept the world, airing on dozens of international TV channels and amassing over a million views on social media. In the weeks that followed, I was swarmed by hundreds of touching letters from people who were deeply affected by our story and the stirring message of hope I delivered within. I can say unashamedly that the message communicated in *The Sea of Trees* is nothing less than supernatural. I take no credit for those words, nor for the obvious presence and power experienced when people hear them. Still, the positive reception of the documentary was a reassuring confirmation that my time in the Aokigahara, as well as my personal pain of losing a loved one to suicide, had not been in vain. God had taken the shambles of my broken heart and the wreckage of a tumultuous production schedule, and used it for His glory, not ours.

I've personally witnessed the profound effect *The Sea of Trees* has on hurting people. During ministry events around the world, I've screened the documentary to packed-out stadiums. I am always flabbergasted by its response. Hundreds of people, young and old, flood to the front of the stage, tears in their eyes, desperate to share their own stories of how suicide has affected them. Tears fill my eyes shortly after as I stand in prayer with these precious people fiercely seeking the same emotional healing God gave me in the Aokigahara, of all places. Like my broken heart, God took the grim nature of the Suicide Forest and turned it around to convey hope and life to thousands throughout the world. That hope has given people the strength to open painful wounds and embrace life once again.

Even years later, *The Sea of Trees* continues to captivate audiences, and the message of overcoming the deception behind suicide has become a cornerstone of my ministry. Every year I host dozens of meetings specifically designed to confront this painful topic. These "Life Events" provide a safe platform for people to shamelessly recognize the lies of hopelessness the enemy has planted in their hearts. After showing *The Sea of Trees*, sharing my own testimony, and exposing the wicked sources of self-destruction, I ask the attendees to stand to their feet if they have found themselves struggling with thoughts of suicide or have lost someone to this epidemic. The staggering response constantly sobers my heart as more than half of the audience rises. The image of a sea of forlorn faces is an irrefutable reminder that the threat of suicide lies just underneath the surface of every society, hiding itself under a heavy veil of guilt and shame.

This isn't an issue that we can continue to sweep under the rug. Yes, it's uncomfortable. Yes, it's messy. But, the need is great and the death toll grows every year. We can't wait for the next tragedy to occur and we don't have to only admit that this is a serious issue when our loved ones are at risk, or worse, gone. We can preemptively attack those deceptions *now* when they're only small whispers, and ever since God healed me from my own wounds of suicide, attacking those lies has continued to be my passion.

Believe me, I never set out to be a minister who confronts the issues behind suicide. I don't have the medical background to examine this subject from a scientific perspective. And let me assure you, there *is* a medical aspect to suicide, and there are trained professionals available to aid us in that physical arena. But as for me, the tragedy of losing my dad to suicide, my emotional restoration while creating *The Sea of Trees*, and my passion for communicating the Gospel created a perfect storm for giving me a voice into the lives of emotionally and spiritually wounded people. I've reverentially accepted this much needed role, knowing that it's not me who can restore wounded people to a life worth living, but Jesus, The One who dwells in me, and desires to dwell in all of us. I continue to keep a mindset that if my testimony can change even one person's destiny, I know that I've obeyed the directive God gave me years ago while I wept uncontrollably in the bedroom of my deceased father.

When it came to finally writing my first book, I knew a story of spiritual warfare, based in the Suicide Forest, *had* to be the subject. Why? Because while *The Sea of Trees* documentary, and the "Life Events" I host, provide tools to confront the people who are *currently* at risk, I found that an additional resource was fiercely needed: A tool to address the wounds carried by those who have lost loved ones. As I can count myself among these survivors, I understand the importance of having practical guidance and spiritual understanding concerning suicide. I have seen firsthand that the message in *The Curse of the Father* is a much needed insight for those who have found themselves in that pit of doubt and unforgiveness.

Numerous aspects of those emotional wounds and that heavy doubt are reflected in the characters and situations in *The Curse of the Father*, while the plot serves to showcase the spiritual battle for our destiny. No aspect of this story was written just for the sake of excitement.

Rather, the concepts exist as signposts for you and me to consider the dangerous mindsets we can find ourselves in when we don't adhere to God's Words of Truth. Some of these parallels are simple fundamentals, others are more abstract. But, each analogy represents a crucial concept when it comes to understanding the spiritual systems at work in all of our hearts.

RESCUE FROM THE FOREST CHAOS

As I begin an analysis of the symbolism in *The Curse of the Father*, the best place to start is with the most commanding of the characters: *the Aokigahara*. The disorienting terrain of the Suicide Forest was unlike any forest I'd ever seen. It's nearly impossible to tell one area from the next! Even the most seasoned hiker could get lost in the maze of twisted branches. Not to mention, finding stable footing on the forest's uneven and collapsible terrain is a laughable act of futility. And yes, compasses aren't always reliable there. The reason isn't because of evil spirits, as Miku had originally feared. Rather, compasses can often malfunction because of the high iron content in the lava coursing underneath the forest floor. That iron literally disrupts the magnetic true north a compass uses to orient itself. Without proper orientation, the inaccuracy of a defective compass can actually get you *more* lost than if you didn't have it at all. How confusing would it be if you were relying on an instrument that keeps shifting its direction! As the iron in the lava continues to distract the compass from what is absolute, you could find yourself walking around in circles, getting nowhere.

Those underground veins of ancient lava act as a direct contradiction to the purpose a compass was created for: to point us in the right direction.

So your compass doesn't work. How about relying on something in nature that can't be upset by the elements around you? What about sunlight? The sun rises in the east and sets in the west. You could use the position of the sun to set your direction, right? Actually, no! Not at all. Frustratingly, sunlight isn't a factor you can count on in the Aokigahara, either. Between the mist and fog that settles at the base of Mt Fuji, and the manner in which the forest's trees grow and spread their leaves, there is created a consistent veil to daylight. This veil makes it very difficult to tell what time it is or what direction you're going. Also, because the forest's canopy diffuses the light so effectively, the descent into night is extremely vague and gradual. If you aren't paying close attention, you could suddenly find yourself lost in total darkness, much like Asuka, Miku and I found ourselves in the clearing, anxiously waiting for rescue.

That rescue was found in the forest ranger, Hiroshi, who filled the clearing with his powerful searchlights. Hiroshi's watchtower was stocked with equipment specifically designed to find lost people. Floodlights, flare guns, loudspeakers and radios. All of these tools, when put into the hands of a trained professional, can mean the difference between being rescued or being lost indefinitely. In fact, the rangers stationed in Aokigahara have spent years stringing dozens of miles of yellow twine throughout the forest. This twine can serve as makeshift trails, lifelines to anyone who finds themselves lost.

Following these strands will lead you either out of the forest, or at least to someone who *can* help you get out. If you can just find *one* of the hundreds of yellow cords, follow it! They are there to lead you out of the turbulence and get you back on track!

Asuka, Miku and I knew how scary it was to be stuck in the Aokigahara, waiting for help to arrive. What would have happened if Hiroshi hadn't come to find us? We might have been trapped in that clearing all night, if not longer! It was only with the help of someone who knew the Aokigahara intimately, and had a high vantage point, that we had any hope of escaping its grasp.

Now, consider how the chaos of the Aokigahara can be mirrored by the turmoil of our own lives. We are fearfully and wonderfully made, but, like the Sea of Trees, untended overgrowth, distracting elements and natural disasters can cause a disruptive anarchy in our hearts. Our lives get messy, plans fall apart, innocent habits grow into serious addictions, and the fear of catastrophe constantly weighs in our mind. It's easy to feel anxious, isn't it? Even more scary, it's easy to feel lost in all that uncertainty. But don't panic! There are small mindsets that we can practice daily to tend to the chaos in our lives.

First, let's talk about an all-out rescue from the forests we find ourselves in. When Asuka, Miku and I were stuck in the clearing, Hiroshi would never have known we were in need of saving if we didn't call out for help. That cry came in the form of Miku's flare gun. Once fired, that orange light signaled that we were in way over our heads. We didn't have the training to navigate the Aokigahara on our own. We *had* to have someone high above our situation and surroundings to intervene on our behalf. The same scenario can be applied when we find ourselves lost in our *own* lives. When overwhelming uncertainty washes over us, we *must* reach out to someone who, not only is positioned above the turmoil, but someone who intimately knows the terrain of our hearts. But, it takes humility to use the tool God's given us to signal for help. Often in life, pride inhibits us from standing up and reaching out for rescue. Insecurity binds us to the attitude that we can navigate the chaos on our own. All the while, roots and weeds continue to spread, further restricting our mobility. Don't wait until you're drowning in despair to call out to The One who can save you. He has given all of us the precise tool to signal for help, it's the Name of Jesus!

> For "whoever calls on the name of the Lord shall be saved."
> – Romans 10:13, NKJV

The Name of Jesus has the ability to not only deliver you, but also restore peace and hope to even the darkest circumstances. And, just like the flare gun Hiroshi gave Miku to signal for help, you can fire off the name of Jesus any time you are in desperate need, and your rescue is assured.

However, the power of Christ's intervention isn't solely to deliver us from the chaos of doubt. If our lives are like an unruly forest, God has also given us the authority to cultivate it! Much like how Ritsuko carved out her own portion of the Aokigahara, transforming it from a forest of disarray into a garden of stillness, God has given all of

...but mine own vineyard have I not kept.
- Song of Solomon 1:6, KJV

us the capability, through His spirit, to take hold of the chaos in our lives and bring it into order. However, cultivating a forest like the Aokigahara takes lots of time, it takes discipline, but most importantly, it takes wisdom to understand which areas of our lives need pruning, which need to be fed, and which areas need to be ripped out by the roots. Ritsuko's exquisite garden didn't happen overnight. It required years of regulation to transform it from an area of disorder into a place of beauty. The same rules apply when looking at the arduous task of tending our hearts. But, if we *don't* tend to that forest, rampant growth will quickly overwhelm us. Years of pain, rejection, and pride, if not examined and removed, can easily mutate into a labyrinth of fear and doubt. The result is a maze where no one can get in, and a more terrifying result, is that no one can get out.

That was the awful consequence Ritsuko found herself in. Despite having cultivated both her garden and her life, she had also built up emotional walls to keep others out. It was those very walls that Auska had to confront when reaching out to Ritsuko, and those same emotional walls were one of the main catalysts for writing *The Curse of the Father*. In the years following my dad's suicide, I too found myself building emotional barriers in my heart. These walls were assembled, piece by piece, with stones of anguish and plaster of insecurity. These barriers became an echo chamber to my deepest paranoia and darkest regrets. I became endlessly riddled with these questions: Did I do enough to reach out to my dad? Was I complicit in severing the last strands of our relationship? What could I have done differently? The manifestation of this torment was what provoked me to pour my heart onto these pages and bring the shaky relationship between Asuka and Ritsuko to life.

BREAKING DOWN WALLS OF ISOLATION

You may find yourself relating to Ritsuko's circumstance. Throughout our life, mental and spiritual strongholds exist to block us from the liberating truth of God's word, preventing us from finding the courage to truly embrace the vital connections God has given each of us. These areas of complacency, although unsettlingly comfortable, if given the opportunity, can become a prison of isolation. We begin to lose our identity and our emotional and spiritual development is certain to become inhibited. We develop behaviors and attitudes that help us deny, ignore, or avoid difficult emotions and difficult people. As a result we become detached from the reality of who we are in Christ and what our role is in the larger perspective of the world. This is a dangerous place to be, it is in this environment that "death" hopelessness and despair will create a nearly unbreakable stronghold, further enslaving us to a cycle of self-pity and fear.

As mighty as Ritsuko's walls were, they were originally created as small barricades. I felt those same small barricades being erected in my heart during my time in the forest. My own insecurities and emotional wounds festered in the fertile soil of the Aokigahara. Those walls pressed and pushed against me, reminding me that, despite the company of the group, I couldn't rely on anyone but myself. It was an attitude that would not only keep the others out, but would viciously attack anyone who would try to get close to me. Soon, the wounds in my heart became a beacon to ungodly thoughts that could have done me and my group serious harm. Just as I pushed my group away throughout the day, Ritsuko also had pushed out everyone in her life over years of misery, and now you may find yourself cutting off loving relationships in your life as well.

Each of us have mental and emotional walls, they're totally *natural*. They are boundaries that, if constructed properly, enable us to operate as healthy members in our family and community. However, in a normally functioning construct, these walls have access points, windows, and doors that serve as entrances and exits. But, in many cases, including Ritsuko's, we look at these access points as areas of weakness that should be shut up and closed off. Ritsuko was operating under that premise and had been for many years. Walls that were designed to serve as a normally functioning attribute of her life, had not only been deliberately closed, but intentionally sealed shut. She had become a prisoner, serving a life sentence of self-isolation. She chose separation from those around her rather than a life of freedom and transparency. It was only the intervention of Asuka and her fortitude of character that provoked Ritsuko to remember the importance of renovating those walls, installing a door and keeping it unlocked to those who matter most.

As much as we can relate to the isolation Ritsuko found herself in, we can also find ourselves in Asuka's position in a relationship. I know I was in her shoes in the final years of my dad's life. What do we do when those strong cords of connection begin to be intentionally severed? How can we understand where those loved ones are when they have given up on reaching out? How are we supposed to respond to those close to us who aggressively keep us away? In many cases, like mine and Asuka's, our first instinct is to echo their rejection. Like two negatively charged magnets, we match the pushback with our own, and thus those walls only grow taller and become continually reinforced. How can we oppose that rejection and break through those barriers? From the mistakes I made with my father, I can tell you that it requires self-sacrifice and humility to reach out to those people, knowing you are going to get hurt in the process. My refusal to take aggressive action with my dad was fueled by the fear of potential hurt. But the pain I felt after the loss of him staggeringly overwhelmed the threat of discomfort I would have felt had I just made our relationship a higher priority in my life. After my dad died, I spent countless sleepless nights creating scenarios of what I could have done and what I could have said to him. However, these superficially cheerful scenarios would always end with the same heartbreaking thought: *it's too late now.* It was a hard lesson to learn. Hopefully, it will be the toughest lesson I'll learn in my life.

Even if the cord of a relationship has diminished to only a single strand, there will always be the chance to reconnect. Be brave! Be humble! Allow your ego to be the sacrifice needed for reconciliation. It's the same sacrifice that God commanded of Christ in order to bring all of us back into relationship with Him. The Bible makes it clear that Jesus would have gone to The Cross for even *one* person.

Through our salvation, that commandment is inscribed on our heart. Even if there is one person in your life who needs you to reach out and intervene. You may be the only person who can discern the battle raging in their mind. You may be the last person who can have a voice in their life. You won't know until you put it all on the line and step out. Tell them they are loved, tell them they have value, that they are appreciated, that they have a bright future ahead of them. Simple words of hope can sometimes mean the difference between life and death. Don't delay in speaking them. Don't let the pride of your own self-preservation keep you from reaching out to those who need to know they're loved. Be courageous!

It takes a lot of boldness for people to step out and admit that they need help. But, even if there's a small spark of courage in their hearts, that bravery can multiply if others are willing to stand beside them. When Miku found herself alone in the Aokigahara, she had the tool, (the flare gun) to signal for help. But the fear brought on by the whispers of that metaphoric demonic creature paralyzed Miku into inaction, leaving her isolated and vulnerable to attack. Without the strength of others to undergird her, she was left alone with her demons. It was the same for *my* encounter with that malicious creature in the Suicide Forest, and I would dare say it was the same for my Dad in the days before he took his life, except the voices inside his head were very real, not metaphoric at all. In the story, it was only when I was alone in the forest, separated from the others, did that demon acquire a voice. And so it is in our lives.

Being isolated is always a very vulnerable place to be. A person, void of human connections will always be compromised by the intentions of the enemy and the strategies designed to isolate us. The strength I needed to conquer that demon and the courage Miku needed to fire off

> *Where there is no guidance, a people falls, but in an abundance of counselors there is safety.*
> – Proverbs 11:14, ESV

that flare gun were both found in the aid from another. In Miku's case, it was only after Asuka and I found her, did she truly know that there was nothing to be afraid of, she was *not* alone. The same applies for my time inside the ancient tree. Without the intervention of someone greater than me, I too would have remained crippled by the lies I was being told.

We are never meant to live our lives in isolation. Cutting ourselves off from human connections leaves us in a very vulnerable position. Every negative feeling, every dreadful thought, every fear, without the stable ground of relationships, can spring to life and grow into exaggerated weeds in our mind! That's why God wants us to live in community. Other people give us mental anchor points to ground ourselves with. These genuine connections not only help to see a world beyond what our mind is telling us, but these relationships can also undergird you when those battles rage in your mind.

It's the *genuine* part of authentic connections that I found myself lacking as I pressed deeper into the Suicide Forest with my companions. The greater my paranoia grew, the stronger my walls became. It wasn't long before I had completely detached from Asuka, Miku and

Paul, replacing genuine interaction with a false persona. The more my fears escalated, so too did my urge to put on a good front, trying to prove to them, and myself, that I had it all together. Maybe you can relate? Let's talk more about how to connect intimately without the crutch of virtual reality (a.k.a., our electronic devices).

CONNECTING WITH REAL PEOPLE IN REAL TIME

If this behavior doesn't sound familiar, it should. Every single one of us operate under this mentality in many areas of our lives. And sadly, as technology continues to evolve, these false personas will only continue to flourish. We live in a modern world of connections. Social media has given us the power to reach out to *anyone* on earth. We use this tool every day to define our identity and bring a sense of purpose to our lives. But this dimension of social interaction can often do as much harm as it can do good. Much like the fears that swelled inside me in the Aokigahara, we all carry fear and insecurities in our daily lives. Just as I walled myself up when those anxieties came, we too, project a false persona to the world, a *digital* wall. In this day and age, it's never been easier to get away with this. We highlight the best, most interesting parts of our lives, we use filters to remove blemishes and brighten our smiles. We present a *version* of ourselves to others, desperately hoping those small notifications of acceptance will muffle the insecurity in our hearts. But, as we all know, those insecurities don't remain quiet for long, do they? Soon, we begin the cycle once again, more makeup, an even brighter smile, and the counterfeit *us* swells.

It's been said that the most socially connected people are often the ones that feel most alone. Why is that? Why do these digital connections fall painfully short when satisfying our need for acknowledgement? Because while the shallow avatar we've created receives an equally shallow level of acceptance, the authentic *us* remains hidden

> *Where there is no (wise, intelligent) guidance, the people fall (and go off course like a ship without a helm). But in the abundance of (wise and godly) counselors there is victory.*
> – Proverbs 11:14, AMP

from others, starving for genuine, loving relationships. Regardless of our social standing digitally, we were not designed to exist in a two-dimensional world. We were created to connect with others, face-to-face, heart-to-heart. In order to do so, we must be humble and be willing to let the people who love us see us for who we are, the good and the bad.

Do you have anyone like that in your life? How many people know the real you? Is there someone who accepts you and loves you in spite of your flaws and shortcomings? If yes, press into those relationships! They're one of the greatest gifts you have, and a great source of strength. If no, then let me assure you there are people in *all* of our lives, although sometimes hard to discern, who are longing to cut through the *uncomfortable* and share that connection with us, no matter what the cost. Ask God to show you who those people are and be aggressive in pursuing them. You have a great responsibility to be present where God has placed you to be. You will never know this side

> *A man who has friends must himself be friendly, but there is a friend who sticks closer than a brother.*
> – Proverbs 18:24, NKJV

of eternity how many people you've encouraged by simply giving a smile, a hug, a prayer, a listening ear, or a lasting relationship. As I've made it very clear, these small connections can sometimes mean the difference between life and death. Don't consider your life pointless and don't assume another person will fill your absence.

No one can replace YOU!

Miku had that lifeline through her genuine relationship with Asuka. The story of how they became childhood friends paints a heartwarming picture of someone, Miku, who desperately needed a true friend in the midst of classmates who wanted to humiliate her. Even at a young age, Miku understood how crucial it was to have even one loving friendship in her life. Despite Asuka's initial reluctance to be that person to Miku, over the years, their friendship blossomed into a pillar of strength in their hearts. Asuka knew the genuine Miku. She knew Miku's weaknesses, her absent-mindedness, and her fear of the irrational. But, Asuka never judged Miku for her shortcomings or insecurities. Rather, Asuka remained as a constant guardian of Miku's well-being, purely wanting to see that small seed of confidence inside her best friend grow into a towering tree of courage. This relationship serves as a great example of the people we need to latch onto in our lives. It also gives a small idea of what God's heart is for all of us! Despite our pride, despite our failings, despite our air-headedness, God will always remain by our side. He patiently shepherds us through our lives, walking us through each adversity we face, knowing that every challenge we overcome will birth a new strength in our heart.

GOD IS ALWAYS REACHING OUT TO YOU

Not only will God guide us through the difficult moments of our lives, He will also passionately seek us out when we try to face our challenges alone, losing our way in the process. When Miku vanished from the group, it was Asuka who selflessly put it all on the line to go and find her friend. She crossed chasms, braved self-doubt, and even shed blood in her quest to secure Miku's safety. Not once did Asuka complain, compromise, or hesitate in her search. Nothing,

> *"I am the light of the world. Whoever follows me will not walk in darkness, but will have the light of life.*
> – John 8:12, ESV

but the well-being of her friend mattered. Her single-mindedness in this mission was absolute and after hours of perseverance, Asuka's persistence was rewarded: Miku was found.

The Bible lends more insight to this thought. In the book of Matthew 18:12, Jesus tells the story of a man who had owned 100 sheep. *One* of the sheep left the safety of the group and got lost. The man then left the 99 to secure the one lost sheep. Jesus, in the book of John, refers to himself as the Good Shepherd, the one who lays down his life for the sheep. What a powerful visual for us to embrace! Jesus knows the importance of finding the lost. So much so that He was willing to leave the comforts of heaven, and come to earth on a mission to find those who desperately needed to be found. His mission cost Him everything, and He gave no regard to His personal safety or reputation. And ultimately, Jesus' sacrifice was rewarded: *We* have been found!

What about you? Are you lost? Are you in need of someone to find you? You may be reading this thinking that no one cares and that your plight is hopeless. But please be assured, you *are* being looked for. Your name is known and your current location has been acquired by a God, who has given everything to secure your safe return, illuminating our path with the light of his word, leading us back into safety.

Jesus uses light to illustrate a simple yet profound truth.

How could we navigate our life without His light to brighten our path? I don't have to tell you that without light, it's impossible to see *anything*. Obvious, I know. But we often forget this basic concept when navigating the dark areas of our mind.

As Asuka, Miku and I were stranded in the clearing, there was very little light. The surrounding darkness made everything around us suspicious. Every vague shadow provoked our imaginations to fill in the blanks with irrational fears of ghost children. Only after the lights from the watchtowers illuminated the clearing did we realize that the threat of ghosts couldn't have been farther from the truth. And boy, were we relieved!

Early humans, in desperation to bring warmth and safety to their cold dark nights, would work for hours just to create a small flame. They knew that if they could get just one flame, *one tiny flame*, it could be fanned into a conflagration, illuminating everything and everyone around them. We will do *anything* possible to light an area that is shrouded in darkness. We consult doctors to shed light on an illness or unknown medical condition. We seek out lawyers to help bring clarity to legal issues. We search the Internet to explain the mysteries of our modern world. But when it comes to exposing the lies and doubt that reside deep in our hearts, often the pain is too great and we would rather relegate ourselves to the murky uncertainty of shadows.

What about you? Do you find yourself lost in areas of your heart that need illumination? Has darkness shrouded your perception of what is real and what is imaginary? Just like when we isolate ourselves, darkness can become a blank canvas for our irrational fears to manifest. Be assured, those fears, those terrors, those monsters aren't as solid as they seem. I guarantee you that with even a little illumination in your mind, not only can you find the way out, but you will have the profound revelation that things aren't as dire as they appear in darkness.

ILLUMINATING YOUR VISION

As it was with the light of the watchtowers, sometimes this light is found through the relationships of other people. Seek the wisdom of trusted others when it comes to the challenges in your life. Don't be afraid to reveal those darkened areas. There are people in your life who have been in the place you now find yourself. Let others help you light the flame and watch those shadows of doubt disappear.

However, even the brightest ray of light can sometimes prove useless when our eyes don't work. Your spiritual eyes, much like your physical ones, are lenses. Without proper maintenance, these lenses can distort our perspective of reality, or worse, leave us completely blind. Consider my colleague, Paul Black, for example. Paul's detailed knowledge of video equipment is a crucial skill I rely on to create television shows. Without his expertise, *The Sea of Trees* would never have come into reality, much less the hundreds of hours of content we have produced before and since then. Just as I have to fight battles of presentation and verbal delivery, Paul fights his own battles of technical details. There is a lot of effort that goes into professional videography. Too much light, too little light, color balance, focus, stability, shutter speed, framerate, aperture, and audio levels are just a handful of dozens of factors Paul has to simultaneously keep an eye on, all while keeping me on point. And what is the endgame of monitoring all these details? To simply capture an *accurate* image!

Capturing accurate colors, accurate details, and accurate sound requires constant supervision and meticulous preparation. Before each recording, Paul will spend up to 20 minutes (sometimes to my frustration) getting the camera's settings locked in. His final step before hitting record and giving me my cue is to thoroughly clean the camera's lens. Paul knows better than anyone that a video shot with a dirty lens, however correct his settings are, will be rendered worthless. No amount of post-production can remove a smudge off a lens. No, Paul has to clean it BEFORE we record, and he has to clean it OFTEN. But, how often do we forget to monitor the complex settings when it comes to capturing an accurate snapshot of our own lives? So many times, we view our feelings and circumstances through a faulty lens. Our mental images are smudged, they're out of focus and even distorted all together. But, unlike when Paul discards that image, we hold onto those inaccurate images, cherishing them and let them define our reality. But even more damning is the fact that we *choose not* to deal with the source of the distortion, the defective lens. As important as it is for Paul to clean his lens before *each shot*, how much more crucial is it for us to evaluate the quality of our "lens on life" *daily*.

> "The lamp of the body is the eye. If therefore your eye is good, your whole body will be full of light. But if your eye is bad, your whole body will be full of darkness."
> – Matthew 6:22-23, NKJV

Jesus explains this with even greater clarity, in the book of Matthew.

Jesus understood the importance of lens clarity and light. You can't have one without the other.

Are you keeping track of the lens you view yourself and others through? Has that lens become dirty? We have to equip ourselves daily with words of truth to be fully confident we're seeing our circumstances accurately. Monitoring our spiritual eyes is a battle of constant vigilance, but the distortions to our perspective can have serious implications.

GUARD YOUR SOUL

Every day, we find ourselves caught in the crossfire of an information war. This barrage of noise and confusion is at times deafening and, need I say, is intentionally designed to cloud our viewpoint and skew our judgement. Some of these volleys are simply distractions in our life, but others have a more malicious intent: to do us harm. Consider the innumerable hopeless people who traveled into Aokigahara to end their lives, equipping their hearts with the same defective lens: *The Complete Manual of Suicide*. The tragedy this one book has brought to thousands of families is sadly inconceivable. There's no greater example of the importance of having an accurate perspective on our lives than this wicked manual.

When Wataru Tsurumi published *The Complete Manual of Suicide* in 1993, he stated that his intentions were to create a text that gave the reader a keen insight into the frailty of life, thus, hoping the reader would assign greater value to the life they had been given. Although his methods were, without doubt, controversial, the audience received the message of this book in a *literal* way. As you now know, people who had the intention of ending their lives flocked to this book to educate themselves on the easiest ways to commit the act. And, yes, each year, hundreds of people *do* go to the Aokigahara to commit suicide on the direct influence of Wataru Tsurumi's words. What a terrible mindset the author unwittingly released on a generation. Consider the count-less souls who must stand before God at the gates of eternity being asked what it was that distorted their perspective so greatly that they chose to take their life. I can only imagine the remorse and regret that they will experience when the truth is revealed, they had believed a lie.

The Complete Manual of Suicide is a book that tells you *how* to end your life, *where* to end your life, and how to keep this dark secret hidden from others. It deceives you into believing that your only viable option to escape a life of pain and isolation is through the pull of a trigger or the taut of a rope.

But, there *is* hope!

Standing in stark contrast to that *damned* book is *another* book—a book that has brought life to billions of people for thousands of years. Its Author's

> "It is the Spirit who gives life; the flesh conveys no benefit (it is of no account). The words I have spoken to you are spirit and life (providing eternal life)"
> - John 6:63, AMP

intention was to bring hope, restoration, redemption, life, joy, and a greater sense of community to anyone who would dare thumb through its pages. We all know what that book is. It's a book that tells you *how* to live your life; it tells you *where* to live it … with others. And, most importantly, it tells you *Whom* to live your life for. Instead of offering a fatalistic uncertainty, framed with the fear of the unknown, this book promises life and life abundantly.

I strongly encourage you to make a thorough inventory of the words you are allowing to populate your heart and mind. Test them. Test their fruit. Is the fruit of those words peace, joy, love, kindness, and goodness? Do they bring you closer to others, or do they push you to isolate yourself, alone with deception. Are they words of life or words of death?

These are the kinds of words we *all* must keep close to our heart. If we do this, nothing can distort our view of life!

THE ANCIENT ENEMY

Now, let's go deeper into the forces at play when it comes to under-standing the value of our lives. I could leave the subject at a cursory concept that our value, or lack thereof, comes strictly from our own mental state. But, I personally don't believe that for one second. I truly believe that there is a greater force behind those negative emotions. No, it's not a belief that many people want to acknowledge. But, I can't ignore the elephant in the room.

Or in this case... the demon in the shrine.

In *The Curse of the Father*, a malicious creature stalked me and my group as we explored the Aokigahara. I intentionally described this creature as something that wasn't just in my head, that it was a real entity in the Suicide Forest. Though I received much criticism about my choice to creatively make the demon being a *real* entity, I felt it crucial to communicate to you that there is a legitimate and intelli-gent enemy after each of us! This enemy has had one goal since the beginning of time: to deceive us to such an extent that we surrender our hearts, our faith, and ultimately, our lives over to it. The demonic enemy has perfected its strategy to take you down. And, I'm sorry to say this but, there is a tailor-made strategy formulated specifically to you!

The demonic creature in the story knew the exact thing, the spe-cific wound from my past that would cause me to crumble under its wicked influence: the loss of my father to suicide. The demon took on the form of my dad, offering to answer many questions I had in exchange for the surrender of my life. This is an example of a strategy specifically made for me. Your weakness may be a similar one or entirely different, but I guarantee you have one, and the enemy *knows* what it is.

But do you, yourself, know what your weakest spot is?

> *For we do not wrestle against flesh and blood, but against principalities, against powers, against the rulers of the darkness of this age, against spiritual hosts of wickedness in the heavenly places.*
> – John 6:63, AMP

I can't answer that question for you. All I can advise is that you take the time to prayerfully ask God to reveal what that frailty is. Secret addictions, insecurities and unforgiveness are open wounds that often serve as doors of entry for the enemy. How many people have chosen to end their own lives because of rejection, bullying, guilt or shame, yielding their will to another who is determined to destroy the last vestige of hope remaining in their hearts.

As I began to look deeper into my unresolved issues concerning my dad's death, I found some unusual correlations between what I was dealing with and a very real condition called survivors guilt or in today's vernacular: PTSD, also known as Post Traumatic Stress Disorder. These symptoms include anxiety, depression, social withdrawal, sleep disturbance, physical pain and dramatic mood swings. This is an accurate description of the physical manifestations in my life. Granted they would ebb and flow much like an ocean tide, but they were always present, and the enemy knew it. I had made a fatal decision to deal with my father's suicide by myself and would violently oppose anyone who tried to scale those walls and expose the source of my pain. I had become so secretive, deceived and self-centered that I even denied God access to this darkened area of my heart.

Have you done the same? Let me tell you, there is only so long that we can hide that pain from others. Inevitably, those wounds will be exposed! The only question is: who will expose them to you? Are you going to wait until those weaknesses are revealed by a force that seeks to destroy you *through* them? Or are you willing to let your loving Father preemptively reveal them, surrounding those areas of fragility with His righteous armor. It's that armor that will give you the power to stand your ground and face your enemy head on, knowing that you have the One in your corner who knows and loves every part of who you are.

LIFE BEYOND THE VEIL OF DEATH

Widening our scope a bit, there is a final riddling character in *The Curse of the Father*, one I haven't brought up yet, and one which I'm questioned about more than the rest of the tale combined: *The Girl.* Yes, she is the figure that will undoubtedly stir the most controversy. And the one that demands a scriptural explanation. So here it is. This is where we step outside of the realms of the supernatural and into the areas of abstract. However, there is a reason I included such a cryptic character. After all, death is a great unknown to all of us, isn't it?

Ever since the beginning of mankind, ever since Adam and Eve sinned in the Garden of Eden, we have lived under the curse of death.

Some of the greatest minds in science and religion have sought to overcome this one, singular constant: everything that eats, breathes, crawls, flies, grows, and feels will eventually cease to be. Death is an element without limit. It doesn't feel, it doesn't discriminate, and it can't be stopped. Whether we can accept it or not, none of us can escape our own natural end. Too forlorn to say? Believe me, I

> *For just as through one man's disobedience [Adams failure to hear, his carelessness and disobedience] the many were made sinners, so through the obedience of the one Man (Jesus) the many will be made righteous and acceptable to God and brought into right standing with Him.*
> – Romans 5:19, AMP

don't intend it to be. Because, the greater significance of death is the existence *beyond* it!

You see, through faith in Christ, there *is* life beyond the veil of death. And that life resides outside the natural laws that you and I currently live by. It is a *new* law! A law written by the tears of our Heavenly Father and signed in the blood of His only son. This new law bypasses death. It proclaims that death from this world is no longer the end of all things, but now a graduation and the beginning of a new life with Christ! It is a life that is beyond the reach of natural death. Consider my conversation with The Girl in the shrine. Her cold indifference is only momentarily disrupted when she considers the only One who has ever been able to rewrite the natural rules to life: Jesus. It is the power of His eternal life that has *swallowed up death forever.*

> *"I am the Resurrection and the Life. Whoever believes in (adheres to, trusts in, relies on) Me [as Savior] will live even if he dies; and everyone who lives and believes in Me [as Savior] will never die."*
> – John 11:25-26, AMP

The Bible declares that there has only been one, the man Christ Jesus, who has overcome death and made void its very nature. His sinless life, sacrificial death and resurrection established His power over life and death.

The Bible explains this in the book of Romans.

The resurrection of Jesus has ensured that those of us who have believed in Him and received his free gift of life need not fear the death we are all destined to face.

Everything in this final chapter has intentionally remained broad. There is much content in this story that applies to *all* of our lives, no matter where we find ourselves. But now, as we come to a close, I'd now like to hone into the specific topic that inspired *The Curse of the Father*: losing a loved one to suicide.

LETTING GO OF GRIEF

I would be remiss if I didn't address the question that I am constantly asked about *The Sea of Trees* documentary, and even more, when I share my own personal experience with suicide. Yes, when I was thirty years old, my father chose to end his life. Reading this book, you already have a vivid picture of the tragedy of that night and the sorrow that I carried in my heart for many years after. I'm not going to recount those events again; they are already here in these pages. But what I do want to address is the hurt that so many people have communicated to me concerning their *own* grief over losing a loved one to suicide. The pain is immeasurable and the emptiness in our hearts is inconsolable. I've spoken with mothers who have lost children, kids who have lost parents, sisters who have lost brothers, and teenagers who have lost their best friends. Each conversation is as gut-wrenching as the next. But there are many common themes that are constantly reiterated in these encounters: the unanswered questions, the grief, the anger, and the guilt; I know these themes all too well.

How do you pick up the pieces of a broken relationship and continue on living the way you did? The truth be told, you *don't*. Believe me, I tried for many years to pretend that nothing had changed. In fact, my father's death was one of the many catalysts that provoked me to leave the United States and become a missionary. I kept the reality of my father's suicide tucked away and unreviewed in my heart. The last place I thought my life would take me was to Japan, to the Suicide Forest, where I, not only had to produce a documentary about the value of life, but had to face my personal demons of suicide that I had kept locked away for many years. How ironic that I, of all people, had been given the task of tackling this issue. But in the months that followed, and after the incredible reception of the documentary, it was clear to me that God had planned this all along; I was meant to use the tragic event of losing my father and turn it into a testimony that could help reach others. My place of weakness had now become a place of great strength. I knew that the shattered pieces of my life, of my father's life, if given to God, could be empowered with the ability to communicate life and hope to those who needed it most. My *mess* had now become my *message*.

But, in order to fully realize that truth, I had to break one final chain binding me to the tragedy of losing my father: I hadn't forgiven him. The chain of unforgiveness held me tightly, restraining me in my struggle to be truly free once and for all. The pain brought from that unhealed wound defined me to such an extent that I didn't know who I would be without it. I spent years avoiding that injury, terrified of the agony that I thought would come if I examined it, all the while its infection spread into every area of my life. But, God continually encouraged me to finally open that wound to Him. I fought that inevitability as long as I could, and God let me combat it on my own until I ended up exhausted and utterly broken.

It was only when my pride had thoroughly been decimated that I turned to the only one who could help me break those chains of unforgiveness and allow Him to attend to the trauma inflicted. His supernatural power transformed that festering laceration into a scar. Just as Jesus still bears the scars of His crucifixion, that wound isn't removed. God didn't make it vanish as if nothing had ever happened. Rather, God *healed* it, sealing that open wound with a stronger tissue. And like a physical scar, that surface is now more durable than the original skin. The pain is gone! No, it's not pretty, but it serves as a reminder of where I've been, the pain I endured and the responsibility I have to help others learn from my suffering.

And it's the same for you. No, you *aren't* meant to continue living your life as it was before your tragedy. Rather, as hard as it is to fathom, you and all of us who have experienced this great pain, now have been given a difficult directive from God: to use this sorrow and hurt, to embrace and communicate a newfound *value for life*, allowing the grace of God to move *through* you, filling that empty place in your heart with compassion, understanding, and peace; a peace that has the ability to not *answer those unanswered questions,* but give you Godly solutions and tools, designed to communicate life and hope to the ones who are at greatest risk.

Communicating that message of hope has been my sole priority for over 30 years. I can say without hesitation that when you step out to help others heal their personal wounds, God will exceedingly tend to yours. *The Curse of the Father* and *The Sea of Trees* documentary are proof that He is always willing to take the pain of our past and turn it into a testimony for others. But these resources are just a few pieces in a vast mosaic of messages needed to address the epidemic of suicide. What is *your* piece? Whether you have struggled with thoughts of self-destruction or have experienced the pain of losing a loved one to suicide, your testimony is desperately needed! Communicate it! Share your story with others! Together, we can bring crucial awareness to this fatal problem.

Before we say goodbye, I'd like you to stand with me and agree in prayer that all of our wounds from the spirit of suicide will, not only be healed, but will be transformed into platforms to reach out and encourage those still struggling. Are you ready to stand up and be counted among the survivors? Are you ready to take up arms against an enemy who wants to deceive and destroy our friends and family? Now is the time to act! So let's agree together.

Father, I come to you with humility and admit that I am lost in my life. I've allowed my pain, my doubt, and my pride to overgrow in my heart. I need your power to rescue me and your authority to rip out those things that are not of you! Jesus, shine your light in the darkened areas of my heart. Reveal to me the places of weakness that can be used by the enemy. Give me the vigilance to clean my lens daily. Help me take an accurate account of the words and thoughts I'm allowing to influence my mind. I ask for Godly connections with others to undergird my life. Give me the courage to break down my walls of self-preservation and the humility to reach out and ask for help when I need it. Give me the wisdom and discernment to know the words to speak when others need guidance. In Jesus' name, I rebuke any wicked influence over my mind, and I command the chains of unforgiveness to be broken off of my heart. Father, I give the pains of my past to you. Heal the wounds of suicide and transform them into scars. Let my mess become a message of hope that I can share with others.

In Jesus' name!

Hey, no matter who you are, your life has value and you are loved! I am so honored to be a part of your journey, and I believe that God has already begun healing your wounds and is daily empowering you to reach others with the words of life!

And now, *my* story of overcoming the pain of suicide is complete.

What will *your* story be?

This is just one of several adventures I have had over the years in an effort to reach a generation with the Gospel of Jesus. Yes, there is more to come. And as always, you're welcome to join me on those future adventures.

– Chad

P.S. If by the end of this story, you find yourself skeptical on what was fact and fiction during my time in the Aokigahara, *The Sea of Trees* documentary we created is *real* and available to view for yourself. The children with the fireworks, my two Japanese guides, the forest ranger, the suicide manual, and the impartation I delivered at the end is all there for your own gratification. After reading this story and watching the documentary, *you* can decide what really happened for yourself.

IN LOVING MEMORY OF

LOUIS EUGENE DANIEL

ACKNOWLEDGEMENTS

Special thanks to Contributor and Editor, my friend, international travel companion, and senior producer, **Paul Black**, for your help in making this book and many other projects come to life. You have dedicated so much to this work and to every project we have created for the past 12 years; I am eternally grateful.

To the artistic genius' at **Atomic Press Inc.** for providing unprecedented visuals to this project.

Special thanks to Senior Editor and Author Coach, **Carrie Glenn**, for your invaluable contributions to this book. You have been enthusiastic, professional, and you are the magic ingredient that helped turn this idea into reality. Carrie, your work is stunning and I am thankful for your contributions.

If you are one of the millions that are struggling with thoughts of suicide, please know that there are those who want to help you find life.

Please call the National Suicide Prevention Lifeline:
1-800-273-8255
suicidepreventionlifeline.org

There is always hope.

SEE THE FILM THAT INSPIRED THE BOOK

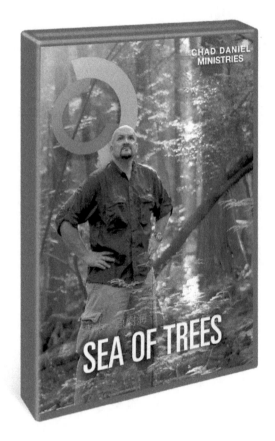

vimeo.com/ondemand/cdmseaoftrees

BRING HOPE TO *YOUR* COMMUNITY

Chad Daniel continues to partner with churches and other community organizations around the world, bringing hope and healing to those at risk.

For more information, go to

ChadDaniel.com

to set up a Life Event in YOUR area.

CONNECT WITH CHAD

youtube.com/
chaddaniel

@chadhdaniel

chaddanielofficial

CHADDANIEL.COM

CPSIA information can be obtained
at www.ICGtesting.com
Printed in the USA
LVHW082336091219
639990LV00019B/1660/P